ANDREAS HUYSSEN is chairman of the Department of Germanic Languages at Columbia University. His most recent book is *After the Great Divide: Modernism, Mass Culture, Postmodernism*. He is an editor of *New German Critique*.

DAVID BATHRICK is Professor of German Studies and Theatre Arts at Cornell University. He is an editor of *New German Critique* and author of numerous articles and two books: *The Dialectic and the Early Brecht* and *The Powers of Speech: The Politics of Culture in the GDR* (forthcoming).

Modernity and the Text

Revisions of German Modernism

Modernity and the Text

Revisions of German Modernism

Edited by
Andreas Huyssen and
David Bathrick

Columbia University Press
NEW YORK

Columbia University Press
New York   Oxford

Library of Congress Cataloging-in-Publication Data

Modernity and the text : revisions of German modernism / edited by
   Andreas Huyssen and David Bathrick.
      p.   cm.
   Includes bibliographies and index.
   ISBN 0-231-06644-9
      1. German prose literature—20th century—History and criticism.
2. Modernism (Literature)—Germany.   3. German prose literature—
Austrian authors—History and criticism.   4. Modernism
(Literature)—Austria.   I. Huyssen, Andreas.   II. Bathrick, David.
PT735.M64   1989
838'.91208'091—dc19   88-38425
                                                                CIP

Printed in the United States of America

Book design by Ken Venezio

Contents

Acknowledgments

The majority of the essays assembled in this volume were first presented at a conference held April 23–25, 1986, at the Center for Twentieth Century Studies at the University of Wisconsin-Milwaukee. We wish to thank the National Endowment of the Humanities for a generous Research Conference grant and the Center for Twentieth Century Studies for its unfailing support and efficiency in preparing and running a memorable conference. The success of the conference was in large measure due to the thoughtful and challenging contributions of respondents and discussants who must be acknowledged here even though regrettably their remarks could not be included in this volume. Our thanks go to Herbert Blau, Giovanna Borradori, Christopher Butler, Miriam Gusevich, Mark Krupnick, Roswitha Mueller, Henry Schmidt, Gabi and Martin Schwab, Ingo Seidler, and Jack Zipes.

We owe special thanks to Kathleen Woodward, Director of the Center, and to the Center's staff, Jean Lile and Carol Tennessen, without whose help and hospitality this project would not have come about. We are also grateful to Laura Roskos who did some of the editing and to Shirley Reinhold who retyped several manuscripts.

Modernism and the Experience of Modernity

David Bathrick and Andreas Huyssen

The study of German and Austrian modernism has a long and venerable history in this country. With the work of an older generation of scholars such as Walter Sokel (*The Writer in Extremis*) and Erich Heller (*The Disinherited Mind*), it has helped shape the American image of Central European modernism in the field of literature. It is no coincidence that Franz Kafka and Thomas Mann, both central figures in this earlier account of German modernism, have become common staples in comparative studies of literary modernism in the United States and still hold a privileged position quite unimaginable today in the German academy.

The point here is not to question the undeniable importance of Kafka and Mann within German modernism; the point is rather to emphasize that as a result of a series of aesthetic and political debates on the nature and tradition of modernism and avant-gardism in Germany, our knowledge of modernist literary movements in Vienna and Prague, Munich and Berlin has expanded significantly. The focus on the few isolated masters of modernism has become too constricting, if not theoretically obsolete. New editions of major and minor authors, including rediscoveries of forgotten texts, collections of documents pertaining to *das junge Wien,* expressionism, the *Neue Sachlichkeit,* and the literature of exile have contextualized the great modernists in a way perhaps not yet possible at an earlier time. In Germany, the more influential books on modernism and the avant-garde since the late 1960s have been those focusing on literary movements in a historical and political perspective, such as Helmut Lethen's study of the *Neue Sachlichkeit* or, very differently, Thomas Anz's work on early expressionism, entitled *Literatur der Existenz.* In a somewhat different vein, more synthetic and encompassing studies like Peter Bürger's *Theorie der Avantgarde* have attempted to draw conclusions from the debates of the 1960s about Lukács and Brecht, Adorno and Benjamin, and the viability of a Marxist theory of literary modernism.

The move away from the isolated masters of modernism toward history and politics is also characteristic of German studies in the United States. It is certainly worth noting that in recent years books on modern German and Austrian culture have come less frequently from within German literature departments. Cultural and intellectual historians such as Carl Schorske, John Willett, Walter Laqueur, and Peter Gay have been more successful than literary critics in shaping American interest in German and Austrian modernism.

At the same time another group of scholars and critics, most of them associated with the intellectual left in this country, have begun to reclaim the heritage of the Frankfurt School for contemporary debates in areas as divergent as social theory, philosophy, media theory, aesthetics, and literary criticism. Of course, the interest in the Frankfurt School has benefited from the general shift toward continental theory that has characterized debates in literary and cultural criticism since the early 1970s, as well as from certain political and theoretical dissatisfactions with deconstruction. But even though the theory of the Frankfurt School, especially the work of Adorno and Benjamin, can be read as a theory of modernity and of modernism, it has rarely been carried into specific readings of modernist texts in the German tradition. It is perhaps symptomatic that Adorno's literary essays, which contain some of his very best writing, still remain largely untranslated.

All of this, then, may be reason enough to put forth a project of rereading German modernist literature. However, the project of this book is also—and perhaps more important—a response to the pressures of the recent debate about modernity and postmodernity, modernism and postmodernism. In this age of the much heralded postmodern, we felt it important to insist that modernism is anything but a dead dog. The reputed exhaustion, decline, obsolescence, and end of modernism may after all have more to do with certain accounts of modernism than with the thing in itself. Of course the very assumption of a modernism as such is highly dubious. A major purpose of this book is to challenge the confining Anglo-American canonization of high modernism into which most of German and Austrian modernism simply does not fit. One of the reasons that earlier accounts for modernism have recently fallen into disrepute is precisely that they have attempted to homogenize a widely heterogeneous field of discourses and practices, to press them into a relatively rigid framework of categories and concepts, the implied ideology of which has increasingly become evident. It is the merit of the current theoretical debates on the nature and politics of language, of gender and subjectivity, of reading and writing, remembering and forgetting, that they have opened up modernist literature to new questions and problematics. They have peeled away layers of scholarly reification of the classics of the twentieth century and have enabled us to read modernist texts afresh, both in their own historical context and in the context of postmodern problematics, the context of the present. What emerges from such rereadings is the insight that rather than being a totally new departure, the postmodern is in many ways involved in renegotiations of the constitutive terms of the modern, a rewriting of the problematics of modernism itself. All the more important then to read modernism in its own historicity, not as something that has been decisively overcome by the postmodern, but as a phenomenon that recedes further and further into the past, assuming an aura that marks its distance from the present. To reject modernism en bloc in order to celebrate a radical postmodern departure is as self-serving a strategy as its flip side, sucking modernism into the postmodern. Both rejection and appropriation deny modernism its own historicity and subject it to the hegemony of the present.

But there are additional problems in the current debate about modernism and postmodernism. Two aspects strike us as particularly noteworthy. While the debate about postmodernism began in certain isolated fields (especially architecture and performance art) in the 1960s and became ever more encompassing, by the early 1980s it had reached a stage of macrotheorizing in which specific texts, paintings, buildings, films, etc., at best served as theoretical objects designed to prove one or another theory about the rupture between modernism and postmodernism. Such macrotheorizing has had its usefulness in forcing the issue of how we can characterize a postmodern condition as against, say, the culture of high modernism (or certain hegemonic accounts of it). But this volume is meant to return us to specific texts, especially narrative and philosophical prose texts, which we seek to read through the prism of contemporary theoretical questions. Fundamentally opposed to reducing modernism to this or that set of criteria from which the postmodern can then be properly distinguished, we are concerned here with the still fascinating heterogeneity of the modernist tradition that will continue to explode any attempt to confine it to restrictive readings, be they Lukácsian, new critical, Adornean, Derridean, or de Manean. This is not to advocate a mindless pluralism nor, for that matter, an ultimate synthesis, but rather to acknowledge the necessity of reflecting upon the historical, political, and aesthetic implications of any approach to modernism.

Writing about modernism in the conservative 1980s is a paradoxical enterprise. On the one hand, the millennarian sensibility of modernism and the revolutionary activism of early twentieth-century avant-gardism fade ever further into the past, and the implications of modernism in the ideology of modernization, capitalist or communist, have increasingly come under critical scrutiny. On the other hand, it seems that the radical potential of modernism's concrete textual practices is far from exhausted, that it is actually gaining steam again in the face of neoconservative attempts to posit a domesticated modernism, the modernism of purely aesthetic "quality," as cultural norm against the experimentations and eclecticisms of the postmodern. Perhaps the fault lines of cultural politics today are no longer between modernism and postmodernism, but rather between aesthetically, theoretically, and politically opposed readings of twentieth-century culture, whether modern or postmodern.

The second problem, more prominent perhaps in current literary theory (especially in deconstruction, but also in variants of reader response theory) than in the postmodernism debate, has to do with the ways in which the historical and the political inscriptions in literary texts have been benignly neglected, if not obsessively blocked out. Thanks to recent scandals involving the political affiliations of Paul de Man and Martin Heidegger (the latter long-known, but dismissed as unimportant in poststructuralist circles), the question of history and politics in the text can be posed with renewed vigor. The pat answers of deconstructive philosophy and literary deconstruction to such questions will no longer suffice. But neither will it suffice to return to older modes of historical or historicist research. Recent literary theory has problematized the relationship between history and text in ways that cannot simply be forgotten. What has to be challenged, however, is the dogmatic ontologizing of the text and the concomitant refusal to engage the historical, institutional, and political implications of textual practices on levels other than that of the text and its language. The question of textual politics is much more heterogeneous and multilayered than deconstruction has tried to make us believe.

But problems exist not only on the side of deconstruction. Certainly, the critics assembled in this volume cannot be accused of programmatic and principled blindness to the historical implications of textual practice. The problem for critics working out of the German tradition, with its strongly hermeneutic and historical orientation and with its emphasis on ideology critique, is rather to evade the objectivist and teleological implications of various historicisms (including both the classical version of historical materialism and the Adornean aesthetic of modernization) and to find alternative uses for the poststructuralist critique of language and representation.

Our own continuing investments in modernism itself will become clear if it can be shown that many modernist texts are more adequately understood in light of contemporary theoretical "advances" than with the rather traditionalist aesthetic categories used to construct the "high modernist" canon in the 1940s and 1950s via existentialism or variants of the New Criticism. As editors, we hope this volume will contribute to an understanding of modernism and the avant-garde and reflect the *Erkenntnisinteresse* of our own times without, however, subjecting the past to the terror of the present.

If the literature of modernism is in some fundamental way linked to processes of modernization (social, political, psychological, economic, technological, etc.), then it becomes important to inquire into the precise nature of that link. The notion of the "experience of modernity" in the title to this introduction is meant to be both programmatic and suggestive in this context. Of course the epistemological and historical, psychological and political problems conjured up by the term "experience" are formidable, and we do not intend here to unravel the complexities of this question. Nevertheless, a few remarks should be in order.

We do not suggest a return to some unproblematic notion of experience as somehow unique, immediate, and spontaneous that would then be adequately reflected or expressed in the artwork. Neither do we advocate a notion of experience that would draw its legitimacy from the accumulated knowledge of past generations, from tradition as codified by the past. If anything, modernity has vaporized this notion of experience as tradition, thereby opening up new relationships to both tradition and experience. The longing for the immediacy of experience, however, may represent the impossible desire of the modern subject to find a substitute for the loss of tradition. We only need to remember Walter Benjamin's work on Baudelaire and Marcel Proust to note that aesthetic modernity may well constitute itself in the gap between an intense desire for experience and the equally intense suspicion that authentic experience is erased by modernity itself. And, of course, the crisis of experience, which plays such a major role not only in Benjamin's thought but in modernist texts in general, is always also a crisis of subjectivity, an atrophy of the bourgeois subject that Adorno never tired of elaborating, whether in his work on the authoritarian, fascist personality or in his writings on Heidegger and existentialism or in his music theory and aesthetics. It should also be clear that the crisis of subjectivity cannot be fully explored unless it is understood as a crisis of the speaking and writing subject, a crisis of language, within language. Take Adorno's lament over the atrophy of the subject one step further and give it an affirmative, Nietzschean twist and you get to the celebrations of the death of the subject in early poststructuralism. Take Benjamin's distinctions between *Erfahrung* and *Erlebnis, Erinnerung* and *Gedächtnis* into the French discourse, especially psychoanalysis, and you get to Julia Kirsteva's distinction between the semiotic and the symbolic in the elaboration of a theory of modernist writing. The basic problematics of modernism, renegotiated to be sure, are still at stake, and it is thus no coincidence that critics have in recent years been tempted to explore in theoretical terms the constellation of poststructuralism and Frankfurt School Critical Theory. Without going into that debate here, we would still want to register a fundamental disagreement with recent attempts to read Benjamin or Adorno (or both) as proto-deconstructionists, as poststructuralists or postmodernists *avant la lettre*. Such attempts only testify to the atrophy of historical and political reflection in the current theoretical discourse.

The problems of experience and subjectivity have recently resurfaced with a vengeance. Both experience and subjectivity are increasingly being understood as social and discursive constructs, subject to historical transformation, bound to class, gender, and race, and modified to a significant degree by place and nationality. The pessimistic lament over the waning of experience and subjectivity, as well as its flip side, the joyful celebration of the ends of man, seems to belong to an earlier discursive constellation and appears altogether as too limiting and one-dimensional. In the light of recent critical debates about subjectivity and experience, there will then be not one experience of modernity but many, just as there is not one modernist text but a wide variety of texts that articulate experiences of modernity in different aesthetic codes, from different subject positions, and with different political affiliations and national contingencies. We need to reclaim such differences in the discursive field of modernism itself in order to open up earlier homogenizing accounts of modernism to what they excluded. Such a critical strategy will also help us resist the pressures of a postmodern discourse that in turn tends to homogenize the past in order to be more persuasive in advancing its own claims to novelty and radical rupture.

Certainly a realignment of the modernist discussion around the linkage of text and history via the experience of modernity must at the very least force us to reinterrogate the designatory categories that have determined discussions up to this point. We have entitled the first part of the volume "The Avant-Garde: Politics and the Text" only to open up questions about the viability of using any such signifiers with a sense of impunity.

For instance, in European as opposed to American discussions, the notion of the subcategory "avant-garde" under the rubric of modernism has served heuristically both to delineate ontological differences and to help map out historical transformations within the modernist tradition. Matei Calinescu's designation of the avant-garde as a second, more politically and ideologically radical phase of modernism is but one way theorists have tried to deal with the seeming disparity within modernism between its activist and its "apolitical" gestures, between an aesthetic that claims to change the world and one centered on language and individual expression.

Peter Bürger in fact used just such a distinction to formulate a theory of the avant-garde in which the historical rupture between "aestheticism" (read modernism) and "the historical avant-garde" became a watershed in the crisis of culture itself at the turn of the century. According to Bürger, aestheticism thematized and thereby brought to extreme awareness the autonomy status of art, which in turn called forth attempts to bridge the distance between art and life on the part of the avant-garde. While Bürger's life-versus-art model is helpful in delineating substantive developments in the diachrony of aesthetic autonomy within what he quite correctly calls the "institution of art," it has been found sorely wanting at the level of reading individual texts in their specific historical inscriptions. Not only has Bürger conveniently limited his prime examples to movements that would easily fit his model, namely dada and surrealism, but his one-dimensional dialectical Hegelianism, combined with a narrow focus on art as institution, represses the largest truth about modernism itself—namely the plurality, the heterogeneity of its response to the maelstrom of modernization.

To be sure, critics such as Bürger are not the only ones to impose constricting historical paradigms in their attempts to reconstruct the modern. On the one hand, there are those on both sides of the political spectrum who would argue that modernism represents at its deepest register a search for a coherent cultural "tradition," for the tradition of the new (Harold Rosenberg); a last effort to establish a unifying cultural-political vision that would grasp the whole—before the onslaught of postmodernist chaos. While such an emphasis upon totality clearly reflects the self-understanding and even political practice of certain movements within modernism—such as Bauhaus, constructivism, futurism, even *Neue Sachlichkeit*—it does not come to terms with the fact that the opposite is also true: that cultural chaos and heterogeneity were also always there, more often than not right within those movements and even the works of those artists who would claim otherwise. What is particularly important about the current methodological impasse is the extent to which it encourages and even provokes a rereading of the modernist canon in light of, indeed as, *the very expression of* its historical and aesthetic diversity.

On the other hand, a dissolving of the facile categorizations such as those between political/apolitical, subjective/objective, collectivist/individualist, or avant-garde/modernist should not and cannot mean a return to the ahistorical designations in which avant-garde and modernism are collapsed to encompass some general notion of the new or the experimental, the "writerly" or the semiotic. On the contrary, what the present collection of essays demonstrates is precisely the extent to which seemingly differing political and aesthetic articulations within German modernism find their linkages and interrelationships when seen as responses to shared experience and historical crisis.

All of which brings us to one central aspect of this volume, namely its face-off between variants of polyglot contemporary theory, on the one hand, and a distinctly *national* tradition on the other. As we look at the Weimar period, for instance, one of the things that makes the German case particularly significant is the role of expressionism rather than dada or *Neue Sachlichkeit* as *the* historical modernist movement par excellence. Viewed within a broader context, German dada was really a short-lived and in many ways anomalous phenomenon. By the time Richard Huelsenbeck "brought dada to Berlin" in 1917, the war and the rapidly evolving political events culminating in the Spartakus rebellion were driving the German dadaists either to the left into the cultural politics of the Communist Party or into seclusion.

In fact, one can even maintain that expressionism is significant as a case example for modernism precisely because it has never yielded to the facile categories and separations that have inevitably been imposed upon it; that as a multifaceted cultural explosion occurring around and within such major political events as World War I, postwar revolution, and civil war, it has steadfastly refused common denominators of classification, be they ideological, epistemological, or aesthetic. It is thus no accident that questions concerning the relation of expressionism to communicm and fascism have triggered fundamental disagreements concerning the nature of modernism that have dominated every area of cultural endeavor—whether that be film, painting, literature, or music; that the efforts of left or right cultural politicians to repudiate or appropriate it for their own cause have inevitably resulted in failure and contradiction. For instance, the famous Nazi exhibition of expressionist art as "entartete Kunst" in Munich in 1937 backfired into a celebration of its glories by an acclaiming public. Similarly, the Communist Party's attack on modernism in the now epochal expressionist debate waged in the journal *Das Wort* during the 1930s threatened to tear asunder the tenuous united front against fascism. In a less volatile context, it is significant to note the differing evaluations of Theodor W. Adorno, Bertolt Brecht, and Walter Benjamin as to the political nature of this movement. For Adorno, these artists were politically radical precisely because of their refusal of resolution or harmony and because their subjective response to the crisis of bourgeois reification drove them beyond subjectivity to reveal in the inner structure of form the increasing dominance of a repressive, instrumentally rationalized social whole. Brecht, on the other hand, repudiated the individualist stance of expressionist *Charakterköpfe* while at the same time embracing their aesthetic advances at the level of technical innovation. Benjamin likewise turned away from expressionist individualism to find in surrealism a collectivist alternative.

The point, of course, if not to resolve these disagreements by settling once and for all the question concerning expressionism's intrinsic political value. Such would remain at best a theoretical solution, which would not even begin to capture the relation of experience to aesthetic response. The point rather is to recast the question in order not only to accept expressionism as one exemplar of German modernism, but to claim its alleged anomaly for an expanded understanding of modernism's truly variegated nature.

Take the response to the experience of fascism. While Fredric Jameson in his study of Wyndham Lewis was one of the first to deal in a more differentiated way with the "modernist as fascist," even his paradigm was marked by the Lukácsian impulse—shared by those who agree or disagree with Lukács's individual evaluations of German expressionism or of Franz Kafka—to decide once and for all the question concerning the real nature of modernism's political orientation: in Lukács's formulation, whether it is or is not "realist." The present volume reveals the methodological irrelevance of such a quest.

For instance, Russell Berman's treatment of Ernst Jünger's texts finds them sharing basic values with what he calls liberal and epic forms of modernism: each proposes homologous alternatives to the terms of the bourgeois aesthetics of autonomy, that is, teleology, identity, and fictionality. This is not to argue that modernism is at heart fascist or Jünger really left-wing, but rather that a reading against the grain of ontologization finds in Jünger an author confronting a crisis of bourgeois culture with shared modernist conceptualizations about aesthetic autonomy, the crisis of culture, and the need for a collective aesthetic to solve that crisis. That his particular project resulted in a valorization of images over the written word illustrates *how* Jünger is able to arrive at an anti-Semitic, fascist ideological construct; it does not argue that he has to arrive there, or that his attack on "the word" is inherently fascist. After all, the left-wing theorist Béla Balázs, writing at approximately the same time, built a whole critical film theory valorizing visual representation over against what he called, quite disparagingly, the reifications of *Lesekultur* (reading culture).

In a similar vein, Peter Uwe Hohendahl's discussion of Gottfried Benn, one of Germany's prototypical modernist poets and the supposed litmus test for the congruity of fascism and modernism, also reveals a kind of undecidability in terms of established categories and traditional readings. In comparison to Hofmannsthal, George, Rilke, or other modernists, Benn would have to be placed in the camp of the avant-garde both because of textual gesture and because of his reception during the pre- and postwar period. And yet, like Brecht, he too never believed in the total sublation of art and life. Hohendahl's reading of the early Benn as a critic of reification suggests a political dimension to Benn's work that gets lost for those who would portray him merely as a self-reflective modernist or as displaying in his "primitivism" overtones of protofascism.

David Bathrick's treatment of the left expressionist Franz Jung and Schulte-Sasse's discussion of Carl Einstein reveal equal incongruities in terms of their supposed status within the left avant-garde. Whereas Jung's development has traditionally been viewed as the prototypical left-wing biography, moving from Munich bohemian modernism steeped in individualist *Lebensphilosophie* to left-expressionism around Franz Pfemfert's Berlin journal *Die Aktion* and then via a transitional dada phase on to Erwin Piscator's proletarian theater, a close reading of a "later" text indicates the extent to which psychoanalytical questions were still central to his notion of a total revolution; indeed, how his focus on the unconsious and upon "common experience" made the "subjective factor" the basis for a more differentiated concept of cultural revolution. But Bathrick's reading also discovers something else: namely, that viewed from the perspective of contemporary theory's questioning of traditional binary oppositions and ideological fictionalizations of subjectivity, Jung's depiction of pathological paranoia in the figure of Anton Gross is not simply a valorization of the outsider. Jung does not just romanticize a position of insight and resistance beyond language and immune from the societal and institutional framework in which it is embedded. His presentation of language as the iron cage within which one must speak is surprisingly consonant with contemporary notions of the power of discourse.

Similarly, Jochen Schulte-Sasse's reading of Carl Einstein's theoretical writings reveals the extent to which his earlier, more subject-centered epistemological rebellion against the reification of contemporary society gave way to an ever more sophisticated institutional critique of the system as a whole. Read through the prism of critical theory (Lyotard's essay on the "sublime" and Adorno and Horkheimer's *Dialectic of Enlightenment*), Schulte-Sasse demonstrates convincingly how the expressionist/modernist Einstein develops from within the conceptual premises of modernism both an epistemological critique of the dominant rationalist discourse and, in a subsequent revision of his earlier utopianism, a critique of modernism's own failure to avoid "diffusion" by virtue of being implicated institutionally in the discourse it wishes to subvert. Einstein as poststructuralist *avant la lettre*? Yes and no. Yes only if one understands the deconstructive process as an intervention that at one and the same time historicizes and materializes the discourse as a whole.

In her analysis of three modernist texts, Judith Ryan also looks to narrative language to elaborate a theory of avant-gardism that would go beyond merely a critique of bourgeois life or the institution of bourgeois art. Far more crucial to the avant-garde movements, she argues, is their explicit consciousness of their own ideologies. This may be the real test that distinguishes the avant-garde from other forms of modernism, which are generally self-conscious, but not ideologically so. Narratives that deconstruct the expectations traditional narratives arouse in readers provide a critique of the assumptions (about discrete subjects, about narratability or knowability, etc.) that are the ideological prerequisites for literature itself. For Ryan, it is not just the thematization of revolt as content that characterizes avant-gardism; not is it merely self-reflexive expression for the sake of expression. Rather, the challenge of the modernist text is political precisely in its assault upon traditional concepts of narrative consciousness such as causality in plot and unity of subject.

When one reflects upon experiences specific to modern life, invariably the city occupies a central space. From Baudelaire and Proust via Döblin and Dos Passos to Calvino and Pynchon, the experience of the metropolis has been crucial in shaping aesthetic perception and narrative articulation. In modernist literature as well as in the visual arts, the city clearly functions as the major challenge to traditional modes of representation and communication. In Part II, "Modernist Cities: Paris—New York—Berlin," Andreas Huyssen, Mark Anderson, and Klaus Scherpe discuss three major modernist novels in which city experiences are treated in radically different ways. At first sight, there does not seem to be much that unites Kafka's imaginary and essentially unlocalizable New York, Rilke's very real Paris, which produces a much more subjective, even autobiographic phantasmagoria, and Döblin's Berlin, which functions as a multilayered discursive space that both creates and swallows up the narrated subject, Franz Biberkopf. Nothing much seems to unite the main characters either. It is difficult to imagine any conversation between Malte Laurids Brigge, Karl Rossmann, and Franz Biberkopf on the subject of their experience of the city. And yet, similarities do emerge when one compares these novels to the discourse of the city in nineteenth-century novels. It seems clear that none of these modernist authors follows the traditional model of the narrated city, as Klaus Scherpe calls it, and as it characterizes city representations in realism or naturalism from Sue and Dickens to Zola and Heinrich Mann. The problems of country versus city, of the social effects of urbanization and industrialization, whether framed in terms of class struggle or in terms of the irreconcilability between the individual and the masses, are no longer central to these modernist texts. Nor are the more traditional reductive symbolizations of the metropolis as department store or whorehouse, as moloch or jungle, as battlefield of class struggle or testing ground for a heroic individuality. Instead, the focus is on problems of perception and vision, language and communication, with Rilke's emphasis on the uncanny and an individual poetic imaginary at one end of the spectrum, Döblin's subjectless and functionalist aesthetic at the other, and Kafka anywhere else but in the center. In different ways, the three essays in this section focus on this question of representation as crucial to the modernist aesthetic and they explore how the much-heralded crisis of representation and of language is linked to the modern city experience and to what one might call a metropolitan imagination.

The final section of the book, entitled "Writing and Modernist Thought," discusses three major writers and critics, none of whom could be claimed for an apolitical and canonical high modernism and all of whom actually insisted on the radical heterogeneity of the modernist project. In Lou Andreas-Salomé's case, this insistence springs from her subject position as woman and the attendant criticism of the totalizing aspects of Freudian psychoanalysis, one of the theoretical master-narratives of modernism itself. As Biddy Martin argues persuasively, Salomé developed an alternative articulation of gender and narcissism within the Freudian paradigm that links her in interesting ways to more recent discussions of the politics of subjectivity, sexuality, and gender in their relation to questions of language and form. Martin uses the case of Salomé to challenge the all-too-simple opposition of a political feminism, derived from the tradition of political enlightenment and allegedly caught in what it opposes, and a self-referential deconstructive notion of femininity that rejects any and all politics of representation.

The final two essays on Ernst Bloch's *Spuren* and the figure of the collector in Walter Benjamin are actually closely connected. Klaus Berghahn describes the Bloch of this work of short prose pieces as a collector of the minute details of everyday life, a collector of the trash of history. Bloch's subversion of the high modernist project begins at the level of the text itself. His dialectical *Denkbilder*, Klaus Berghahn argues, appropriate this Benjaminian anti-genre to combine everyday narratives from the garbage pit of popular culture with philosophical commentary so as to make the prose of life visible and readable. Theory, prose, and image, avant-garde and mass culture, Hegel and Karl May—the philosophical flaneur's montages are as rich in perception as they are disdainful of the high modernist prerequisites of aesthetic unity and cultural coherence. In his focus on Bloch's technique of constructing thought images, Berghahn discusses this specific form of modernist prose as a kind of small-scale epic montage, tied to the avant-gardist project of closing the gap between high art and popular culture. Perhaps the Ernst Bloch of *Spuren* can be seen as a modernist storyteller. At the same time, one would have to recognize that both storytelling and its social function have undergone a fundamental transformation if compared with the storyteller of premodern times so vividly evoked in one of Benjamin's seminal essays.

Benjamin, finally, one of the key voices within German modernist thought, always maintained the tensions in his work between Marxism and Jewish messianism, between a relentless advocacy of the march of modernity and an intense longing for a kind of *Erfahrung* that modernization itself seemed to have obliterated. Where Berghahn analyzes a specific genre of short prose, to which Benajmin—like Brecht, Musil, Adorno, and others—contributed in those years, Ackbar Abbas discusses Benjamin's figure of the collector as a fundamentally contradictory figure within modernity. The collector, whose gaze is turned to the past, even to the eventual pastness of the present, seems to fall outside of the parameters of modernity's privileging the present, the new. And yet, it is precisely the culture of modernity itself that creates the collector as a type, as one who preserves experience in the objects he collects, for a time when authentic experience no longer seems possible, when only a semblance of experience is still possible via the collected objects. Just as in Benjamin's work the figure of the storyteller stands back to back with that of the operative avant-gardist writer or the author as producer, the collector, as Abbas shows, is tied back to back to the modernist. For Abbas, the figure of the collector becomes a paradigmatic figure of modernity, one who tells us more about the fate of experience in modernity than the celebrated figure of the flaneur. The gaze of the collector at the object is, in Abbas's words, not one of mastery but one that opens the object up to interpretation. The flaneur is located in a present, the present of modernity; the collector finds himself in a position of posteriority, a position of desire and fascination vis-à-vis the unfulfilled promises the objects hold.

In a certain sense one might suggest that we today are in the position of the collector vis-à-vis the texts of modernism. Modernism has become a tradition, much of it already forgotten, much of it reified beyond recognition or reduced to pop cliché. Like Benjamin's collector, we too stand at a crossroads, looking to a past, telling a story with the texts from that past. Rereading as collecting, collecting as producing a new gaze at the objects, a gaze that refuses to subject the object to preconceived notions, a gaze that opens up the texts of the past to the queries of the present and discovers new visions, new layers in a body of works that remains as alive as ever.

PART I

The Avant-Garde:
Politics and the Text

Speaking the Other's Silence: Franz Jung's *Der Fall Gross*

David Bathrick

Some if not most American readers will never have heard of Franz Jung—not to speak of *Der Fall Gross*. And for that reason mv'initial strategy will be to exploit this ignorance in order to construct and reconstruct several biographies—of a literary text and of its authors—and in so doing to reflect upon the reasons for their somewhat bizarre status within the pantheon of the Weimar avant-garde. Of central concern will be what such constructions tell us about the modernist/avant-garde canon itself; and why the more recent rediscoveries of Jung, first in the early 1970s as a left radical and more recently as a classic of literary modernism, have inevitably foundered upon the methodological grounds of their self-proclaimed rescue operation.

But first let us outline, if only briefly, Jung's biography. And to that end there is nothing like the Marxist-Leninist-Maoist rendition of a poor soul's *Bildungsweg* to political edification. It is provided in this instance by Walter Fähnders and Martin Rektor, who in a chapter devoted entirely to Jung in their *Linksradikalismus und Literatur* (1974)[1] mark the pathstones of this classical left radical biography from petty-bourgeois expressionist to his finding of the Proletariat.

Born in 1888 in Neiße, Jung went to Munich in 1911 where as a writer and bohemian he involved himself in the anarchist politics of Erich Mühsam's "Gruppe Tat" and immediately became a devotee of the left Freudian Otto Gross. It was the writings and political practice of Gross in particular, an amalgam of anarchism and psycho-analysis, of Landauer and Freud, that were to influence an entire generation of expressionist writers in their antiauthoritarian struggles against partriarchy. And it was Gross as a friend whose close collaboration with Jung theoretically defined the latter's creative work in this his expressionist phase. Jung's novels and writings of this period reflect strongly the themes of artist individuals in their struggles against authority and for community, and in so doing articulate politically what Fähnders and Rektor call his "flight into Bohemia."[2] Franz Jung's move to Berlin in 1913 saw a broadening of political perspective. His desertion from the army after a brief stint of military service led to imprisonment for six months, during and after which time he was a regular contributor to Franz Pfemfert's left expressionist journal *Die Aktion*. Jung's further involvement in the antiwar movement and the increasingly politicized atmosphere of the industrial metropolis included affiliation with the Berlin dadaists, involvement with Erwin Piscator's proletarian theater, active participation in the Spartakus uprisings and the workers' movement, brief membership in the KPD (Communist Party of Germany), and finally to the founding, together with Franz Pfemfert, of the left oppositional Communist Workers' Party, the KAPD. It was during this later period that he both wrote his major proletarian plays and novels and also managed to pirate a ship to the Soviet Union, where he met with Lenin in an effort to get recognition for the KAPD.

Little wonder then that such a biography would lend itself ideally to an almost hagiographic presentation of Jung as a model for left radicalism. A listing of the signifiers alone tells the story of an artistic and political transformation embedded in the telos of revolutionary history: from the bohemian *Kunststadt* Munich to proletarian Berlin, from Freudian id to Marxian superego, from narcissistic individualism to the enrichments of the collective, from expressionism via dada to revolutionary-proletarian drama. And all that within ten brief years.

While the recounting of such a dramatic narrative, as with all vanguard narratives, is at one level quite true, one need not probe too deeply to find fissures, to observe the neatness of it all begin to crumble. For instance, Jung's obsession with psychoanalysis and the theories of Otto Gross, as the dates of his works attest, does not diminish during his later "revolutionary" period, nor is it, as Fähnders and Rektor would have us believe, subsumed and *aufgehoben* under the larger rubric of proletarian politics. For instance, his major theoretical work entitled *Technik des Glücks,* with its Bachofian plea for matriarchy as the basis for any new society and its anarchistic call for the abolition of *all* political states, is clearly an elaboration of ideas that come straight out of the Munich phase, just as *Der Fall Gross,* published in 1920, is a direct attempt to realize the political dimensions of the psychoanalytic relationship in the writing of the modernist text. In fact, the very disjuncture between the Marxian and, if you will, the Freudian Jung, the bifurcation of style and strategy—proletarian realism on the one side, psychoanalytic modernism on the other—speaks profoundly to the struggles and contradictions of both the Jungian project, and our reconstructions of it. The subsequent reading by Fähnders and Rector of a linear path from Freud to Marx, with its attendant repression of the unresolved conflict between Freud and Marx, is itself a latter-day manifestation of a larger problem: namely, the need inherent when constructing the avant-garde prototype to reduce complexity and aporia to the monolithic truth of one deep structure.

But let us move on to our second biography, that of *Der Fall Gross,* as a text with its own history embedded in a larger history. And to tell this story we must return to Otto Gross and to 1913. Certainly *Der Fall Gross* by Franz Jung reverberates with associations at the level of names alone. For instance, it is important to establish initially that although the Gross in the title is not Otto, but the engineer Anton W. Gross, Otto is clearly in the center of the text at a number of levels. The main character in question was a psychoanalytic patient of Otto Gross at an asylum in Troppau, Austria, and the latter's written analysis of the case forms one of the seminal texts upon which Jung based his telling. More important, Otto Gross was at Troppau not as an analyst but as a patient, having been arrested and commited there by his father Hans Gross, a famous Austrian scholar of criminology. Angry at his son's irresponsible use of drugs and notorious treatment of patients, the father enjoined the Berlin police to abduct Otto from the house of Franz Jung and illegally transport him over the German-Austrian border. The struggle for his release immediately became a cause célèbre for expressionist and left-wing intellectuals throughout the land, who saw in Otto's imprisonment a symbolic reenactment of the worst forms of patriarchal authoritarianism by the older, Wilhelminian generation. Not surprisingly, Franz Jung orchestrated the successful campaign for Gross's liberation and it was on the occasion of Otto's release that Jung met Anton and became acquainted with his case. Clearly, Otto Gross's fascination with and subsequent analysis of the paranoiac Anton was a clear case of projection compulsion, by a man who himself had once been analyzed by Carl Gustav Jung as having severe moments of paranoia.

Carl Gustav Jung? The name adds another intriguing nominal association, which in turn necessitates further explication in the development of our text, another important accretion in the complicated genesis of this tiny novella. Otto Gross and C. G. Jung were both students of Freud at the turn of the century, and it was Freud who referred Gross to Jung after Otto's first major breakdown in 1907. It was also during this period that Gross was to launch a critique of Freud that came to mark the broadening differences between the two and to establish Gross as the progenitor of a left-Freudian tradition, which anticipated such later figures as Wilhelm Reich and Herbert Marcuse.

While Gross shared with Freud and Jung basic premises concerning the importance of psychoanalysis and the primacy of sexuality as a locus of psychic disturbance, he also went on to argue that the cause of such disturbances must ultimately be attributed to the demands made by "larger social organizations." This relocation of emphasis from a natural to a social scientific grounding of psychoanalysis drove Gross eventually to a further articulation of three major positions that were to earn him enmity and eventual ostracism from the entire psychoanalytic community.

The first concerned his revision of Freud's instinct theory. Where Freud saw the repression of instinct by reason as the precondition of civilization, Gross denied that aggressive behavior and the closely related phenomena of sadism and masochism were instinctual in the species. The aggressive-sadistic character of the male and the passive masochism of women, far from innate, were to be attributed to deformation by the existing organizations of society, in particular the male-dominated bourgeois family. Monogamous marriage, Gross provocatively asserted ahead of his time, was founded upon principles of legalized rape, the subjugation of women, and the destruction of children.

This historicizing of Freudian instinct theory and concomitant critique of the authoritarian family, anticipating in many respects a similar position later developed by the Frankfurt School, led Gross to expand his theory into a critique of the cultural premises for patriarchal domination in Western society as a whole. Inner psychological conflict, he argued, is the struggle of one's nature against the internalized values of a repressive society bound on crushing that nature (*Der Kampf des Eigenen gegen das Fremde*). But unlike the Frankfurt School, which saw no alternative to internalization for the formation of a healthy critical ego, Gross called for an overthrow of all male-dominated institutions and a return to matriarchy, to a social order in which the male will to power would be supplanted by a "will to love and relationships."

And how to bring about such a society? Gross's final revision of Freud was clearly his most controversial one and concerned the role of psychoanalysis in the process of revolutionary struggle. If the penultimate seat of oppression lies beyond and below the economic and political infrastructures of the given social order in the internalization of norms, then the struggle for a new society must begin with the resistance to such norms at the moment of their socialization—and for that there was needed a new, revolutionary psychoanalysis. "The psychology of the unconscious is the philosophy of revolution; it has been called to become the ferment of revolt within the psyche, as the liberation of an individuality bound by its own unconscious."[3] Where Freud grounded the therapeutic process in the relationship between psychoanalyst and patient, in which the latter would be led to adjust, Gross called for a social therapy to attack the order that brought the illness about. For him the psychoanalytic relationship reproduced the very authority patterns that had caused the problem in the first place. It was from there but a step to a sexual politics aggressively advocating free love, communes, and orgies, one that earned him opprobrium and finally ostracism from friend and foe on the left and the right.

Having reviewed the central tenets of Gross's theory and perused the impact of his thoughts and life upon a generation, we are now in a better position to understand how Jung's *Der Fall Gross,* published in the same year as Otto's death owing to an overdose of drugs and starvation on the streets of Berlin, clearly reverberates back upon a whole series of events, debates, and ideological gestures that cluster around the myth of Otto Gross during and after World War I. The case of Otto Gross was a political rallying cry for an entire generation, mirroring "the contrast between bohemian and bourgeois, expressionism and Wilhelminian 'Zeitgeist,' son and father, psychoanalysis and psychiatry."[4]

But what, one might rightly ask, does all this have to do with the text in question and the problem of the avant-garde? Haven't we really taken an unconscionable digression, seeing that the hero of our story is Anton and not Otto? In the following, I shall indicate the ways in which the whole political "meaning" of the persona Otto Gross provides us with a historical and philosophical mediation for understanding this text in its context—the connective glue that holds together its disparate political and aesthetic parts.

If we look first at the narrative strategy of the text itself, we note how the discourse of psychoanalysis and the psychoanalytic relationship are central to its constitution. In fact, Jung's initial knowledge of Anton Gross came from a detailed case report by Otto Gross, which was later published in an essay entitled *Drei Aufsätze über den inneren Konflikt.*[5] Otto's narrative reconstructs a world of imagined persecution and paranoia. While living in New York, the engineer Anton Gross begins to hallucinate that he is suspected of a series of sex crimes, which are being committed throughout the city. After months of increasing imagined persecution, during which time he moves from city to city, withdraws from public life, and experiences even a physical assault upon his person, Anton boards a ship to return to Europe. Here he experiences further surveillance and harassment, and upon arrival in Germany retreats to an obscure hotel, where he barricades himself in a small room in a desperate attempt to escape his tormentors. The end result is a shoot-out with the police that leads to Anton being wounded and subsequently admitted to Troppau. Here the plot thickens. Anton believes that the director of the asylum is in reality the head of a band of persecutors called telepathics who are abducting women to deep catacombs under the earth and who wanted to kill Anton because he knew their secret. At the conclusion of his report, Otto offers the following diagnosis: Anton is a sadist who in his psychosis fulfills his unconscious sadistic desires. That Anton also reveals signs of masochism shows that he has tried to escape from his sadism into the opposite sexual feelings.

Franz Jung uses the Anton material, which consists of Otto's report and Anton's own descriptive notes, to produce two fictional versions of the Gross case. The first, entitled *Die Telepathen,* published in 1914, remains close to Otto's case report and even incorporates some of its language. The second version, *Der Fall Gross,* relies much more heavily on Anton's writings and traces the beginning of Anton's persecution to his life in Poland prior to leaving for the United States. More importantly, it clearly indicates a shift in narrative strategy. Whereas in the earlier version we are given a much more objective, analytical, if not psychoanalytical third-person account of Anton's struggles, in which the narrator himself remains seemingly impartial to the information conveyed, *Der Fall Gross* condemns such a stance from the very outset: "I must say that today I condemn my earlier attitude. Perhaps something could have been done."[6] *Der Fall Gross* then is not just a second version, it is a confrontation with, a rewriting of, the first in which the author employs a bifurcated narrative strategy in order to enhance the political significance of what he is telling.

Through one of the modes of narration, we experience a diminishing of authorial presence and overview in the careful recounting of Anton's plight. Jung's *erlebte Rede* in the inner narration leaps over the bounds separating narrator from narrated to recreate in *total* detail the complicated but absolutely logical and consistent web of occurrences in Anton's life. I offer an example: "In the Wirtshaus owned by Barbara Schreiner on Bretterplatz in Bielitz-Biala, Anton is made drunk by a swig of wine so that a big fight erupts with the Herzlikas, the Werners, and a Seidel, who is standing behind the bar. A legal clerk with very thick glasses and slightly built jumps between them but was unable to help—according to Anton, a brother of their former maid, who belonged to the Rosenkranz club and whose two brothers looked very much like the Seidels: one of them had stolen 40 Kroner from Anton the last time he was at home."[7]

Although using the third person, and punctuating his account with such phrases as "according to Anton," the narrator here is at one with Anton, refusing to weed out irrelevant data from the confusing wealth of reported trivia, meticulously withholding judgment as to the potential hallucinatory nature of what is being told. Jung later acknowledged that the writing of the story was an attempt to express "what Anton could not release from his consciousness in order to put into words. The inner tension, prior to the formation of the word, had overcome him."[8] On the occasion of their brief and only meeting at Troppau, Jung remarks on Anton's inability to express himself verbally: "An actual conversation never took place. Anton Gross spoke too quickly, the words just tumbled out, I could only understand half of what he said."[9]

Der Fall Gross represents Jung's effort to speak Anton's silence. Freud has written of the paranoiac that he builds up the world, "not more splendid, it is true, but at least so that he can once more live in it. He builds it up by the work of his delusions (*Wahnarbeit*). *The delusion-formation, which we take to be a pathological product, is in reality an attempt at recovery, a process of reconstruction* (Freud's emphasis)."[10] Jung's faithful reconstruction of Anton's belabored scribblings narratively reenacts the latter's *Wahnarbeit*. And Freud is right; it is indeed not a splendid world, fragmented and hopelessly bureaucratic in its convoluted structures and entanglements—but it is inhabitable.

It is also painfully familiar—as the narrator reminds us at the outset—and this is where Jung's retelling adds a Weberian touch to Freud. In an analysis of Anton's original "notations," Günter Bose and Erich Brinkmann have asserted that the counterpoint to them can be found in the organizational matrix of police files. From very different starting points, both are concerned with the burden of proof. "The matrix of expression that this demand adheres to is no longer centered on an axis point, which explicitly or implicitly is called I or author, but rather is bound to a meta-logic, whose anonymous subject links up the terms of a logical marshaling of evidence."[11] Jung's *Der Fall Gross* elaborates a metonymic discourse that indeed engulfs and diminishes the individual subject. What emerges is a power web of "metalogic" in which the impulse to produce proof consumes the very subjectness that would be constituted by it. Its mimetic moment articulates at the level of language the Byzantine entrapments of the Weberian iron cage in which mediations have been destroyed, in which fragment produces fragment, in which the prisonhouse is not that of language per se but that of the language of reification.

The narrative technique in *Der Fall Gross* is particularly interesting for the way it situates itself within the larger spectrum of modernism in the Weimar period. Its representation of insanity and psychosis differs significantly from many other such presentations within the European avant-garde tradition.[12] For the German expressionists, such as Ernst Stadler, Johannes R. Becher, Carl Einstein, Georg Heym, etc., the figure of the insane came to be identified with forms of social ostracism or outsiderness. This delination of psychopathic otherness took on both positive and negative representations.[13] The figure of the mad artist or genius, for instance, was often seen to transcend the status quo, to posess a special kind of perception that in its opposition to the hated bourgeois represented all that was hopeful or utopian about a new and emerging human being. In 1914, Wieland Herzfelde wrote in *Die Aktion* that "the mentally ill are artistically gifted. Their works show a more or less unexplained but honest sense for the beautiful and appropriate."[14]

Conversely, the psychopath also became an emblem for the existential suffering of social ostracism, for otherness as a locus of Angst or alienation from which to sense one's calling as a member of the downtrodden. The expressionist Ludwig Rubiner numbers "religious lunatics" among "the scum, the offal, the despised," who make up what he called the "holy mob."[15] Whether positive or negative, the expressionist avant-garde model for madness itself contained at its core a basic dualism that has marked the discourse on the insane since the appearance of asylums in the fifteenth century. On the one side, we find the theoretical and practical reason of the bourgeois, with an assumption of absolute normalcy; opposed to that, the madman as its incarnate negation. "As for a common language," writes Foucault, "there is no such thing; or rather there is no such thing any longer; the constitution of madness as a mental illness, at the end of the eighteenth century, affords the evidence of a broken dialogue, posits the separation as already effected, and thrusts into oblivion all those stammered, imperfect works without fixed syntax in which the exchange between madness and reason was made."[16]

In *Der Fall Gross* Jung seeks to renegotiate the broken link from within. By recreating the paranoiac discourse itself and thus participating in the "building up" of Anton's world, Jung has shifted the focus from subject to language. In so doing, he moves away from those romanticizations of madness that have characterized the avant-

garde. We no longer have two worlds, two languages, two ontolog-
ically separated systems of subjectivity. Here the subject himself constitutes and is constituted by the language system as a whole. What
evolves out of such a narrative strategy is a very different kind of
modernist text with a very different message about madness and pathology. In place of literary innovations such as paratactic speech,
unconnected exclamations, etc., all of which simulate the language
of the insane and suggest the affinity among insanity, textual exper-
imentation, and genius, we find ourselves here immersed and engulfed . . . and struggling within the discourse of the everyday. The
clear-cut bounds between reason and unreason have been dissolved
in language as they have in the social world. The experience of reification, of anxiety, of persecution is not something reserved for the
outsider, but is registered as the experience of quotidian modernity.
Thus in keeping with the teachings of Otto Gross, Jung has recreated
narratively the link between neurosis and societal deformation. There
is no text outside and beyond, just as there are no longer pathological
outsiders to speak it. As the narrator makes very clear at the outset,
"The threat to existence in everyday life marches on. In this seemingly simple draughtsman of the Garrison foundry in East Pittsburgh
there unravels the fate of everyone, to be threatened in the nets of a
band of robbers and murderers, whom no one knows and whose
crumbling effect everyone can hear every day of their life."[17]

In our reading of his paranoiac reconstruction, we have stressed
that the narrator is not just a teller but a listener as well. In order to
speak the other's silence, he has had to be able to hear it. The relationship between Jung/narrator and Anton is at one level of its
structure a psychoanalytic one. For as we have seen from the Freud
quotation, "The delusion-formation, which we take to be a pathological product, is in reality an attempt at recovery, a process of reconstruction." But is must also be stressed that the narrative strategy
employed in *Der Fall Gross* is not only one of reconstruction; the
case of the draughtsman Anton Gross is not just a literary illustration
of Freudian *Wahnarbeit*. The Gross case is part of a polemical, political project as well. Through its articulation of fury and engage-
ment, we see the text expand and break out of the bonds of its psychoanalytic discourse in order to enter upon the terrain of revolutionary
struggle.

Repeatedly, the narrator interrupts his detailed narrative to register his rage at what is unfolding before him and his solidarity with the beleaguered Anton. "All of us may indeed just be pigs, but at least we ought to experience the suffering of another. The torturings of a friend eat into your brain and rip your bones apart."[18] In the course of the text, these narrative interjections become longer and more prevalent, and increasingly lack direction. "Tell me with whom you consort and I will tell you who you are. A coward. . . . If someone murders a woman, he works faster than when he marries her. The tempo of the work is everything."[19] The final exhortation raises the fate of Anton to the level of manifesto: "There's no sense in spinning out the tale of Anton Gross any further. I assume he has kicked the bucket in some corner. That is not the important thing.—Wait! But rather: That terror finally reign triumphant That everyone continually smash himself in the jaw That a power be unleashed from one to the next to a third"[20]

The bifurcated narrative voice of *Der Fall Gross* articulates the gap between the individual victim of oppression and those who would help overcome it. Nestled in this gap, in its most elemental and inchoate form, lies a fundamental challenge to avant-gardism: how to negotiate at the most personal level the move from individual to societal revolt. The attempt and finally the failure to solve the paranoiac crisis within the therapeutic framework of Freudian *Wahnarbeit* is nevertheless a prerequisite step in making conscious the need to explode outward.

In an essay written commemorating the work of Otto Gross, Franz Jung characterized his own goal as wanting to transform Otto's "technique of thinking" from a means of therapy to a weapon for attack—"not in order to help or to heal, but in order to destroy . . . to destroy the obstacles that stand in the way of human happiness."[21] The "obstacles" to which Jung refers are the internalizations of societal power. "The decisive element is not the organization," he wrote, "decisive is one's belief in it, the construction of authority in the life of the lonely individual (*Einsamkeitsleben des Einzelnen*), the will to allow oneself to be dominated. Absolutely vital is the technique of casting off one's own fetters."[22]

What was important for Jung about Otto Gross's technique of thinking" and the notion of revolutionary psychoanalysis was that it offered a means by which to negotiate the link between societal and personal liberation. The role of analysis was not to "cure" individual neuroses or delusions, Jung argued, but to make unbearably conscious the searing connection between collective and individual suffering and thereby provide the individual a means "to work on the total process, to commit his life, that is, his continually becoming conscious, and in so doing to experience himself."[23]

In the wake of Reich, Marcuse, Adorno, and the Frankfurt School, Jung's somewhat watered-down pop version of Gross's considerably more sophisticated theories sounds neither very profound as a theory of human behavior nor even very convincing as a strategic program for revolutionary struggle. However, what Jung *does* draw together under the rubric of the unconscious and psychoanalysis is a constellation of concerns and themes that speak directly to the political-cultural avant-garde as it was emerging in and around the communist parties at an absolutely crucial moment of development in the period between 1917 and 1921.

The first concern dealt with making use of revolutionary psychoanalytical principles at the level of the production of the avant-garde text. Here it must be emphasized that Franz Jung was not the only artist to be influenced by Gross's theories. In 1915 he and Richard Öhring founded a journal called *Die Freie Straße*. Its collaborators included the dadaist sculptor and poet Raoul Hausmann, the painter Georg Schrimpf, and Otto Gross, whose psychoanalytical writings were already having a profound influence upon the entire dada movement. Hausmann called Gross "the psychological basis for dada" and was himself instrumental in bringing the Grossian notions of the "opening up of the unconscious" into theoretical discussions about art and literature. Both in the simultaneity of fragmented sound basic to the dada *Lautgedicht* and in the broken montage of the dadaist paintings, Hausmann argued, there is evoked a thrust into the realm of the precategorical, "which is the only valid form of communication as something commonly experienced."[24] Hausmann's use of the term "commonly experienced" (*gemeinsam erlebt*) is an obvious borrowing from the Grossian system. The montage artwork, he wants to say, reorganizes and breaks through the commodifications of everyday representations to release repressed potential for shared experience and community. This use of Gross and psychoanalysis to understand the formal principles of dada as a critique of instrumental representations and as a means for igniting a shared unconscious provided Hausmann and Jung with the psychoanalytical starting point for the juncture between individual and society at the level of the avant-garde text itself.

In *Der Fall Gross* the montage of bifurcated narrative culminates in a gap, in a disjuncture, out of which explodes rebellion. The carefully constructed pieces of the *Wahnarbeit* reach a breaking point in which the analytical discourse breaks down and opens up into revolt. In this way, the modernist literary text transcends the overly objective, narrowly contoured bounds of official psychoanalytical discourse. Jung's work is at once a call for revolt and a critique of the discourse of categories and analysis, which in its scientistic manner of speaking the other's silence contributes to its repressions.

But all this has broader implications as well, which brings us to our second major point concerning the confluence of psychoanalysis and political revolution. Jung and Hausmann's use of Gross and Freud at the textual level was expanded in their political writings into a strategy for analysis and organizational work. What was common to both men was the conviction that the communist revolution then apparently in progress would remain dangerously incomplete if it did not expand the economic sphere into the personal and the sexual. In Hausmann, the Freudian and Marxian revolutions had to go together. "The world economic revolution alone is insufficient," he wrote in 1919, "the total condition of man in the psycho-physical sense must be fundamentally changed. . . . The doctrine of Freud (and Adler) is ultimately as important as a means for the understanding of petty-bourgeois individualist society as the economic doctrine of Marx-Engels."[25]

In Jung's writings of the same period, it was also clear that the psychoanalytic question was absolutely vital both as a critique of existing notions of social change and as a means to conceive of the new society. As a critique of Marxism and socialism in the 1920s, it served to thematize questions of subjectivity and psychic need that were being ignored by the more economistic policies of both the communist and social democratic parties. In this regard, his efforts to theorize a collective, psychological realm of experience (*Erlebnis*) and community (*Gemeinschaft*) anticipated in fundamental ways Oskar Negt and

Alexander Kluge's later theoretical elaboration of proletarian "experience" as the basis for a postbourgeois public sphere. Experience (*Erfahrung*) in their definition, much in the spirit of Jung, meant areas of life beyond the realm of industrial production or organizational party life that would encompass such things as sexuality, psychic structures, individual needs, fantasy, etc.—a *Lebenszusammenhang*, which, while stunted by capitalist incursion, would nevertheless provide the socio-psychic basis for forms of total political resistance.[26]

It has been my contention that Jung's political writings, a vague and undifferentiated amalgam of Otto Gross, J. J. Bachofen, and Karl Marx, derive their significance more as a critique of existing left theory and practices than as a blueprint for a better world. In the spirit of that insight, let us return to Jung and the literary text *Der Fall Gross*, using both to draw together some concluding critical generalizations about the "historical" cultural avant-garde in Germany between 1914 and 1922.

The first point to be made is that starting even within the prewar expressionist avant-garde, one notes from several quarters a certain tension if not outright hostility toward the discourse of psychoanalysis. For instance, in 1914 the left expressionist-anarchist Ludwig Rubiner, in a series of articles published in *Die Aktion*, ridiculed the theories of Otto Gross and suggested that psychoanalysis was effeminate and useless. "Take a look at whom psychoanalysis really affects: not creative (*gesetzgebenden*—lawgiving) people. But rather those into whose life nature can intervene; impressionistic artists, people who love the sea, and women,"[27] Rubiner's bravado not only reveals a phallocentric bias remarked upon often of late as characteristic of historical avant-gardism but locates as well a coalescence of otherness that on occasion has led an uneasy existence in the value system of the avant-garde. The feminine, the natural, the mimetic—linked by Rubiner with psychoanalysis and subjectivity—stand, not only in Rubiner's mind, as incompatible with the more instrumental (think of constructivism), antipsychological (think of Brecht), productivistic (think of *Neue Sachlichkeit*) features of historical avant-gardism. Hence the Jung/Gross critique of the patriarchal dimensions of established socialism finds its corollary culturally in an unmasking of similar structural biases even within the framework of experimental avant-gardism.

All of which brings us back to the literary work of Franz Jung and to *Der Fall Gross*. As we have already noted, the reception of Jung's own work reveals similar tensions and unresolved antinomies. Where his Marxist critics look to Jung's psychoanalytic writings as temporally early, and ideologically bohemian in comparison with the writing of the materialistically centered work of the "red years," more recent Lacanian and literary modernist readings have sought to invert the paradigm, and heap praise on his literary "modernism." In both cases, the definition of avant-gardism is taken out of its context to be judged in accordance with an abstract system. *Der Fall Gross* offers perhaps the best example of this. For the Maoists Fähnders and Rektor, its forms of protest and resistance, because they emerge from the experience of an individual, result in *freischwebende Radikalität* (free-floating radicality) rather than concrete political action. On the other side of the ledger, it can also be noted that for years this text was read *in isolation* as an example of "expressionist prose" anthologized in a volume with the title *Ego und Eros: Meisterwerke des Expressionismus* (Ego and Eros: Masterworks of Expressionism).[28]

As an important counter to both these receptions, it should be kept in mind that *Der Fall Gross* appeared in the journal *Die Erde* in 1920 at a time and in a place where the whole question of combining individual and collective, sexual and economic, Marxian and Freudian revolution was of central concern. At the center of this turmoil was the figure of Otto Gross.[29]

And what, finally, did Otto represent? Most profoundly, perhaps, a repudiation of any political avant-gardism that would exclude the individual, the idiosyncratic, the psychological—the other—from the realm of the political. Positively, a notion of avant-gardism that would locate the cutting edge of the new at the intersection of the individual and society. Whether such a position offers ultimately a self-critique of the avant-garde or some "post" variant thereof was not for Gross or Jung to decide. One assumes they didn't even care.

Notes

1. Walter Fähnders and Martin Rektor, *Linksradikalismus und Literatur* (Hamburg: Rowohlt, 1974).

2. *Ibid.*, 165.

3. Otto Gross, "Zur Überwindung der kulturellen Krise," in Otto Gross, *Von geschlechtlicher Not zur sozialen Katastrophe*, ed. Kurt Kreiler (Frankfurt am Main: Robinson, 1980), 13.

4. Thomas Anz, ed. *Phantasien über den Wahnsinn: Expressionistische Texte* (Munich: Carl Hanser, 1980), 43.

5. Otto Gross, *Drei Aufsätze über den inneren Konflikt* (Bonn, 1920).

6. Franz Jung, *Der Fall Gross*, in *Gott verschläft die Zeit: Frühe Prosa*, ed. Klaus Ramm (Munich: Edition Text + Kritik, 1980), 78.

7. *Ibid.*, 242.

8. Franz Jung, *Akzente II*, in *Gross/Jung/Grosz*, ed. Günter Bose and Erich Brinkmann (Berlin: Bose & Brinkmann, 1980), 244.

9. *Ibid.*, 242.

10. Sigmund Freud, *General Psychological Theory* (New York: Macmillan, 1963), 41.

11. Günter Bose and Erich Brinkmann, "Paranoiawelt," in *Grosz/Jung/Grosz*, 184.

12. For an excellent discussion of the relation between artistic creation and madness, see the chapter entitled "The Mad as Artist" in Sander L. Gilman, *Difference and Pathology: Stereotypes of Sexuality, Race and Madness* (Ithaca: Cornell University Press, 1985), 217–39.

13. A number of these distinctions are worked out carefully in: Thomas Anz, *Literatur der Existenz: Literarische Psychopathographie und ihre soziale Bedeutung im Frühexpressionismus* (Stuttgart: Metzler, 1977).

14. *Die Aktion*, (October 24, 1919): 1251.

15. Ludwig Rubiner, "Man in the Center," in *An Anthology of German Expressionist Drama: Prelude to the Absurd*, ed. Walter H. Sokel (Garden City, N.Y.: Doubleday, 1963), 4.

16. Michel Foucault, *Madness and Civilization: A History of Insanity in the Age of Reason* (New York: Random House, 1965), x.

17. Jung, *Der Fall Gross*, 78.

18. *Ibid.*, 84.

19. *Ibid.*, 95.

20. *Ibid.*, 98.

21. Franz Jung, "Von geschlechtlicher Not zur sozialen Katastrophe," in *Grosz/Jung/Grosz*, 108.

22. *Ibid.*, 137.

23. *Ibid.*, 124.

24. Raoul Hausmann, "Synthetisches Cino der Malerei," in *Dada Berlin: Texte, Manifeste, Aktionen*, ed. Carl Riha (Stuttgart: Reclam, 1977), 31.

25. Raoul Hausmann, "Schnitt durch die Zeit," *Die Erde* (October 1, 1919): 542–43.

26. See Oskar Negt and Alexander Kluge, *Öffentlichkeit und Erfahrung:*

Zur Organisationsanalyse von bürgerlicher und proletarischer Öffentlichkeit (Neuwied and Berlin: Luchterhand, 1972).

27. *Die Aktion* (May 7, 1913): 483.

28. Ed. Karl Otten (Stuttgart: Gouverts, 1963), 201–20.

29. Gross's programmatic essay "Protest and Morality in the Unconscious" was published in *Die Erde* in December of 1919.

Carl Einstein; or, The Postmodern Transformation of Modernism

Jochen Schulte-Sasse

In slightly altering the distinction between "the nostalgia for presence felt by the human subject" and "the jubilation which result[s] from the invention of new rules of the game" that Jean-François Lyotard attempted in his essay "Answering the Question: What Is Postmodernism?" I would like to distinguish between two modes of aesthetic modernism. Both modes presuppose a radical critique of social modernity, particularly of the instrumentalization of reason and language in the course of the civilizing process, of the alienation of people from one another, of the development of increasingly agonistic identities, and so on. But while one mode of artistic response intersperses nostalgic, utopian images of a better, reconciled world into its critique of civilization, the other insists on the necessity of an epistemological critique from within existing discourses and on the development of a deconstructive rhetorical praxis that can breach those discourses. Among the examples he cites, Lyotard locates "on the side of melancholia, the German Expressionists, and on the side of *novatio* Braque and Picasso."[1]

Both of these modes of aesthetic reaction to social modernism have existed ever since early German romanticism, with the first one dating back to the enlightenment. In spite of its historicophilosophical conception of itself, the "side of melancholia," of "nostalgia for presence felt by the human subject," has always tended to offer merely compensatory aesthetic experiences in the functionally differentiated world of capitalism. Friedrich Schlegel saw the difference quite clearly when he wrote in his *Literary Notebooks:* "There exists a twofold derivation of literature (*Poesie*). For the practical, utilitarian man [art is important] as play, festival, semblance (*Schein*), allegory.—The other derivation [of art] is for the philosopher, it [comes] from the side of phantasy and its orgies."[2] For Schlegel fantasy/imagination is an absolutely necessary epistemological weapon, the most radical means conceivable, in the human spirit's battle against the petrification of thought in modernity. Literature in which a radically deconstructive fantasy is at work does not merely compensate in the imaginary realm for what is missing in reality, as sentimental literature does. Rather, it "chaoticizes" (*LN,* 171) the mind to prevent intellectual atrophy and to pave the way for a new critical beginning.

In the following pages, I will outline the contours of an intricate and complex, but to a large extent still undiscovered artistic and cultural-political project that was conceived in the tradition of the second mode of artistic production Lyotard speaks of and that eventually transcended the idealistic limits of romanticism: the aesthetic theory of Carl Einstein. Einstein, the novelist, art critic, and art historian, friend of Picasso and Braque, discoverer of African art, and political activist, was born in 1885 in the German Rhinelands and committed suicide in 1940 in southern France while trying to escape the Nazis. After 1907 he periodically lived in Paris where he became friends with Picasso, Braque, and Gris. In 1912 he published one of the most important novels of the historical avant-garde, *Bebuquin oder die Dilettanten des Wunders.* In 1915 he published *Negerplastik,* a book on African sculptors that revolutionized the understanding of African art and that he turned into a cultural weapon against the central perspective prevalent in European art since the Renaissance. In November of 1918 he became a leader in the revolutionary uprising in Brussels and, for a short time, served as "secretary of state" of the Belgian workers' and soldiers' council. In 1928 he emigrated to Paris where he founded the journal *Documents* with Georges Bataille and became co-editor of *Transition.* In 1936 he joined the Syndicalists in the Spanish Civil War and fought in a column led by the anarchist Durruti.

I stress that Carl Einstein eventually transcended the tradition of imagination's "orgies." In the 1930s, that is to say, Einstein's experiences with Stalinism and fascism influenced his turn away from a merely "chaoticizing" strategy and toward a materialistic foundation for his writing. Thus, his statement—"Modernism contains within itself romantic chiliasm. One believes in the better, more imaginative human being who can oppose reality and disprove it. This rejection of the real reminds one of the old obsession with original sin" (*FF*, 24)[3]—sounds like a critical, negative response to Schlegel's still positive, chiliastic assessment of fantasy: "When fantasy has won its battle with human reflection, then humanity will have achieved perfection" (*LN*, 211). Yet Einstein, to my mind one of the most interesting of the literary figures of German modernism, conforms completely in the main body of his work to the early romantics. Since this influence can still be felt after his materialistic turn, I will start with a rather detailed account of his earlier writings.

Einstein begins, just as Schlegel (and Lyotard) does, by differentiating between fantastic-deconstructive art, which he views positively, and sentimental art, its negative counterpart, and he continues the early romantic epistemological critique while radicalizing it. He regards sentimental art as the dominant form of art in modernity, one that fulfills an important compensatory function within the established system. Hence, a further essential aspect of his work is the critique of intellectuals and their social function in modernity. He sees them as nostalgics, whose task within the system is limited to compensating aesthetically for newly emerging modes of alienation. He dismisses expressionist artists like van Gogh and Gauguin as "Dionysian house-painters" and "paint-drunk semi-peasants" (*W*, 2:264). According to Einstein they belong to the dominant group of modernist philosophers and artists who "transform an atavistic romanticism into counterfeit modernism" (*FF*, 227). His second Bebuquin novel, which he began twenty years after the first one of 1912, and which remained a fragment, was conceived of as a novelistic deconstruction of this type of intellectual. At least before the materialistic turning point planned for him in the course of the novel, Bebuquin is "a kind of messiah of the new reality; a lost chiliast/a doubter who nevertheless keeps searching for paradise/with an insane sensibility for what is dead" (*P*, 32).

Aesthetic modernism *reacts* to social modernity. Every reactive critique runs the danger of constructing an opposing view, posited as a kind of antithesis, which locks the critique into a radical epistemological dependence on the very thing it criticizes. Einstein believed that the second mode of aesthetic modernism, that is, the one carried out by nostalgic, nondeconstructive representatives of aesthetic modernism, had fallen victim to just this danger, and he saw nostalgia where others believe they have located a radical critique of society. He himself tried to avoid the danger of a fixation on established systems by offering an epistemologically radical critique of oppositional figures of thought. These he defines not only as language and visual forms but increasingly as the differential system of social institutions, which he also sees as semiotic structures that determine human thought. All of these transcendentally powerful figurations—which for Einstein are inexorably linked to the negative development of modernity and thus unredeemable—can be dislodged, he believes, only by an immanent, deconstructive rhetorical strategy. Especially in light of his decision to join the anarcho-syndicalists in the Spanish Civil War, it is extremely important to realize that the quasi-anarchistic moments in Einstein's thought are the result of his epistemological insights; they cannot simply be dismissed with an exclusively political critique of anarchism. For Einstein "revolt" is a principle of deconstructionist rhetoric; it is for purely epistemological reasons the only "form of emotion or thought" justifying the hope that aesthetic modernism could also have a political effect. However, Einstein cautions: "Most people forget this principle [of revolt] for reasons of social integration, etc.; for many it degenerates into a dialectical opposition" (Wl:122). The first part of my essay will be a reconstruction of the epistemologically critical aspect of Einstein's work. Starting from the Schlegel-Einstein-Lyotard distinction between two modes of modernism, it will ask if modernist writing based on an epistemologically radical critique of language and of language's role in cognition can escape the compensatory functionalization of art in modernity.

II

To begin, let me anticipate my answer on a relatively general level: for a while Einstein overlooks the fact that a radicalization of the early romantic epistemological critique solely on a linguistic level is not enough. When it is assigned to a specific locale or to a specific institution that stands in opposition to other institutions, such a critique can also become compensatory. In other words, a danger arises when, in the process of differentiation that constitutes the emerging social organization of modernity, this particular critical discourse is relegated to a separate, aesthetic realm where it takes on a narrowly circumscribed function. The reason this can happen is that the oppositional images and figurations to which the critique repeatedly turns may themselves become so dominant in a given culture that their structural effect reaches beyond the content of individual texts. They start to determine the very order, the hierarchy of discourses in that culture, and the hierarchy, which is a semiotic as well as a social fact, regulates both the process of signification and the course of human interaction. Thus a rational, logical, and instrumental discourse may, on the level of societal differentiation, be opposed by an emotional, alogical discourse, which as as "public" and as institutionalized as its instrumental counterpart. Judicial discourse, for example, belongs to the former group; the discourses of music or love to the latter. To put it still differently, the structuring effect of the restrictive fixation on a particular opposite, which is characteristic of thinking in binary oppositions (such as instrumental reason versus aesthetic intoxication), is seldom limited to a mesmerizing fascination with binary figures of perception on the level of the word and the sentence. The same is true on the level of formal or institutional differentiation. Thus an aesthetic revolt that is determined by purely oppositional images and figures of thought (intoxication versus rationality) affects both the structure of individual texts and the text of a culture, especially the differential system of a culture's discourses. If this happens, the gesture of revolt may be defused on the level of social differentiation rather than on the level of the individual text. Any discourse that is structured around social critique and opposition, and that is also functionally differentiated as an aesthetic discourse, ultimately runs the risk of only taking on religious or compensatory functions, no matter how radical its contents may be. For whether a discourse is determined by socially critical oppositions like identity and dissolution, rationality and irrationality, alienation and a classless society, the worldly and otherworldly, myth and logos, primary and secondary processes, that discourse is always in danger of stylizing the mental constructs it opposes into nostalgic, utopian images, thus achieving an imaginary reconciliation of the opposition, and defusing its critical content by making it merely aesthetic.

In understanding art's reactive dependency on modernity, the concept of the sublime that Jean-François Lyotard has reintroduced into aesthetic theory has recently gained renewed importance. Lyotard's starting point is Kant's aesthetic. He notes that Kant's aesthetic theory—like most theories of the enlightenment—revolves around the notion of community; Kant circumscribes the aesthetic as the presentation of a utopian projection of an ideal society, the only possible contemporary representation of that ideal. "But this community is yet to be. It is not realized. For the first time, maybe, communities begin to conceive themselves in terms of promise, in terms of obligation, and in so doing they are conscious of not being real. . . . Nobody has ever *seen* a beginning. An end. . . . In this case, can we have a sensory intuition of what these questions are about? The answer implied in the critical approach (in Kant's sense) is, no, its impossible, they are Ideas of Reason (of *Reason,* they are no phantasms). We must consider these Ideas *as* Ideas if we are to avoid illusion: they are like guiding threads, and this is, in particular, the case for the Idea of freedom. . . . an Idea in general has no presentation, and *that is the question of the sublime.*"[4] For Lyotard, the sublime results from an artist's or a thinker's *insight* into the impossibility of presenting a utopia. Only a sublime work of art into which an awareness of this impossibility has been incorporated has a chance to transcend its compensatory institutionalization.

Lyotard's theory of the sublime is the philosophical precipitate of postmodernism's intent to call the aesthetic (and social) project of modernity into question. The insistence on the sublime nature of all artistic representation is—as an initial move that has to be followed by others—designed to remove art at least perceptually from its self-inflicted linguistic and institutional closure. The argument that an idea such as the future golden state of society can have no presentation opens up a more adequate understanding of the social function served by the illusory claim that the aesthetic can indeed represent such an idea, that it can foreshadow the political realization of that idea. For as long as the impossibility of the aesthetic representation of a future state of affairs does not affect art's traditional premise that it is in fact capable of achieving precisely what it cannot, this indicates a distinct need to hold fast to this illusion—a need that can only be rooted in the actual organization of bourgeois society. Lyotard's theory of the sublime reflects a comprehension of modernity that is not based, as is Habermas's theory of modernity, on an acceptance of the latter's premises; it is compatible with a more sociohistorical analysis of the compensatory function of the aesthetic in modernity.[5]

The postmodern theoretical context is very similar to the one Einstein unfolded seven decades earlier. From the late nineteenth century on, artists slowly started to comprehend the impact that the institution-alization of art in modernity, that is, the separation of art from life, has had on art—an insight that was basically epistemological and that considerably changed the practice of art in this century.[6] Einstein was one of the first among those who became aware of the problem-atic status the arts had gained in modernity. My thesis is that the degree to which artists gained such an insight determines the differ-ence between modernism and the avant-garde/postmodernism. The modernist gesture of *épater le bourgeois* claims to be able to criticize society as a whole from the detached point of view of a critical in-tellectual. To be sure, modernists reject the revisionist optimism of the enlightenment project of improving society by critiquing and moralizing it. But the lack of a teleological philosophy of history does not affect the rigor and epistemological self-confidence with which they critique society. A prevalent figure of this critique in modernism is irony (in contrast to parody in postmodernism), a prototypical fig-ure for a stance that lacks a philosophy of history but still shares the epistemological premises of that philosophy; the best example being, of course, Thomas Mann. Modernism's epistemological claim is that the artist can inhabit a place outside of society and the discourses institutionalized in society; modernism thus perceives itself as being its own agent of linguistic and perceptual renewal. (Cultural) mod-ernism attacked (social) modernity without ever reflecting on how its critique was defused by the autonomous institutionalization of its artistic practice. In other words, modernism is the cultural comple-ment of social modernity without ever understanding its own posi-tion within modernity.

Unlike modernists such as Thomas Mann, Carl Einstein radically challenged the legitimacy of the organizational demarcations consti-tuting modernity. Furthermore, he doubted the possibility of an epis-temologically stable and independent vantage point from which an affirmative, productive critique of society leading to meaningful reforms could be launched. In this sense, Carl Einstein belongs to the historical avant-garde. He rigorously expounded those theoretical and artistic issues that were to resurface in the cultural movements of the last two decades; he belonged to those artists who developed a growing awareness of the epistemologically constitutive effect that media of expression have on human perception and cognition. More persistently than anybody else he shifted the aesthetic debate in a consumer culture from questions of linguistic or formal renewal, of the replacement of worn-out stereotypes with "fresh" expressions, to the epistemological inadequacy of simply renewing language and to strategies whose intent is to deconstruct established patterns of perception without hastily replacing them. In my estimation, Einstein's intellectual and artistic project amounts to an early transformation of modernism into postmodernism. Modernism's predominantly revisionist critique of established linguistic and institutional boundaries in bourgeois society always presupposed that language, logical categories, and figures of thought exist outside of and independent from history and society; that is, that they are neutral tools that can be utilized for various critical purposes without affecting the very nature of those purposes. Since modernism still shared these epistemological premises, they offer an appropriate, albeit not singular, category by which one can distinguish between modernism on the one hand and the historical avant-garde and postmodernism on the other. In accordance with his epistemological premises, Carl Einstein attempts, as do the avant-garde and postmodernism, to be critically effective from within established boundaries by deconstructing these boundaries. Through his artistic strategies of intervention he hopes to open up a space, even if only for fleeting moments, from which a reflection of modernity undetermined by its established demarcations will become possible.

In a first phase, which lasted until the early 1930s, Einstein's accent lay on a critical epistemology and its effects on aesthetic forms, while in a second, short phase, which ended with his suicide, an analysis of the institutionalization of the imaginary as a kind of cultural lightning rod and system stabilizer created the prerequisite for a materialistic transformation of aesthetic modernism. Yet, instead of rejecting the results of his epistemological critique in the process, he integrated the two phases. In order to show the nevertheless marked difference between the two phases, I later will examine the very different significance that his concept of myth had in each phase. His concept of myth is, however, only a kind of litmus test for a more general development, and I could just as easily, and probably more correctly, have entitled my essay "The Metamorphosis of Romanticism in Modernity—from Epistemological Criticism to Leftist Radicalism: The Paradigm of Carl Einstein."[7]

III

Einstein's epistemological critique is historically oriented. That means that he proceeds from the assumption that subject and object were increasingly separated from each other in the course of historical time, an idea that he derives psychogenetically and ontogenetically from the process of civilization. The separation is the "result of recent social differentiation."[8] Premodern thought "was much more complexly structured than its modern counterpart because it included the irrational obverse side of the logical." Modernity, in contrast, "is dominated by the prejudice for continuity and qualitative unity and by the unequivocal nature of knowing," whose psychological function in the formation of agonistic identities Einstein describes as follows:

Human beings defend themselves against overpowering impressions and experiences, against the flood of forces, by rationalizing and conceptualizing their experience. . . . Every conceptualization is carried out in order to accommodate concrete experience and control it. . . . One overrates . . . the rational for the purpose of self-preservation. . . . Such positions are attained through a renunciation of the integrated and intertwined nature of the world; instead one strives for spherical borders and divisions. The juxtaposition of an inner and an outer world is only a question of perspective, or of power, just like the assertion of the closed human form and fixed objects. We can also recognize these repressive and displacing methods in the way causal relationships are posited; one rationalizes on the basis of fear, that is, one diminishes things. The conscious human being lives at the edge of the world, confronted with hostile or indifferent powers that he attempts to capture ever more firmly in his conceptual net. (P, 70 f.)

The constitution of the ego "means murdering all the others" (Oe, 13), and the forces experienced as hostile include not only that part of nature that can be contrasted with the subject but also his or her own unconscious nature. According to Einstein, the logicalization of thought must curtail "the important, visionary zone of experience. . . . One attempts to displace the mass of activity into the conscious ego. . . . However, with the overemphasis on the conscious ego, and on concepts that destroy formative powers, a static picture of the world arises. What happens is paralyzed by reason, and deadly systems are constructed. People are afraid of ideas, while experience grows old and gray from them" (P, 72).[9] All the important insights contained in Horkheimer and Adorno's *Dialectic of Enlightenment* seem to me to be present or at least suggested in Einstein. In fact, his analysis of conceptualization as the reduction of experience (*Erfahrung*) to what can be repeated and controlled through its repetition is considerably more advanced than the analysis in the *Dialectic of Enlightenment*.

These ideas have two decisive implications for a theory of modernism: first, Einstein includes the traditional model of the organic, closed work of art in his diagnosis of paralyzed thought. In his essay "Form and Concept" he writes: "Knowledge like every fixation is a sign of exhaustion, functional constipation, and of closing the files. Its separation from dynamic processes . . . is always characterized by its result becoming autonomous and independent. One can observe the same process when works of art become independent" (P, 74). Art viewed as a closed, timeless construct is just as endangered by the fatal process of repetition as the concept; in both cases the process of repetition ends in semantic atrophy.

Second, he sees the imposition of grammatically correct speech as a result—to be sure, one that must be overcome—of the phylogenesis of the civilizing process, for "grammatically regularized speech enforces the regularization of experience and restricts complex experiences."

The conclusion that follows from both ideas is that neither language nor art can be mimetic: "The world lies beyond language and the word. The word is not imitative" (FF, 234). For Einstein, the impetus toward mimesis at the level of the word and of the work of art has the same psychic cause, the drive for self-preservation, which cannot achieve its goal because dominance through fixation is transformed into death: "Knowledge like everything that is fixed, including images, is a symptom of the continuing death of the heavens (*Gestirne*), and the earth's fatal tendency gradually overshadows its vital strivings" (*P*, 80).

At this point Einstein begins to define the contours of a resisting art within modernity. Art should allow the individual "to oppose the deadly generalizations, the radical impoverishment of the world, and to sever the chains of causality and the world's net of meanings (*Netze der Versinnung*)" (*P*, 91). The dominant stylistic principle in such art is hallucination or fantasy/imagination. In the first phase of Einstein's development these three terms are more or less synonymous. They are all located in the unconscious and are the expression of its "constantly changing, active, creative force" (*Oe*, 19), which is expressed stylistically as the "free connection of discrepant functional signs"; as a result, the unconscious oversteps "logical causality and connections" (*P*, 28). "In hallucinations the recent, differentiated ego dies; recently acquired conscious levels fall off, and all learned or habitual memories sink away. The observer becomes unhistorical; ordered variations, secondary facades disappear, yet the observer now gains an uncommon freedom vis-à-vis tradition and history" (*Oe*, 60). The binary opposition underlying this thought is similar to the difference between primary and secondary processes in Freudian thinking. The rejuvenation of the decentering experiences associated with the primary process initiated by art does not—as is frequently the case with Benn—simply aim at an aesthetic experience of dissolution (*Entgrenzung*); it is viewed rather as the only possible means of hindering atrophy.

If Einstein's diagnosis of the atrophy or paralysis of thought in modernity is correct, then the project of initiating a cultural revolution that would take its cue from this diagnosis has to consider the conditions under which such a project is possible. For Einstein the question of the possibility of a cultural revolution was decided relatively easily. In his eyes it is no longer merely a project but something that is already operational, something that has already been started to a degree in modernism. He explains its realization as follows:

We have to ask how the hallucinatory could have broken through so stormily and so strongly. Quite simply: The mechanization and intellectualization of life was so overdeveloped, and a mass of repressions had been saved up—from forces that could not be utilized in the rational course of events. Life proceeded according to clear rules, but the mind is composed of various layers, and it is not satisfied with a simple explanation. . . . the great portion of mental processes do not correspond to rationalization in the way science has conceived of it for us. (P, 55)

The question posed for me here, one that I intend to discuss more fully later, is whether the dichotomy between the conscious and the unconscious, between the instrumentalized and the noninstrumentalized realm of psychic life, does not ultimately also have to degenerate into nostalgic, utopian thinking. Whether, in other words, Einstein's and other modernist thinkers' intended epistemological radicalism was not undermined so long as they felt the need to provide a space for salvation—however secularized or psychologized. For the early Einstein this space is an unconscious untouched by the civilizing process. It is a pure, positive force, the "prerequisite and source of future existence." He calls it a "nothing" because it is not logically determined; as such it is "identical with the compulsively hallucinatory." As a "logical nonentity" it is "the primary part of the mind and at the same time the earliest phase of the real" (P, 89).

It seems to me that one of the dangers of aesthetic modernism that has been reflected upon far too little becomes visible here. However, among the few modernists who gradually overcame this danger one has to reckon Carl Einstein, along with Brecht and Benjamin. But before I turn to Einstein's gradual realization of this danger, I would like to examine more closely another oppositional figure of thought or mental image, that Einstein ultimately also employed, using as an example the concepts of fantasy and myth.

In a fragment from his planned novel, *Bebuquin II,* Einstein composed a critical but precise review of his early ideas: "Imagination—irrational = individual—therefore unprovable and incommensurable—therefore mythical situation through individualism, regress. . . . myth . . . without dogma, structure, and a social foundation—therefore unchained fantasy, one expresses no more than the irrational, asocial functions of humanity.—infantile behavior—insanity—the dark side, etc." (P, 33). For the early Einstein the existence of myth was a condition that aesthetic modernism should reestablish. "People are presently busy," as Einstein wrote in an early, positive summary of developments in modern painting, "inventing mythical figures and objects. Something is therefore coming again, romantic valorization, the return to fairy tales, just as with primitive peoples. These mythical forces are now achieving their due place, and people no longer want to be subjected to the inhibitions of selective reason" (P, 59). The "need to . . . construct myth" is for Einstein an "expression of the difference between man and reality," which emerged in the process of civilization (P, 89). Myth is a positive regression, because the "metamorphosized identity" of subject and object, which it creates, together with fantasy, momentarily overcomes the historically recent separation of subject and object within the civilizing process. In modernity, according to Einstein, myth cannot be reestablished collectively; it can only be rejuvenated as the product of individual fantasy. For after the phylogenetic separation of subject and object—which includes, according to Einstein, alienation between subjects—a collective myth is no longer possible, or— as was the case in National Socialism—only possible as a pseudo-myth. In the artistic achievements of individual fantasies, that is, in "the vision, resolutely out of nothing, reality finds the growth of mythical forms, without which it would perish" (P, 91). The "mythical in the present" is therefore ostensibly not just "an atavism" (P, 55) but an epistemologically critical means of overcoming the alienation of subject and object, subject and subject.

This train of thought makes it clear that, for Einstein in his early stage, reality was never something independent of the subject; it was never an opposite that affected a subject, but rather a form of seeing that the civilizing process gradually enforced as a transcendental a priori and that therefore had to be overcome. These transcendental forms of apperception, historically induced in the civilizing process, constitute the conscious ego. Through myth, and that ultimately means through all of "hallucinatory" grounded aesthetic modernism, "the conscious ego [with its alienated forms of apperception] is destroyed, and this eliminates the dualistic position of subject and object" (P, 99).

What interests me here is that this mental image, which is motivated by a radical, epistemological critique of human signification, seems to lead necessarily to an egocentric isolation and overvaluation of the activities of the fantasy, while orienting them toward individual pleasure. The Sisyphus-like labor of a constant epistemological critique through art becomes, in other words, nothing more than a constant "high" achieved through asceticism and "self-denial." Note the pathetic tone in Einstein's description of life in the following quotation; in addition, Einstein applies a dialectical, oppositional image here, against which he constantly polemicized in other connections:

Since a person, in order to live at all and not be completely victimized by the negative and impoverishing processes of logic, has to throw himself repeatedly into logically senseless and irrational processes, every sensible unity is destroyed, immediately and without interruption. In so doing, a movement that opposes the tendency to view the world as a continuum is formed; one is namely driven to thin out, separate, and remember the world as something erratically discontinuous. This happens when the conformist and rationalized world is constantly bombarded with visions that are not logically determined. (P, 90)

IV

My intent here is of course not to critique Einstein but to note the point at which Einstein's own critique and his subsequent transcendence of his earlier position began, a position that can, so far, be taken as paradigmatic of an epistemologically critical version of modernism. His later position augments the earlier one by adding a materialist, leftist-radical base. His critique starts with the insight that once it had been relegated to an autonomous institutional framework, that is, to modernism as modernity's institutionally independent aesthetic sphere, even a radical epistemological critique had to take on a compensatory function within the range of differentiated discourses in society. In other words, modernism's fragmentary, discrepant, or hermetic aesthetic form offered no guarantee that it could avoid the fate suffered by the autonomous, closed, organic work of art, that is, of being a discourse whose potential as a medium of social critique is always already defused, and which provides imaginary satisfaction for residual needs not met in bourgeois society. However, since Einstein did not return to an aesthetic of mimetic representation—that is, since he remained true to the epistemologically critical project of his earlier years,—he could scarcely have resorted to the affirmative system-

theory solution of accepting this differentiation as a positive achievement of modernity, as is typical of Habermas's work. It is for this
very reason that Einstein turns, in *The Fabrication of Fictions,* his
monumental work from the 1930s, to a reflection on the consequences of the institutionalization of a separate aesthetic sphere. But
before analyzing his conclusions, I would first like to address Einstein's
diagnosis of the civilizing process as the differentiation of social sub-
systems. In the course of modernization, scientists and technologists
had "refined life and force into elegant calculations. Life seemed to
roll precisely along bright tracks; yet existence was only technically
normalized. . . . Now people were escaping from the clear-cut nature of the mechanized world, which hardly permitted any further
differentiated reactions, into the regions of imaginative wonders, into
the vision" (*FF,* 56).

For Einstein, the normalization or standardization imposed by industrialization leads, on the one hand, to differentiations between
individuals and institutions, and, on the other hand, to differentiations within the psychic life of individuals:

The bourgeois sat during the day in the office or factory. Thus he was dependent on people who occupied themselves with procuring the material for
forming and nourishing his special personality. This is what intellectuals were
paid for. The bourgeois became fabulous (*fabelhaft*). Increasingly insub-
stantial (*luftige*) superstructures were dumped onto his shoulders; he lost the
feeling for every concrete milieu. Bankers and manufacturers juggled between bookkeeping and phantasms. (*FF,* 166)

In reference to psychic differentiation he speaks of the "romantic,
reactionary double existence" of the individual, which resulted in a
"schizoid division" (*FF,* 97 f).

Einstein is thus convinced that the art of social modernity, regardless of whether one means "high" art for individualists or kitsch for
the masses, fulfills a necessary function within the organizational
structure of society—one that, to a certain extent, can be explained
in terms of system theory: "Imaginary modernism achieved its success by offering romantic compensation for rationalized daily labor.
Now the driven calculators rested in infantile regression and produced a private, facilely utopian dream-personality" (*FF,* 88). Of decisive importance is that Einstein never perceives this compensatory
function for art as coincidental or dispensable; nor does he believe

that it could be overcome by changing the attitudes or the behavior of individuals. His concept of revolt changes accordingly. If for the early Einstein the revolt of the individual against the mechanization and standardization of reality was both practically implementable and politically and morally imperative owing to the existence of a non-colonized and noncolonizable unconscious, it is always already institutionally defused in the system-theory perspective of the later Einstein. "It hardly need be said that the dreamer Schulze was incapable of revolt. He had let off steam aesthetically, and had satisfied his secret self-consciousness theoretically. Schulze's compensation came in poetry and he felt sublime bliss in the ideal realm" (FF, 97). And since the purgation achieved by the aesthetic is socially institutionalized on the interpersonal as well as on the psychic level, Einstein is afflicted by the "tormenting question whether the poetic does not represent a regression per se" (FF, 111).

In his essay "Form and Concept" Einstein had already laid the foundation for his understanding of the effect of this differentiation of the aesthetic subsystem on artistic contents. There he had seen the phylogenesis of modern subjectivity as responsible for the idolization of concepts, for the rational constriction of the person into a conscious self, and for the isolation and identifying circumscription of objects juxtaposed to the conscious self as "rigidly defined." At the same time he pointed toward the psychic consequences of the process. The fixation of concepts and conceptual systems can, in Einstein's assessment, lend a sense of pseudo-security to the individual, but the simultaneous displacement of the nonstandardizable "psychically immediate happening" engenders a fear that arises from the phylogenetically determined isolation of subjects. For the distancing of the individual from nature, and of individuals from other individuals, which is so constitutive of social modernity, whose epistemological sign is the "conscious self and the rigid object," forces "metamorphotic sexual identification" to dissipate (P, 75). This term, which Einstein uses frequently, refers to forms of dissolution (e.g., aesthetic intoxication; the enjoyment of music; happenings) and to the de-centering of psychic experiences between individuals and others, between people and things (e.g., erotic experiences; sensual pleasures). For the *early* Einstein the importance of this form of experience was that he used it to develop his concept of myth, and his

concept of imagination was a means of achieving the mythic condition. He considered the "hallucinative" and the imagination capable
of changing reality to such a degree that the anxiety created by the
civilizing process would be alleviated and finally eliminated. On the
basis of his institutional critique the *later* Einstein insists that, at best,
anxiety can be weakened and compensated through the "metamorphotic sexual identifications" portrayed in art. Therefore, the results
of his institutional critique simultaneously destroy his concept of myth
and inspire him to analyze carefully the role of sexuality in art.

Before considering the erotic side of Einstein's ideas, let me first
touch on his conception of the overall function of the imaginary in
modernism. In his *Fabrication of Fictions* Einstein writes: "The lit-
erati want to make up for lack of community with symbolic ties."
While symbolic ties could be experienced fictionally in nonsexual experiences—for example, in the pseudo-myths of people's community
(*Volksgemeinschaft*),—Einstein maintains that the sexualization of
art in modernity was a necessary step, expressing its system-differential function in an immediate way: "The intellectuals worked off
their sexuality through the imaginary. . . . Thus an increase in the
preponderance of the sexual was ensured; sexuality became the center of the modern myth" (*FF*, 309). For Einstein the "broadening of
the imaginary zone" in (social) modernity has to be ascribed to
"growing, unrealized displacements," that is, to the repression or displacement of individual erotic needs that necessarily accompanied the
development of agonistic and "one-sidedly and technologically standardized" selves. The system-differential institutionalization of the
aesthetic is in his eyes an achievement of sublimation during the process of modernization; as such it helps determine the collective psyche. It was this achievement that first created the conditions necessary for the institutionalized displacement of erotic fantasies of
dissolution into the aesthetic sphere. And it alone permitted those
intensifications of experience needed to counterbalance the excessive
cultivation of the rational self. "Love had become metaphoric; it's
not coitus that counted, but its symbolism. The client was wonderfully sublimated, his love life became indirect and laden with symbols. Engaging in coitus became poeticizing, the dream became coitus" (*FF*, 158).

The socio- and psychogenetic derivation of the imaginary as a mode of institutionalized compensation led Einstein to a new definition of the epistemological achievement of art. From now on he separates the mythic from the imaginative. In this latter stage he only employs the term *myth* pejoratively, in contrast to the terms *hallucination* or *imagination*. Thus he remarks critically: "The myth, which had been an expression of magic collectives, was to have redeemed individuals in a technological age [from total standardization]." The effect was a "romantic dualism as cleavage" (*FF*, 144), which did not change reality at all, but stabilized it. Owing to the autonomous institutionalization of aesthetic activities, the new mode of seeing aesthetically was confined to the aesthetic sphere; it did not extend to other spheres.

In a similar fashion Einstein derives a new concept of reality from his reflections on the institutionalization of art. He defines reality not only as transcendental, that is, as a form of apperception against whose standardization and normalization the artist must work; reality has now become independent of its possible cognition—reality is that which affects and effects humans, which can be worked through experientially. Einstein now conceives of the institutional differentiation of society and, as part of the same process, the functionally differential exclusion of the aesthetic, in a manner similar to his earlier view of conceptualization—as a fixation through form, as the "fatal tendency of the earth" hindering an adequate comprehension and working-through of the concrete. Fixation is thus seen as a process that also occurs at the level of functional differentiations within the social system, that is, at the institutional level. In other words, the specific form of institutionalization enforced upon the aesthetic sphere in modernism contributes as much to the semantic expropriation of individuals as does, for example, the standardization of language through commercials. As Einstein put it: "The romantic utilization of archaic residues [in the psyche, as they are employed by modern art] led to the collapse of the fact-building, concrete individuality. . . . In the final analysis reality dies off from the growth of the imaginative and archaic factors" (*FF*, 271).

Einstein is aiming here at something very important in his diagnosis of (social) modernity and (cultural) modernism. Ever since the aesthetic theories of the eighteenth century, the *general* nature of science had been juxtaposed to the *particular* nature of art. But the general as contrasted with the particular was from the outset more than just a category applied to scientific theory and to scientific methodology; moreover, the interest in this opposition was by no means merely theoretical. For already in the eighteenth century, the general was conceived of, albeit in a vague and associative way, together with the "generalizing" process of abstraction that characterizes modernity. A number of thinkers already associated everything with conceptual abstraction, from the political centralization and economic planning activities of the absolute state, to the codification and standardization of the laws, the abstract nature of exchange and the abstracting power of money, and the demand for logicizing thought and for rational behavior; they saw both modes of abstraction, the conceptual and the "real" one (cf. the Marxist term *Realabstraktion*), as a side-effect of the process of modernization. All this necessarily led to a hypostatization of art as the sole refuge in a context that was otherwise dominated by abstractions.

At first it seems as though Einstein's thought is also structured by this opposition. He writes, for example: "In the liberal society money and amassed capital were valued more highly than productive forces. The capitalists had deconcretized the economy by means of their accumulated wealth. . . . Money was valued as the prerequisite of all production and was considered to be the only measure of value and the only standard. . . . Accordingly, one grew used to placing abstract formulations masterfully above doing and above positive experiences. Liberal culture was of an abstract mode. Idealistic intellectuals believed that the abstract concept possessed the same power as money, and they used the former as a surrogate for the collective" (*FF*, 79). Yet, in contrast to his early phase, in which the particular forms of fantasy and of mythical experience were intended to defend against modernity's pressure toward abstraction, Einstein now sees quite clearly that the opposition of the general and the particular is illusory and incapable of grasping the process of abstraction to which art was also subordinated. Thus he draws a parallel between the abstract circulation of money and the circulation of aesthetic signs in art. For the "neutralization of concrete things or persons," which the capitalist achieves by deforming "humans and objects with the power of abstract money," is also achieved by the poet through the autonomization of his signs, that is, by the failure of his language to work through concrete experience: "Poet and capitalist are dynamicists, and they seek a maximum of mobility. The poem seems successful to the poet when his small sensation—distant reflection of a fact— has hurried through a hundred signs. The speculator would like his money to change places as often as possible. Both types are meta- morphotically obsessed. Money, as well as [poetic] metaphor, changes mimically and dissolves concrete facts" (*FF*, 311).

Einstein also derives the specific use of language in art from the particular form the autonomous institutionalization of art imposed upon the aesthetic in modernity. Since art becomes the locale for the redemption of individuality and is juxtaposed in a utopian and nos- talgic manner to the modern process of abstraction, it is therefore dependent on its opposite, namely, on the social process of abstrac- tion, through which the dialectical opposition of art and reality is overdetermined. This abstraction necessarily carried over into art and changed the status of the particular within the aesthetic realm. At first, the determination of art through its opposite had the effect of making the aesthetic attitude contemplative; however, from the non- location of art, reality could indeed only be grasped contemplatively. Thus for Einstein contemplation and abstraction signify essentially the same thing. Both stifle the will for change since they have lost contact with the concrete. This is not altered by the fact that it is precisely the "contemplative intellectuals" who responded to "the limited possibilities of existence" with the creation of a "whimsically mobile ideal world" "dualistically" opposed to a "positive reality" and who believed themselves to be "incredibly revolutionary." For Einstein their conviction that they were opposing social reality with a critical alternative was always already institutionally disproven: "In fact they misdirect important energies into the aesthetic sphere, in- stead of allowing the artistic experience and its energy to flow into life" (*FF*, 284). Thus language, too, was ultimately and necessarily "filled with increasingly numerous contemplative aestheticisms alien- ated from action" (*FF*, 601), accelerating the "tempo of reality's dis- appearance" (*FF*, 216).

V

These last comments recall the avant-garde project of leading art back into life. Yet in individual points Einstein deviates considerably from the avant-garde's program. For him, leading art back into life means working together "in the production of a new reality" (*FF*, 327). For him, this is inconceivable without experiencing the existing, dominant form of reality in a sensuous, material way. The contemplative intellectual, who is constitutive of modernity, "avoids subjecting himself to the happening" (*FF*, 192). Einstein appeals for action in the sense that the artist should first actively subject himself to what he wants to describe, allowing it to be inscribed in his body as everyday experience before attempting its verbalization. He contrasts the proletariat with the intelligentsia, whose experience has become abstract: "The proletariat was superior to the intellectuals despite all their privileges. The former lived and worked within a constraining reality and possessed a clear destiny. Out of this grew proletarian thought, which was not based on subjective speculation, but was grounded in the conditions of working-class life" (*FF*, 93). To be sure, owing to the institutionalization of semiotic praxis in modernity, Einstein concedes that proletarian thought could never really unfold. "The masses, working concretely, were disarmed through *Abstrakta*" (*FF*, 80). *The* means of domination par excellence are, for Einstein, "formulations laden with contemplation but leading to no action since concrete, activating moments are excluded."

Within Einstein's culture-revolutionary project the intellectual of the future should attempt to help the masses "form their own appropriate conventions for the real" (*FF*, 315), thereby reviving the social function that art had had in premodern times, namely, organizing a social group's "common impressions and experiences in images and poems" (*FF*, 81). This task, however, is still defined on the basis of the epistemologically radical position of Einstein's early phase. For since all "ideal figurations," regardless of whether they refer to closed aesthetic forms or to conceptual systems, "in the final analysis" address "questions of power" (*FF*, 213 and 218), neither a conceptual nor an aesthetic insight can ever be final: "A revolutionary insight, for example, is only a useful link between an outmoded phase and a new one. Such knowledge is never artistically dissociated from its concrete preconditions. A practically effective insight provides a transition between two actions; in other words, abstract activity is only a secondary interval between two phases supplanting one another. Only in this sense can thinking be productive" (*FF*, 192 f). Here, too, Einstein insists on the paradoxical double-sidedness of all cognition, claiming that every individual insight means "a stoppage of functions," a "resting point," a fixation of ongoing events. "The dying happening is transformed into abstraction [form]. One distances oneself cognitively from positive reality, in order not to be absorbed" (*FF*, 204). Art can never be mimetic. When it succeeds, it makes one conscious of historic, concrete experiences and simultaneously—by dissolving itself in this practical effect—perishes.

VI

To be sure, this redefinition of the function of art in modernity poses a problem that Einstein does not tackle. Human action that is not purely anarchic has to be organized on the basis of an *Entwurfsstruktur,* that is, on the basis of some kind of meaningful design oriented toward a future (even if that future should be limited to tomorrow), toward change, or toward the interpretation of historical structures, past, present, or future. A purely anarchic action, be it in the linguistic or the political realm, could never organize a social group's "common expressions and experiences in images and poems." For any human action intended to surpass the stage of merely dislodging existing structures, both consciousness and interpretive acts are necessary. Such consciousness and the interpretive acts it engenders need not be conceived of in terms of presence and self-identity, or—in Lyotard's terminology—as nostalgia for a community that does not exist. They could, for example, take into account the fact that any human *Entwurfsstruktur* can never do more than approximate an individual's or a group's being or experience. Its interpretive acts would then be a necessary, albeit never-ending, always only approximating, and, to a certain degree, always already obsolete semantic organization of their own human experience. Since such an *Entwurfsstruktur* has to have a temporal structure, it must necessarily be structured as a narrative. To the extent that this touches upon the current debate surrounding Derrida's concept of *différance,* that is, the possibility of meaning and subjectivity, I follow Manfred Frank's detailed critique of Derrida as developed in his *What Is Neostructuralism?*[10]

I only hint at these difficulties here. In my view, they are to a large extent identical to a similar difficulty posed by the practice of deconstruction in the context of contemporary theoretical debates. Nevertheless, since the epistemological critique put forward by Einstein, which in this respect might be less radical than Derrida's related critique, does not exclude accepting the necessity of an *Entwurfsstruktur* guiding human self-understanding and action, I still hold that Einstein's later work represents one of the most consistent models of a leftist-radical, grass-roots democratic theory of art to date. Like that of the Russian proletcult and the culture-revolutionary projects tied to the KAPD (particularly that of Franz Jung, whose work Einstein obviously did not know), Einstein's project was based on his reflections on the conditions under which the rise of a collective consciousness and a working-through of experience that is not always already caught in the pitfalls of a system may be possible. As early as 1914 Einstein said of social democracy: "one evolutionizes from protest to protest until the theory is thoroughly ingrained in all members. A club of rationalists will never revolutionize; they'll only order things somewhat more" (W, 1:230). More radically than Jung or the Russian proletcult, Einstein tied his political ideas to reflections on the epistemological status of language and to the institutionalization of art in modernity. In this he approached the theoretical presuppositions of Brecht's *Lehrstück* project and of Benjamin's *Passsagenwerk*. It is thus all the more unfortunate that his work is still so poorly edited and that it has until now received so little critical attention. Moreover, the very limited renaissance that Einstein's work enjoyed in the 1970s concentrated almost exclusively on the early, epistemologically radical Einstein. This may relate to the fact that the early Einstein is more compatible with the branch of poststructuralism that has had increasing influence on younger Germans. Perhaps this is why the editors of the three-volume edition of Einstein's work published by the Medusa Verlag between 1980 and 1985 were content to print only those works that appeared in Einstein's lifetime. Nowhere has such an editorial policy been more disastrous than in the case of Einstein, whose other literary remains in Berlin and Paris have—with the exception of *The Fabrication of Fictions*—only been published in very fragmentary excerpts. Einstein, the postmodern modernist, has still to be discovered. He would deserve discovery as much as Walter Benjamin, whose life-story bears an uncanny resemblance to

Einstein's and whose intellectual project has many elective affinities with the one introduced here.

Notes

1. Jean-François Lyotard, *The Postmodern Condition: A Report on Knowledge* (Minneapolis: University of Minnesota Press, 1984), 80.

2. Friedrich Schlegel, *Literarische Notizen 1797–1801* (Frankfurt am Main, Berlin, and Vienna: Ullstein, 1980), 184. Henceforth quoted within the text as *LN*.

3. The works of Carl Einstein will be cited according to the following symbols: *W*: Carl Einstein, *Werke*, Bd. 1–3 (Berlin: Medusa, 1980–85); *P*: Sibylle Penkert, *Carl Einstein. Existenz und Ästhetik: Einführung mit einem Anhang unveröffentlichter Nachlaßtexte* (Wiesbaden: Steiner, 1970); *FF*: Carl Einstein, *Die Fabrikation der Fiktionen*, ed. Sibylle Penkert (Reinbek: Rowohlt, 1973). The few cases in which I cite unpublished material quoted in Heidemarie Oehm, *Die Kunsttheorie Carl Einsteins* (Munich: Fink, 1976), are indicated by the symbol *Oe;* Oehm's is by far the best publication to date on Einstein.

4. Jean-François Lyotard, "Complexity and the Sublime," *ICA Documents 4: Postmodernism* (London: Institute for Contemporary Art, 1986), 10–11.

5. Cf. my two essays in the special issue of *Cultural Critique* on "Modernity and Modernism, Postmodernity and Postmodernism" (5, Winter 1987).

6. For a detailed discussion of this impact see Peter Bürger, *Theory of the Avant-Garde* (Minneapolis: University of Minnesota Press, 1984), and my "Avant-garde/Postmodernism" in *Encyclopedia of Communication* (Philadelphia: University of Pennsylvania Press, 1988).

7. This is the title I chose for a shorter and somewhat different German version of this essay in *kultuRRevolution: zeitschrift für angewandte diskurstheorie* 12 (June, 1986): 62–67.

8. Carl Einstein, "Aus der Einleitung für den Russischen Maler," in *alternative* 75: 255.

9. In regard to the historicity of such statements, see Jochen Schulte-Sasse, "Imagination and Modernity; Or the Taming of the Human Mind," *Cultural Critique* 5 (Winter 1987): 23–48.

10. An English version was published in 1988 in Minnesota's THL series.

Written Right Across Their Faces: Ernst Jünger's Fascist Modernism

Russell A. Berman

If the will triumphs, who loses? *Triumph of the Will,* Leni Riefenstahl's cinematic account of the 1934 Nazi Party convention at Nuremberg, is one of the few aesthetic monuments of German fascism that have attracted serious critical scrutiny. In scene after scene one finds evidence of the ideological self-understanding of National Socialism: Hitler's descent from the clouds, the cathartic applause welcoming the charismatic leader, the visions of the medieval city, the presence of the unified folk including contingents of peasants in their traditional costumes, the rough-and-tumble life in the encampment, the mass chorus of the Work Front, the demonstration of the Hitler Youth, the celebratory display of banners, torchlight processions, and a soundtrack that mixes Wagnerian strains with patriotic songs and martial anthems. The list could be extended, and each item could be decoded and explained within the constellation of the right-wing populism, the *völkisch* ideology, on which German fascism thrived. That sort of investigation can have a compelling explanatory value in regard to the political content of the film. However, I should like to eschew the ideological-critical stance and investigate the rhetorical grounding of Riefenstahl's énonciation, an investigation that can shed light on a politics prior to ideological contents, that is, the politics of fascist representation. It is this rhetorical politics that will concern me later when I turn to Ernst Jünger's construction of a fascist modernism, and it is the examination of rhetoric that may allow me to answer the question posed initially: if the will triumphs, who loses?

Triumph of the Will begins, like most films, with script, with words on the screen, but this opening gesture takes on particular importance within fascist rhetoric. Elsewhere titles name the individual work, give credit to individual artists, and, perhaps, locate the precise historical setting. Here, by way of contrast, the writing on the silver wall invokes the history that has passed—history, or historiography, the writing of history, as past—in order to introduce the agent of its supersession: in the cloudy heavens emerges an airplane, the paradigmatic modernist vehicle, bearing the body of the divine leader, the guarantor of national resurrection, whose arrival on earth signifies the miraculous incarnation of the will triumphant. Henceforth history is overcome, and the jubilant folk rejoices in a redeemed present provided by the presence in flesh and blood of the visible savior. The point is not that Hitler lands in Nuremberg; the point is that Hitler lands in Nuremberg and is seen. "Wir wollen unsren Führer sehen" (We want to see our leader), cries the crowd, and the film, *Triumph of the Will,* defines itself as the proper medium of a fascist privileging of sight and visual representation. The will triumphs when it becomes visually evident, and it triumphs over the alternative representational option, cited at the commencement of the film, writing and an associated culture of verbal literacy. When the will triumphs as image, it is script that is defeated: the verbal titles of the cinematic preface, henceforth displaced by Riefenstahl's shots; the written signatures of the "November traitors"; the Versailles Treaty, denigrated as just so much paper; and the volumes that disappeared in the conflagrations of May 1933.

Triumph of the Will defines a fascist rhetoric as the displacement of verbal by visual representation: the power of the image renders scripture obsolete. This contention may be tentatively, although not conclusively, confirmed by two pieces of evidence. I draw the first from the folklore of fascism, the infinitely repeated vernacular attribution of Hitler's success to the unique power of his eyes that allegedly fastened his interlocutors and fascinated the captivated masses, as if the force of fascist rhetoric depended less on words than on the energy of vision (cf. the parallel claim that no one ever "read" *Mein Kampf*). I return to the film for the second piece of evidence, the self-effacing signature of the director. After Hitler's triumphal arrival and the evening demonstrations outside his window, the cinematic

narrative proceeds to the next morning, crack of dawn in Nuremberg—sleeping streets, the city walls, the ancient bridges—and for
a brief moment one catches a glimpse of the shadow cast by the photographic apparatus. Note: not a glimpse of the apparatus itself
(technology is excluded) but its shadow projected onto the wall as a
metaphor of the cinematic screen. The signature announces the age
of the film and the priority of visual representation as the rhetorical
practice of fascism. Hitler turns out to be precisely the enigma described by the subtitle of Hans-Jürgen Syberberg's cinematic investigation of National Socialism: "a film from Germany."

Much more could be said about the specifially rhetorical problems
posed by *Triumph of the Will,* especially with regard to the status of
speech in the film: the political speeches at the convention, Hitler's
several addresses, and the text of the mass chorus. Briefly, I would
argue that its verbal character is always secondary to the visual spectacle and the image of the present speaker, and that it therefore differs fundamentally from the initial script, the writing whose author
is necessarily absent. A considerably more difficult problem involves
the role of radio and loudspeakers in National Socialist Germany, an
obvious case of disembodied speech, on which the power of the re-
gime indisputably depended. Rather than pursue these matters, however, I will conclude these introductory observations, having used
Riefenstahl's film in order to isolate a crucial conflict between visual
and verbal representation, in particular the insistence on the priority
of image over writing as a stratagem of fascist power. I call this a
crucial conflict because it turns out to be the central rhetorical principle in Ernst Jünger's formulation of fascist modernism as described
in his 1932 volume *The Worker,* bearing the telling subtitle *Herrschaft und Gestalt,* which I render inadequately as *Domination and
Form.* For it is visual form that will, in Jünger's modernist account,
displace an obsolete culture of bourgeois writing and guarantee the
authority of fascist domination.

Jünger's proximity to the problematic isolated in Riefenstahl's film
is evident in the first paragraph of the 1932 preface. I will cite it now
and later comment on its rhetorical self-positioning, its claims regarding competing modes of representation, rather than on its ideological contents, that is, the significance of his terminology, such as
"worker."

It is the plan of this book to make the Gestalt of the worker visible, beyond all theories, all parties, and all prejudices—to make it visible as an effective mass, which has already intervened in history and imperiously determines the forms of a transformed world. Because this is less a matter of new thoughts or a new system than of a new reality, everything depends on the sharpness of the description, which demands eyes capable of a complete and unclouded vision.[1]

It is nearly unnecessary to underscore Jünger's insistence on the urgency of visual representation. The project of his book amounts to a making visible (*sichtbar zu machen*) of a form (*Gestalt*); this in turn leads to a presentation that demands eyes (*die Augen voraussetzt*) with an unclouded vision (*denen die volle und unbefangene Sehkraft gegeben ist*). The desideratum of sight and form, the image of images, pervades the text, which consequently defines its rhetorical mode as *descriptio*—to be understood less in terms of the etymology pointing toward writing (*be-schreiben*) than as a project of visualization to be carried out by writing. Imagistic vision is then set in contrast to an alternative constellation of theories, parties, and prejudices, a domain of ideas, defined as mere ideas, that is, separate from reality. The descriptive representation of Gestalt has powerful practical consequences (*die bereits mächtig in die Geschichte eingegriffen*), as opposed to the ultimately powerless ephemera of "new thoughts or a new system." "System"—a standard Nazi pejorative for the Weimar Republic; Jünger is suggesting in 1932 that a new order of power, structure, and form will replace an anachronistic amalgam of empty theories, political parties, and effete idealism. This paraphrase points out the underlying diachronic presumption, the transition from a bourgeois age of subjective interiority, the site of literary culture, to a postindividualism of visible power. This transition is central to Jünger's political ideology, his hostility to democracy, and his totalitarian preferences. It is, moreover, central to his aesthetics; the disparagement of a powerless culture of idealism and the advocacy of artistic formations (*Gestaltung*) with life-practical ramifications are homologous to the terms of the modernist attack on the bourgeois institution of autonomous art such as Peter Bürger has presented in his *Theory of the Avant-Garde*.

In *The Worker*, Jünger undertakes myriad permutations of these themes, but the overriding concern remains the Gestalt, the visual

form or structure: "The Gestalt contains the whole, which encom-
passes more than the sum of its parts and which an anatomical age
could never achieve." Here Jünger borrows from a reactionary strain
in German romanticism running through Wagner and Langbehn that
denounced the analytical intellect and the individuation of bourgeois
society; in the Gestalt, Jünger discovers synthetic power. "It is the
sign of an imminent epoch that one will again see, feel, and act in
the thrall of Gestalten." Again Jünger declares an epochal transformation and emphasizes the practial ramifications (*handeln*) of the
Gestalt. "In politics too everything depends on bringing into battle
Gestalten and not concepts, ideas, or mere illusions."[2] The force of
the Gestalt is set in contrast to the forms of subjective consciousness,
denounced for their irrelevance. Thus the Gestalt is capable of to-
talization, it is practical, and it is therefore superior to the verbiage
and concepts of autonomous culture. The visual Gestalt displaces the
terms of writing. The fascist Gestalt displaces the bourgeois who was
never a Gestalt but only an individual, a mere part, in an "anatomical," which is to say, analytic or atomistic age. It is finally the heroic
Gestalt, the will incarnate, plain for all who have eyes to see, whom
Riefenstahl brings to Nuremberg, to wipe away the writing and
everything that writing represents.

Before proceeding with my discussion of *The Worker* and the particular character of the descriptive rhetoric of fascist representation,
I want to explore some aesthetic and aesthetic-historical aspects of
the problem of fascism and modernism. Fascism and modernism—
that is a touchy combination. Postwar criticism, at least in the West,
was eager to exclude from serious discussion literature complicitous
in fascism. A conservative humanism attempted to escape the political turbulence of the twentieth century by turning its gaze toward
the values of an unimpeachable occidental tradition with which one
could hope to overcome the political catastrophes of the present. The
same exclusionary move could of course be repeated on the left, for
example, Sartre's reading Céline out of the French literary tradition.
A further case that makes the issue clear: the efforts by the defenders
of Ezra Pound to separate his poetic from his political imagination
in order to canonize the former while relegating the latter to the domain of insanity, as if modernist innovation were necessarily separate
from or even opposed to fascist totalitarianism. Meanwhile, during

the first postwar decade in Eastern Europe, when the Lukácsian paradigm held sway (before the Hungarian Revolution of 1956), an association of modernism and decadence tended to lead to a collapsing of modernism and fascism *tout court*. That may overstate the case and do the critic Lukács some injustice, but it certainly corresponds to widespread political judgments associated with the aesthetics of socialist realism in that period. Classical critical theory, anxious to develop a general account of fascism, did little better in formulating a specific account of fascist aesthetics, although it provides a wealth of insights and comes close to an answer in the exchange on surrealism.

Recent critical work has begun to move beyond both the absolute separation of fascism and modernism and the thorough identification of fascism and modernism. Several preliminary points can be made. First, against efforts to prohibit a thematization of fascism within literary criticism, one notes that a considerable number of authors, whose works are irrefutably embedded in modernism, were drawn to various models of fascism: Marinetti, Céline, Maurras, Pound, Lewis, Hamsun, Benn, and Jünger. Second, against (socialist realist) efforts to collapse fascism and modernism, one notes the plethora of clearly modernist authors to whom it is patently absurd to ascribe an association with fascism: Brecht, Kafka, Mann, Döblin, Proust, Sartre, Joyce, and Woolf. Therefore if one were to endeavor to set the poetics of the modernist authors attracted to fascism in some resonance with their political proclivities, then the resulting model (or models) would not be adequate as accounts of modernism in general. A fascist modernism would have to be distinguished from competing versions that, as also modernist, are likely to display certain affinities or homologies, but that will be clearly distinct variations of the modernist problematic. Finally, the aesthetic profile of models of a fascist and a leftist and a liberal modernism ought to highlight aesthetic features and not concentrate on the political deeds of the historical individuals. Writers near political movements may always tend to be eccentric figures, outside of the inner circle of institutionalized political power. The proper question for literary critical inquiry has to do with the extent to which the political imagination of the author or the text (which may be extraordinarily eccentric when measured against the standard of the established political power) contributes to the construction of an aesthetic project and, in particular, one that can be labeled characteristically modernist.

In order to describe three competing models of modernist aesthetics—all of which are initiated by political motivations—I begin by limiting the term to its normal usage, parallel to the connotation of the term "modern art," that is, the radical aesthetic innovation that commences around 1900. Whether the proper dating begins somewhat earlier (with Heine and Baudelaire) or later (the generation of 1914) is less important than distinguishing this sense of the "modern" from the larger usage of a postmedieval modernity suggested by the German term *Neuzeit*. In his *Theory of Communicative Action*, Habermas works with this second, epochal model and, drawing on Weber and one strand in Adorno's thought, describes the differentiation of a particular aesthetic value-sphere undergoing a linear progress of autonomization. More sensitive to the vagaries of aesthetic representation in the twentieth century, Bürger insists on a rupture in the trajectory of autonomization produced by the historical avant-garde movements. In this context, I cannot even attempt a critique of Bürger's analysis of that rupture and I cite him only in regard to his insistence on the distinction between, on the one hand, an aesthetic culture of the eighteenth and nineteenth centuries, and, on the other hand, one of the avant-garde and modernism (I will also bracket a discussion of the exaggerated distinctions between modernism and the avant-garde).

These reflections on the theoretical construction of a category of modernism indicate the need for a nonmodernist foil, a countermodel of bourgeois culture against which one indeed finds all the aesthetic innovators of the early twentieth century railing: the art of the Victorian or the Wilhelmine establishments is regarded as just so much philistinism, historicism, sentimentalism, ornamentalism, and so forth. The key features of that countermodel include: (1) a developmental teleology, especially in the linear narratives of the Bildungsroman as well as in the bourgeois drama; (2) a thematics of identity-construction for the bourgeois subject undergoing the development; (3) an aesthetics of fictionality guaranteeing an autonomy, that is, a separation of the work of art from immediate life-practical concerns. It is this third point that Bürger underscores, singling it out as the object of attack by the historical avant-garde movements in order to sublate art and life-practice. That attack also leads, I contend, to a revision of the other aspects of the model—teleology and subjectivity—and all three aspects are lodged in an ostentatious antibourgeois gesturing that often induced an explicit politicization, particularly in the context of World War I and its aftermath. The moment of modernism was marked by the belief in the confluence of aesthetic and political change. The optimistic and perhaps self-serving assumption of modernist writers was the claim that literary innovation stood in some easy correspondence with political innovation. Hence the political motivation behind the competing modernist models.

Modernism was constituted by what it perceived to be the bourgeois aesthetics of autonomy, that is, teleology, identity, and fictionality. I identify three ideal types of German modernist aesthetics—fascist modernism, epic leftism, and liberal modernism—each of which proposes homologous alternatives to the terms of autonomy aesthetics. In place of bourgeois teleology, fascist modernism operates with iteration, a perpetual repetition of the same, suggesting the eternal return of a cyclical history. In place of identity-construction, it offers the spectacle, unnuanced and unquestioned, the authoritative presence of Jünger's aestheticized battlefields; in place of fictionality, it denounces escapism and claims for its texts a curious pseudodocumentary status. Hence Dinter footnotes his *völkisch* novels with alleged proofs, and Jünger prefers the memoir; he does not turn to the novel form until the mid-1930s, when, as in the case of Benn and Heidegger, a disappointment with the reality of the fascist revolution began to induce minor revisions of the positions held earlier.

Epic leftism replaces development with static examples of false consciousness (Döblin's Biberkopf), identity with dialectical constellations (Brecht), and fictionality with an operative aesthetics of documentary literature (Ottwalt). For liberal modernism, the corresponding features are seriality (Mann's *Doctor Faustus*), ambivalence (Broch's *Bergroman*), and the objectivity afforded by essayism (Musil). This map is of course only a map and would need extensive elaboration. I mention it in order to locate a fascist aesthetics within the modernist field next to alternative versions of German modernism. This is a necessary task, since Jünger himself underscores only the diachronic component, fascist aesthetics as a critique of an obsolete autonomy aesthetics, and does not recognize simultaneous but alternative critiques of the same autonomy aesthetics. Nevertheless this map has in fact only placed modernism as a catalogue of aesthetic categories. It has not yet led us much closer to the answer to the question that I began to examine before regarding the rhetoric of fascism: is there a specifically fascist politics of representation? Now I add an additional question: how does fascism subvert its own claims? Do immanent contradictions erode the flaunted stability of fascism? To find the answers, it is necessry to return to *The Worker* and to investigate a rhetorical micropractice in Jünger's text.

In the second part of *The Worker,* sections 58–67 bear the title "Art as the Formation (*Gestaltung*) of the World of Work." Since the whole book is devoted to the project of producing form as visually evident, the question of representation is not at all restricted to these passages. Everywhere the grand theme is the imposition of contours and the description of surface structures. There is no longer any inside and outside; there is no longer any above and below but only a ubiquitous constellation of power as form. Therefore the whole book enters a plea for the projection of the categories of art onto everyday life, an "aestheticization of politics," to use Benjamin's designation of fascism. In sections 58–67, Jünger consequently does not articulate a separate aesthetics, describing instead the separation of a sequestered aesthetic realm as itself anachronistic. Autonomous art is an expression of the obsolete bourgeois world view, that is, in place of an explicit aesthetic theory, Jünger provides a fascist version of the end-of-art theorem.

For Jünger, bourgeois conceptions of aesthetic autonomy are corollaries to the modern, that is, postmedieval (*neuzeitliche*), constructions of individuality. Despite the fragmentation of the universalist claims of the Catholic Church and a sweeping process of secularization, bourgeois individuality remains grounded in the tradition of the Christian soul. The constitutive categories of the autonomous personality recur in the autonomous work of art as the discourse of the individual genius: "The history of art appears here above all as the history of the personality, and the work itself as an autobiographical document."[3] As the bourgeois individual loses legitimacy—Jünger counterposes him to the soldier in his war memoirs of the twenties and to the worker in 1932—so does the bourgeois understanding of art. In the era of total mobilization, autonomy in no field can be tolerated. To the extent that bourgeois culture still plays a role, it merely provides an escapist refuge for a privileged few, while impeding the urgently necessary decisions in the ongoing state of emergency. Jünger has nothing but contempt for the manner in which the Weimar state draped itself with signs of culture, the portraits of writers and artists on stamps and currency, as compensation for its inability to master the political crisis. "It is a kind of opium that masks the danger and produces a deceptive sense of order. This is an intolerable luxury now when we should not be talking about traditions but creating them."[4] Bourgeois autonomy has run its course and can no longer claim the allegiance of the generation of the trenches: "Our fathers perhaps still had the time to concern themselves with the ideals of an objective science or an art that exists for itself. We however find ourselves clearly in a situation in which not this or that but the totality of our life is in question"[5]—thus the fascist version of the modernist hostility to the culture of the philistine nineteenth century. In place of philistinism and autonomy aesthetics, Jünger advocates a postautonomous, postmodern culture that structures life-experience within an overriding Gestalt of authority. He identifies public practices likely to organize the masses and abolish private identity: film, architecture, urban planning, *Landschaftsgestaltung*—practices that are inimical to the victims of fascist modernism: subjectivity, privacy, and writing.

I turn now to a passage that I consider particularly important, not only because it again repeats the critique of autonomy aesthetics— such repetition corresponds to the iterative aspect of fascist modernism—but because it does so with a phrase that will allow me to unravel the textual web and explore the politics of fascist representation. Jünger first identifies a parasitic artistry (*schmarotzendes Artistentum*) that, like standard bourgeois art, sets itself apart from life-practice but that, in addition has lost the genuine values of earlier generations. Clearly the object of attack is contemporary innovative art, which, for Jünger, is not only bourgeois (which would be bad enough) but epigonic as well.

Jünger then proceeds to associate these degenerate artists with the advocates of an aesthetics of autonomy. Recall that, for Jünger, the insistence on the autonomous status of art represents an impediment to resolving the political emergency. He therefore accuses the proponents of autonomy of treason in a remarkable turn of phrase: "Therefore in Germany one meets this artistry with dead certainty (*tödlicher Sicherheit*) in close connection with all those forces on whom a hidden or overt treasonous character is written right across their faces (*denen ein verhüllter oder unverhüllter verräterischer Charakter ins Gesicht geschrieben ist*)."[6] Why does the accomplished stylist Jünger choose this phrasing? Whose faces does he envision and what is written across them? And what does this figure of speech tell us about the status of writing in fascist rhetoric?

Let me first complete the recapitulation of the passage in order to indicate the importance of the matter for the history of fascism and the status of literature within it. Jünger goes on to predict or, better, to look forward to the wrathful retribution these treasonous aesthetes will soon meet:

Fortunately one finds in our youth a growing attention for these sorts of connections; and one begins to understand that in this domain even just the use of abstract thought is tantamount to a treasonous activity. A new sort of Dominican zeal has the nerve to regret the end of the persecution of heretics—but have patience, such persecutions are in preparation already, and nothing will hold them back, as soon as one has recognized that for us a factual finding of heresy is called for on the grounds of the belief in the dualism of the world and its systems.[7]

Clearly Jünger is not, as he has recently claimed in retrospect, merely describing an objective historical process but rather applauding the impending initiation of a new inquisition in order to purge Germany of the heresy of dualism, that is, the claim that autonomous dimensions of human activity might operate outside the structure of power. The general heresy exists in several versions; he speaks of materialist and spiritualist positions that appear to be mutually exclusive. He must be referring to Marxist materialism and conservative idealism, the twin opponents of fascism that the Nazis would name with the crude alliteration of "Rotfront and Reaktion." Despite their apparent antagonisms, Jünger insists that both have a fundamental hostility to the survival of the German Reich: November treason in art. Both are implicated in an ultimately bourgeois discourse of an emancipatory narrative; both propagate the enervating nihilism of dialectical thought, shattering the totality into an endless series of antinomies; and both are blind to the *Gestalt* of *Herrschaft*.

The passage, especially the description of opponents with treason written right across their faces, immediately suggests several points. Recall that their crime involves the advocacy of autonomy, that is, the separation of art and, more broadly, all representational practices of culture from life-practice. Jünger's image denounces that belief by reducing the distance between writing and the body to nil. The body of the text is transformed into the body as the text, as if Jünger were already preparing to tattoo the victims of the emerging Dominican zeal. Jünger metes out a punishment fit to the crime: the proponents of bourgeois idealism learn about the materiality of language, as script branded in their flesh, across their faces.

In addition to this corporealization of writing, homologous to the appearance of Gestalt and the incarnation of the will in the body of the leader, the passage betrays a simultaneous hostility to particular identity. The victims are guilty not simply of treason but of having treason written across their faces, thus rendering them identifiable. Because they emerge as particular, they are fair game for particular persecution. Jünger does not like *their* faces because he does not like faces, that is, the representation of an individual personality, at all, especially those that are constituted by writing. The vision of persecution to which he looks forward anticipates the book-burnings of 1933, which can be considered not only as political demonstrations but as literary acts, the fascist realization of the generally modernist posture of iconoclasm toward a literary culture deemed traditional.

Beyond these explicit ramifications of Jünger's figure of the inscribed physiognomy, the passage is implicated in fundamental aspects of fascist representation. I want to isolate three points and comment on each of them: (1) the moment of recognition and the priority of vision (sight and the faces); (2) the perception of particular identity through a characteristic marking (writing as scar); and (3) the antipathy toward a symbolic order and the imaginary desire to escape writing.

1) Throughout Jünger's oeuvre, a series of descriptions defines the dimension of sight and its counterpart, physiognomy, in both negative and positive versions. The sentimental bourgeois, with sight clouded by emotion, is out of place in the age of total warfare, for "it is not the time to read your 'Werther' with tearful eyes."[8] Eyes trapped in the darkness of bourgeois interiority cannot provide the

clarity of vision demanded at the outset of *The Worker*. Moreover it is writing, a founding text of German bourgeois culture, *Werther*, that leaves its traces on the cheeks, traces that mark the individual as such, while they simultaneously distort his vision.

The positive *Doppelgänger* of the lachrymose bourgeois stares out from under the *Stahlhelm,* a physiognomy devoid of literacy or emotions but toughened by modern warfare into a calloused clarity:

[The face] has become more metallic, its surface is galvanized, the bone structure is evident, and the traits are clear and tense. The gaze is steady and fixed, trained on objects moving at high velocities. It is the face of a race that has begun to develop in the peculiar demands of a new landscape, where one is represented neither as a person nor an individual but as a type.[9]

The right-wing critique of bourgeois individuality could not be more explicit; it announces the end of interiority and the emancipation of vision. The new man has unimpaired sight, just as the contours of his face take on the sharp and clear lines of Gestalt. Yet no lines of age deface the complexion of the eternal youth invoked by fascism. Ambiguity disappears. The face of the hawk-eyed soldier is the diametrical opposite of the image of a spectacled intellectual, a rigid mask without nuance.[10]

Jünger's moment of recognition privileges the clear image of the soldier and then doubles the point by attributing to it a clarity of vision. Conversely, the bourgeois, who cannot see through his tears, is embedded in a literary culture of writing. Hence the treason of those whose faces are marked by writing: they disrupt the presence of the image with the mendacity of words. Jünger's fascist modernism promises to liberate the imaginary from the Jacobin tyranny of the symbolic order. It draws on a long-standing reactionary tradition, a Wagnerian formulation of which can help us identify Jünger's traitors. Polemicizing against the actor Josef Kainz, Wagner writes: "One's impression is as though the Saviour had been cut out of a painting of the Crucifixion, and replaced by a Jewish demagogue."[11] It is not Christ but Christ's image that concerns Wagner, but the point is moot since Christ as the visible incarnation is image and is threatened by the Jew as language and the people of the Book. Based on the Old Testament prohibition of graven images, the aporetic construction of Wagnerian anti-Semitism contrasts the visible Gestalt with an alternative defined as verbal and hence inimical to visual appearance. Wagner's logic is perversely consistent when he continues: "A race whose general appearance we cannot consider suitable for aesthetic purposes is by the same token incapable of any artistic presentation of its nature." Because their God is invisible, Wagner denounces the visible appearance of Jews and considers them a threat to any representative images. The legacy of Wagner's anti-Semitism recurs in Jünger as the contrasting physiognomies and the agonistic confrontation of Gestalt and writing. Figures with writing in their faces are Jews: "And thou shalt bind them for a sign upon thy hand, and they shall be for frontlets between thine eyes" (Deuteronomy 6:8). The phylacteries, the sign of treason, have become the mark of Cain by which the fascist modernist recognizes the enemy. The French racial anthropoligist and fascist collaborator Georges Montandon entitles a pamphlet *Comment reconnaître le Juif?* Jünger's answer must be: by signs of writing.

2) Signs of writing in the face mar the image and make it particular. The scar produces identity, be it the wound received by Rotpeter in Kafka's "Report to an Academy" or the vernacular understanding of the significance of the tattoo, as expressed in an advertisement: "Who you are/ What you stand for/ On your skin/ If you like—forever."[12] Scarring the face in the ritual dual, the *Bestimmungsmensur,* a key element in German student culture, survived despite an imperial prohibition of genuine duels in 1883, various papal encylicals, and the agitation of the Deutsche Antiduell-Liga, founded in 1902; if the social function of the *Schmiss* had to do with the production of the signs of an elite, its expressed purpose involved the preservation of individual honor and the strengthening of the participant's personality.[13] Jünger could recognize treason "written right across their faces" because that writing, the scar, produced individual identity, which was anathema, as we have seen, for fascist modernism.

This connection is confirmed by the discussion of the scar of Odysseus in the first chapter (written in 1942) of Erich Auerbach's *Mimesis* (1946). When Odysseus returns to Ithaca, the servant Eurykleia, who had nursed him as a child, recognizes him by a scar on his thigh, as if the marking on the body were the locus of the personal identity that Jünger detests. Auerbach describes how Homer interrupts the narrative at the moment of recognition in order to recount how young

Odysseus, visiting his grandfather Autolykos, received the scar. The wound marks the body and marks the rite of passage from a preliterate infancy to a symbolic maturity associated with writing and language. This suggestion goes beyond Auerbach but is compatible with his argument that the interpolated incident does not heighten suspense; instead it testifies to the mimetic impulse in the Homeric text to encompass the world with language and to omit nothing from the verse. The scar on the body that grants Odysseus identity and personal language also generates the expansive agility of poetic language.

Auerbach juxtaposes the story of Odysseus' return with the sacrifice of Isaac in order to contrast Homeric and biblical narration. Critics have however pointed out the fundamental similarity, the thematic concern with the production of male identity in barely hidden practices of ritual scarring.[14] When Jünger denounces the marked bodies of his opponents, he participates in a sublimated anti-Semitism by articulating a displaced critique of circumcision. His critique of identity is a fascist critique of *male* identity. Patriarchal culture depends on the symbolic order of law and language; fascist anti-patriarchy, which is always implicitly an attack on the patriarch as Jew, is an attack on the practices of writing in order to resurrect the imaginary as Gestalt, the visible body without stigmata, descending from the clouds over Nuremberg.

3) "Written right across their faces"—the scar in the face is a long-standing topos of the writer. It is because of a scar of irresolution that Montaigne, in his essay "Of Presumption," chooses a private life of writing and abjures the courtly public where kings are represented in portraits.[15] The writer Jünger abhors that bourgeois privacy and casts constant aspersion on "the desks of Europe" where the culture of literacy takes place.[16] The fascist modernist denounces identities constituted by language, while expressing a desire for the image freed from verbal mediation. Of course both this denunciation and this desire are themselves lodged in language. Jünger's prose searches for the Gestalt, which is outside of language, by means of language. Its descriptive *parole* is committed to the abolition of *langue*. Similarly Jünger hopes to be able to recognize the new post-bourgeois type who, by definition, can have no identifying features. This slippery rhetorical situation can be analyzed through the parameters of the trope of ekphrasis.

Ekphrasis was the primary technical option in the speech of praise (epideixis or panegyric) that, during the Roman Empire, overshadowed the other two objects of classical rhetoric, judicial and deliberative speech. It profoundly influenced the poetry of late antiquity and the Middle Ages.[17] For Ernst Robert Curtius, ekphrasis is above all laudatory description, accounts of beautiful persons and landscapes, leading to the topos of the *locus amoenus,* in the tradition of which the sensuous spectacles of Jünger's battlefields have to be placed. However, as a description of beautiful objects, ekphrasis has a somewhat more precise usage, which Leo Spitzer articulates with reference to the definition of the trope provided by Théophile Gautier, " 'une transposition d'art,' the reproduction through the medium of words of sensuously perceptible *objets d'art* (ut pictura poesis)."[18] Classical examples include the descriptions of the ornamental shields of Achilles (*Iliad,* 18.478 ff.) and Aeneas (*Aeneid,* 8.626 ff.) and of various cups, garments, and sculptures. The term is occasionally extended to include descriptions of poetic renderings, e.g., the interpolated narrations included in the *Metamorphoses,* although this usage certainly goes beyond the limits suggested by Spitzer.[19] In either the limited or this extended sense, ekphrasis has to do with the verbal representation of aesthetic representation. It functions either to interrupt the course of the narrative (like the account of Odysseus' scar which is ekphrastic only if one accepts my suggestion that the scar is an instance of writing or aesthetic marking) or as an allegorical interlude: Achilles' shield reproduces the cosmos and Aeneas' shield predicts the future. "Its images of Roman history chart the course of destiny in which the hero must play his inevitable role and illumine the similarity between his own deeds of violence and those of his descendents."[20] The proximity to Jünger's military fatalism is evident.

However, the connection between this aspect of classical rhetoric and fascist modernism is not merely thematic. Jünger's descriptivism and his fascination with the visible Gestalt are ekphrastic in a new and revealing manner. The authors of antiquity devote special attention at particular moments to works of art, as if art were already a relatively autonomous sphere, separate (no matter how integrated) from the rest of the narrative, to which the author would return at the conclusion of the aesthetic description. For Homer the whole world and all its details can of course be mastered by poetic representation, and Auerbach could therefore contrast the Homeric text with the sparse abstraction of the biblical epic. This does not mean that the Homeric cosmos is always aestheticized in advance or that the work of art is indistinguishable from all other dimensions of human activity. Yet this is precisely the case for fascist modernism where the aporia of bourgeois autonomy is sublated through a universal aestheticization. The writer approaches a cosmos that is only art, and he can only recount its aestheticized Gestalt. Ekphrasis becomes the sole option of a literature that takes the classical admonition to an extreme: ut pictura poesis.

I have tried to demonstrate the ekphrastic character of Jünger's rhetorical stance not only to identify the continuity of certain topoi— from the shield to the *Stahlhelm,* from *locus amoenus* to *Langemarck*—but to investigate the politics of representation in fascist modernism. Ekphrasis necessarily implies a double dialectic: it invokes as present a missing object, and it appropriates speech to produce a visual image. Each of these points is worthy of consideration with reference to Jünger's writing.

Ekphrasis conveys the desire for an absent object, which Jünger attempts to redeem as Gestalt, just as the Gestalt of Hitler arrives in Riefenstahl's Nuremberg as the vehicle of national resurrection. A regenerative aesthetics pervades much of European fascist ideology: the object that is missing has to be retrieved from death. Jünger's writing constitutes an extended project to overcome the mass death of World War I. In *The Worker* he asks: "What kinds of minds are these that do not know that no mind can be deeper or wiser than that of any of the soldiers who fell on the Somme or in Flanders?"[21] Jünger, the intellectual, is prepared to sacrifice intellectual identity in order to revivify the anonymous cadavers of the war. Ekphrastic writing becomes an exchange, a sacrifice of atonement as payment for the absent bodies. Because bullets have robbed them of their subjectivity, Jünger makes a career of denying his own and repressing his pain. This self-denial and repression account for the banality of his contributions to the controversy around his receipt of the Goethe Award: a fundamental inability to give serious consideration to the consequences of his fascist advocacy. Reminiscent of Hannah Arendt's Eichmann, Jünger's mental blockage is due to the trauma of the trenches. He is marked by the guilt of the survivor who cannot account for his having escaped death. When asked by an interviewer if he was sad to to have survived 1914, he only objects to the coarse phrasing and adds that he "agrees with the ancient Greeks: those who fall in war are honored by men and gods. That would have been a good ending."[22] He refers to his refusal to flee into a bomb shelter during a British air raid on Paris in 1944 (the incident is described in *Strahlungen*) as a "toast with death" (*ein Bruderschaftstrinken mit dem Tode*). Similarly when critics complain that he did not resist the Nazis adamantly enough after 1933, his testy response that opposition would have led to execution in a camp has all the earmarks of a classical psychoanalytic denial: as if he knew he should have acted differently and had met his death long ago.

His ekphrastic rhetoric is therefore both a desire for the absent object and a desire for the absence of the author. Jünger simultaneously undertakes resurrection and enacts his own death. In this gruesome exchange, the idealized physiognomy of the new man is the *facies hippocratica:* for Benjamin a critical tool to pursue the mortification of the artwork with an eye to redemption, for Jünger a prescription for the aestheticization of life as death mask without transcendence.

Jünger's version of the death of the author can be treated as one item in the history of German intellectuals responding to the catastrophes of war and holocaust. It is also implicated in the second dialectic of ekphrasis, the effort to appropriate language in order to surpass it with the production of image. This tension is a constitutive moment of the trope but comes to the fore in the ekphrastic rhetoric of fascist modernism. It corresponds to the displacement of writing by image in *Triumph of the Will* and to the emphatic prescription of *The Worker* where "it is no longer a matter of a change of styles [i.e., modes of literary expression] but rather of the becoming visible of another Gestalt (*das Sichtbarwerden einer anderen Gestalt*)."[23] Fascism as the aestheticization of politics transforms the world into a visual object, the spectacular landscapes of industry and war, and this first renders writing solely descriptive only to proceed to the denigration of writing as not-visual. The author's hatred for identities constituted by the presence of writing in their faces is also a self-hatred of the author as writer. It is a writing trying to escape writing. In fascist modernism, the imaginary rebels against the symbolic order of language where the author, dependent on language, is necessarily at home. It is literature at the moment of the auto-da-fé, always about to go up in flames along with the identity of the writer. If Jünger's military thematics recall Virgil's account of Aeneas' shield, his constitution of a self-subverting writing is closer to the Ovidian version of ekphrasis, the perpetual destruction of the second-order narrators in the *Metamorphoses:* Jünger's decimation of his own subjectivity repeats the slaying of Marsyas, the death wish of the descriptive poet, fleeing language.

Fleeing language, the fascist rhetorician also flees time. The classical ekphrasis interrupted the linear progress of the surrounding narrative, drawing attention to a particular *locus* apparently impervious to the vagaries of temporality. In fascist modernism, ekphrastic representation resonates with the antiteleological bias that all versions of modernism share in their rejection of traditional bourgeois culture. I want to conclude with a remark on the organization of time associated with autonomy aesthetics and its critique at the moment of the modern.

Horkheimer and Adorno's account of Odysseus and the Sirens in the first chapter of *Dialectic of Enlightenment* describes the moment of birth of bourgeois aesthetic culture. It is a process of autonomization, insofar as the local myth, still embedded in primitive religious cult, is subjected to the force of enlightenment secularization and robbed of its apotropaic power: the song of the Sirens becomes the song of art. Henceforth art has no life-practical consequences, although the nonoperative character is experienced in different manners by the opposed classes in heteronomous society. Art is simply denied the slaves whose ears are plugged with wax, while the bourgeois adventurer can partake of aesthetic expression only at the price of binding his hands to the mast. This cultural autonomization is located meanwhile within the context of a victory over space: Odysseus, the first hero in the age of discovery, navigates unknown seas and subdues them, while his body, which is separated from art, also escapes danger. Mastering the globe, he lives to tell the tale, and this is the birth of history, the victory over the lyric entreaties of forgetfulness, which allows the constructions of narratives of teleological practice.

Because historical memory and aesthetic autonomy are consanguineous, the modernist attack on autonomy aesthetics begins to pull apart the intricacies of the Odyssean nexus. The distance between body and text is radically reduced, and experience undergoes a re-spatialization: Odysseus could traverse every dangerous terrain, while Jünger's hero remains in the field with neither personal past nor individual future. The optimistic temporality of linear progress is frozen, but each version of modernism records the end of history in a different way. Liberal modernism, as a rhetoric of irony, critiques structures of representation and explores the immobility of the present. Epic leftism, with its anticipatory hopes of radical revolution, operates as prolepsis and explodes the continuum of history. The ekphrasis of fascist modernism asserts the immutable presence of Gestalt and exalts the luminous positivity of visible power that will shine for a thousand years, uncorrupted by the infectious nihilism of writing. It glows with the light of the image; "the fully enlightened earth radiates in the sign of disaster triumphant."[24]

Notes

1. Ernst Jünger, *Der Arbeiter*, in *Werke* 6 (Stuttgart: Klett, n.d.), 13.

2. *Ibid.*, 38–39.

3. *Ibid.*, 227.

4. *Ibid.*, 219.

5. *Ibid.*

6. *Ibid.*, 250.

7. *Ibid.*

8. Ernst Jünger, *Der Kampf als inneres Erlebnis*, in *Werke* 5 (Stuttgart: Klett, n.d.), 41–42.

9. Ernst Jünger, *Der Arbeiter*, 119.

10. *Ibid.*, 129.

11. Richard Wagner, "Judaism in Music," in *Stories and Essays*, ed. Charles Osborne (London: Peter Owen, 1973), 27.

12. On the cover of Albert Parry, *Tattoo: Secrets of a Strange Art* (New York: Collier Books, 1971 [1933]).

13. See Konrad H. Jarausch, *Students, Society, and Politics in Imperial Germany: The Rise of Academic Illiberalism* (Princeton: Princeton University Press, 1982), 244–49.

14. See John Freccero, "Manfred's Wounds and the Poetics of the 'Purgatorio,'" in *Centre and Labyrinth: Essays in Honour of Northrop Frye*, ed. Eleanor Cook et al. (Toronto: University of Toronto Press, 1983), 69–71. I am grateful to Elizabeth Statmore for this and other references.

15. See Philip P. Hallie, *The Scar of Montaigne: An Essay in Personal Philosophy* (Middletown: Wesleyan University Press, 1966).

16. Ernst Jünger, introduction to Richard Junior, ed., *Hier spricht der Feind* (Berlin: Neufeld and Henius, n.d.), 11–12.

17. Ernst Robert Curtius, *Europäische Literatur und Lateinisches Mittelalter* (Bern: Francke, 1948), 75–76.

18. George Kurman, "Ecphrasis in Epic Poetry," *Comparative Literature* 26:1 (Winter 1974):1.

19. Eleanor Winsor Leach, "Ekphrasis and the Theme of Artistic Failure in Ovid's Metamorphosis," *Ramus* 3:2 (1974):104.

20. *Ibid.*, 105.

21. Ernst Jünger, *Der Arbeiter*, 221.

22. Interview in Der Spiegel, No. 33 (1982):160.

23. Ernst Jünger, *Der Arbeiter*, 225.

24. Max Horkheimer and Theodor W. Adorno, *Dialectic of Enlightenment* (New York: Seabury Press, 1972), 3 (translation modified).

The Loss of Reality: Gottfried Benn's Early Prose

Peter Uwe Hohendahl

In 1915 a young German physician and officer, stationed as a member of the German occupation forces in Brussels, wrote a number of prose pieces, among them the novella "Gehirne." In this text he created the figure of Rönne,

the physician who could not endure the real world, who could not grasp reality anymore, who knew only the rhythmic opening and closing of the Ego and the personality,

as the author commented some twenty years later in his autobiography.[1] When these short prose pieces, presenting Rönne as their central character, appeared first in the journal *Die weißen Blätter* and later in a collected edition entitled *Gehirne* (1916) they were for the German world of letters what James Joyce's *Ulysses* was to become for English literature—a text that could no longer be interpreted in terms of traditional narrative fiction. However, the significance of this break was not fully understood at that time. While the broad literary public hardly acknowledged the Rönne pieces, those critics who grasped their innovative character read them as a radical form of literary expressionism. They interpreted them, in other words, in the context of the currently most advanced literary movement, which had appeared on the horizon of German literature around 1912. Since Gottfried Benn, the author of these prose pieces, had made his literary debut with a collection of poems (the famous *Morgue* poems) that shocked the audience through their unfamiliar, sometimes cruel themes and their radical metaphors, his early narrative prose elicited similar responses. It was seen as a part of the general attack of the young generation of expressionist writers on the values of the middle class, especially on the limitations of the scientific mind. Yet this view (which was later reinforced by literary historians and has guided much of Benn criticism until rather recently) does not, at least in my opinion, do justice to the force and the historical meaning of Benn's early prose. When we read the Rönne pieces primarily as a radical articulation of German expressionism we implicitly marginalize their aesthetic significance by limiting their literary and social context to the German situation during World War I. Therefore, I want to argue that we should rather choose a broader and at the same time historically more specific literary configuration as the proper parameter, namely, the European avant-garde movements of the early twentieth century. This shift in focus would allow us to interrogate Benn's prose with more precise questions. As soon as we place Benn's oeuvre within the context of the avant-garde movements, our attention is drawn to a number of problems that have not been addressed adequately by Benn specialists.

My intention is twofold: by bringing together the category of the avant-garde and Gottfried Benn's early prose I want to probe both the narrative structure of Benn's texts and the theory of the avant-garde. In particular, I want to raise two questions: (1) What do Benn's novellas, as he calls his early pieces of narrative prose, contribute to the articulation of the European avant-garde? (2) what can we learn about the nature of the avant-garde from these texts? The meaning of these questions, particularly of the second one, will become clearer only when we look more closely at the present debate over the relevance of the avant-garde.

The concept of the avant-garde has been used in various ways. As long as the term is understood as being more or less interchangeable with the concept of modernism, a usage that has been predominant in this country, it will not be a very useful tool for our analysis. Since the formal innovations of Benn's poetry as well as his prose have been recognized, nobody will seriously deny that he belongs to the same group of writers as T. S. Eliot, Ezra Pound, Kafka, Thomas Mann, Proust, and Gide. Using modernism as the decisive category, various critics have argued that Benn as a disciple of Nietzsche fully understood the literary implications of radical aestheticism and therefore in his poetic practice consciously explored textual formations that transcend the realm of realism. Only when we clearly differentiate between modernism and the avant-garde can we focus on those elements of Benn's narrative prose that articulate the specific literary response of Benn to his predecessors and distinguish his achievement from earlier attempts to break away from a realistic mode of presentation.

In his study *Faces of Modernity*, Matei Calinescu, on the one hand, has suggested that the avant-garde movements of the early twentieth century should be understood as a second, more radical phase of modernism—a phase characterized by ideological and political commitments that Calinescu finds less appealing and ultimately aesthetically less successful than the original impetus of modernism.[2] On the other hand, Peter Bürger in his *Theory of the Avant-Garde* (1974) has stressed the importance of this radical gesture. For him the avant-garde is more than a continuation of modernism. He defines the avant-garde as a movement that subverts the traditional basis of aesthetic production and reception. The avant-garde movements of the early twentieth century, according to Bürger, are involved in a radical self-critique of art, a critique that goes beyond the negation of specific established norms and practices. Calling the institution of art into question—this was the task that movements like dadaism and surrealism set themselves. "With the historical avant-garde movements, the social subsystem of art enters the stage of self-criticism. Dadaism, the most radical movement within the European avant-garde, no longer criticizes schools that preceded it, but criticizes art as an institution, and the course its development took in bourgeois society."[3] Following Marx's notion of self-criticism, as it was developed in the introduction to the *Grundrisse*, Bürger advances the thesis that the protest of the avant-garde movements against bourgeois art and bourgeois values was aimed at the reintegration of art into life. "Only after art, in nineteenth-century Aestheticism, has altogether detached itself from the praxis of life can the aesthetic develop 'purely.' But the other side of autonomy, art's lack of social impact, also becomes recognizable" (22). This self-criticism of art as a social subsystem, Bürger argues, allows for the first time an objective understanding of the evolution of past stages of literature and the arts. Realism, for instance, appears no longer as the ultimate principle of aesthetic production but rather as a historically limited system of norms and procedures governing the institution of art. What distinguishes Bürger from Calinescu is his insistence on the radical break between aestheticism, that is, modernism, and the avant-garde. This emphasis is grounded in his reading of romantic aesthetic theory as the decisive turning point in the history of European literature. Autonomy of art, as it was proclaimed by Kant and his romantic followers in Germany and England, dominates the institution of literature between 1800 and 1900. Autonomy means detachment of art from the life-world; it implies the *Herausdifferenzierung* (crystallization) of this special realm of experience. Only when the separation of art and life reaches its radical end, when substantive concerns in art are canceled by purely formal concerns during the years of late-nineteenth-century aestheticism, so Bürger argues, has the stage been prepared for self-criticism. Literature begins to undermine its institutional basis by calling into question its autonomous status.

The prime examples of Bürger's *Theory of the Avant-Garde* are dadaism and surrealism. But what about Gottfried Benn? To what extent does his early prose confirm Bürger's understanding of the avant-garde? Can we speak of an attempt to reintegrate art into social life?

A closer examination of "Gehirne," the first story of the collection by the same name, should possibly give us some clues. When one comes to Benn from earlier realistic fiction one is more aware of the experimental character of his prose. In this case the critical response would have to be formulated primarily in negative terms. This "novella" hardly conforms to the model set up during the nineteenth century. There is, for instance, no plot that leads to the famous turning point required by earlier theory. It would be difficult indeed to capture the sense of the piece by summarizing the plot and describing the characters involved. The reader finds only fragments of a story, kept together by a narrator who moves from factual report to the articulation of consciousness with great ease, frequently without indicating that there is a shift. Yet compared with Benn's later prose, "Gehirne" still contains a number of conventional features. We confront a narrator who sets up the parameters of the events in terms of time and space. Likewise, there are references to the world as we ordinarily experience it. Rönne, the central figure, takes up a new position at a sanatorium where he is expected to supervise the staff during the absence of the senior physician in charge of the hospital. Special references that help the reader to orient himself/herself are given. For instance, events leading up to the dismissal of Rönne are presented roughly in their traditional time sequence. The prose piece, in other words, provides a framework with some traditional elements of narrative prose. On this level we can read "Gehirne" as a "case study," narrating the inner development of the hero who is increasingly unable to cope with his social environment. Rönne is portrayed as the man who loses reality, who experiences a growing rift between his consciousness and external reality, a rift that makes it more and more difficult for him to act. A few years later, in *History and Class Consciousness* (1923), Georg Lukács was to develop the theory of reification, which analyzes the very phenomena that Benn's novella foregrounds.

Without any doubt, Benn's analysis of the pathological state of Rönne's mind is fascinating, the contrast to the normalcy of the bourgeois world illuminating, but is this thematic polemic enough evidence to conclude that Benn's text destroys the institution of literature? Can we speak of a self-criticism of art?

In 1934 Benn offered a perceptive interpretation of the Rönne novellas. He wrote:

In Rönne the decomposition of natural vitality has reached a degree that looks like decadence. But is it really decadence? What is decaying? Maybe it is no more than a historically superposing layer, uncritically accepted for centuries, while the other is the primal essence? (4:36)

For Benn the Cartesian Ego and the rationalist construction of reality have come to an end. Consequently, the narrative structures built on the epistemology of the enlightenment, as it is still present in nineteenth-century realism, have become insufficient for the purpose of aesthetic presentation, particularly for the presentation of consciousness.

It is in this area that we observe the most significant changes in "Gehirne." The traditional dichotomy of Ego and outer reality, the character and the social and natural environment, is collapsing. In "Gehirne" Benn uses a variety of techniques to present new forms of consciousness. Both narrated and quoted monologue are applied. Yet, as Dorrit Cohn has shown, these techniques are by no means limited to the twentieth century.[4] What makes their use striking and novel in Benn's prose is the easy and rapid shift from one mode to another. The transition from the third person to the first occurs several times in the short story. The result is a deliberate obscurity and opaqueness of the text. The narrator does not provide the traditional signals that allow the reader to differentiate between the consciousness of the character and the commentary of the narrator. Thus, the attempt of the narrative to penetrate the mind of the central character, to unfold the process of mental destabilization, leads to the fragmentation of the plot. While this tendency is still checked in "Gehirne" by the imposition of a narrative voice offering a perspective of the mental process from the outside, stories like "Die Reise" or "Die Insel," written almost at the same time, no longer provide the reader with a narrator who consistently explains the difference between external and internal reality, between the presentation of things and events on the one hand and states of mind on the other. Hence, relations of time and space become increasingly blurred. This narrative strategy indeed decomposes traditional reality; it brings into the foreground the fact that the mode of reality underlying nineteenth-century fiction is a *construct* that was grounded in institutionalized narrative conventions.

In "Die Insel" we find a similar configuration—again Werf Rönne, the problematic individual who has to face alienated reality. His world is one in which the visible and tangible phenomena are close and distant at the same time. Rönne's consciousness, as it is presented throughout the narrative, can register these phenomena, but it is unable to put them together into a meaningful whole. Reality consists of heterogeneous elements that resist the traditional move toward synthesis. At least, the consciousness of the hero lacks the power to construct a meaningful totality that would provide metaphysical security. The factual details are stronger than the notion of a whole that would guide the search of the subject for truth. Yet it would not be enough to point to the dichotomy of the subject and the phenomena, the tension between the pure subjectivity of the hero and the reified heterogeneity of things with which the subject comes into contact. The *abstractness* of the relationship has to be emphasized. In spite of the objective tone of the narrative, the text is not presenting a neutral reality *an sich*—a reality that can be separated from the consciousness of the central character. Clearly, the subjectivity of the hero provides the novella with its organizational focus. Still, "Die Insel" cannot be reduced to a straight presentation of the hero's consciousness. Rather, the narrative contains a number of interconnected levels and relies on a variety of methods. Most important, the voice of the narrator transcends the consciousness of the hero. This voice is sympathetic to Rönne's existential problems, but it is at the same time distant to, and critical of, the reified subject-object dichotomy. This is the locus of the intrinsic reflexivity that the early Lukács in *The Theory of the Novel* called *irony*. Unlike the use of irony in Goethe, however, Benn's narrator does not assume that the reader of the text will naturally find the proper perspective that will enable him/her to understand and thereby to overcome the problematic nature of the hero. Benn's narrator seems to be involved more in a dialogue with the consciousness of the hero than in a dialogue with the potential audience. In other words, the space of the implied reader is not clearly defined. This opaqueness is of course one of the reasons why Benn's early prose has remained highly esoteric.

Benn's prose is certainly critical of the epistemological model of the enlightenment. But is it self-critical in the sense of Marx? Does Benn attempt to undermine the very core of fiction? Do the Rönne novellas tend toward a negation of art, closing thereby the gap between the aesthetic and the social realm?

The deconstruction of conventional notions of reality and the decomposition of the traditional fictional character as a closed unity to which thoughts and actions can be ascribed lead in the case of Benn to textual structures that ultimately valorize the aesthetic sphere. In this respect the last paragraph of "Die Reise" is suggestive. The journey of the hero ends in a park. After watching a movie (which serves as a surrogate epic with "real" characters and "real" action) Rönne finally achieves, momentarily at least, the lost unity:

It was dark and threatening, covered with clouds and horrific, with a sense of being asleep, a sleep into which one plunged without even leaving a whirl above oneself, one ceased to live, positive only in the sense of a point of intersection; but he still walked through the spring and created himself vis-à-vis the bright wind flowers, he was leaning against a herm, deadly white, eternal marble, dropped at this place from the quarry which for ever contains the mediterranean sea. (2:36)

Rönne moves toward a regressive, dreamlike state of mind where the rationalist dichotomy of subject and object has been canceled.

This state of mind negates the conventional category of reality but it does not, I think, negate art. If we accept this thesis, we have to rethink either the position of Gottfried Benn within the German avant-garde movements or the theory of the avant-garde. We could, for instance, reconcile our findings with Bürger's theory by arguing that Benn is still a modernist and not part of the avant-garde. This thesis could be supported, for example, by the argument that the dadaists openly rejected the expressionists precisely because they failed to critique the institution of art itself. I suspect that Bürger would choose this explanation, but I am not certain whether Benn's prose, given its radically subversive character, could still be labeled as modernist in the same sense as one would define the prose of Hofmannsthal and Rilke as modernist. Hence, if we insist on the *difference* between Hofmannsthal and Benn, if we understand Benn as part of the German avant-garde, we are led to a crucial conclusion: the theory of the avant-garde has to be reformulated. Especially the notion that art would be reintegrated into the life-world must be reconsidered. Bürger's theory relies primarily on dadaism and surrealism, leaving it open whether the expressionist movement would support his argument. This cautious gesture, however, does not protect the theory against criticism.

In the case of Gottfried Benn's prose two arguments speak against Bürger's theory. First of all, in the Rönne pieces Benn uses narrative strategies to critique not only specific social phenomena but also the given construct of reality. He explodes the fabric of our life-world—a move that leads to regression and solipsism rather than to a reorganization of social praxis. Similarly, the critique of traditional art forms in Benn's experimental prose, possibly against its own intentions, upholds the very autonomy that it supposedly wants to destroy. To put it differently, the use of *new techniques* does not automatically cancel the autonomous status of art. Despite the obvious break, as it is stressed in Bürger's theory, there is also continuity (and thus a connection with modernism). I would argue that the avant-garde, including Benn, continues to rely on the romantic paradigm of sublation and with it the concept of aesthetic autonomy. It is not the self-critical abdication of art vis-à-vis reality that motivates Benn but the insistence that the *radical and subversive use of aesthetic means* can and should bring about a process of reconceiving and reexperiencing the fabric of life. This explains why Benn in 1934, looking back at his early prose, connected the figure of Rönne with art rather than with its destruction (see 4:37). Benn never saw a contradiction between his claim that in his youth he belonged to a rebellious and destructive literary movement and the belief that the aesthetic realm had to be autonomous. He shared with the avant-garde movements the *utopian* notion that through the radical deconstruction of conventional forms the aesthetic project would ultimately overcome the reified structure of modern capitalist reality.

During the 1920s Benn pursued this project in various forms. In his poetry motifs of regression and return, frequently using the color blue as an overdetermined signifier, hint at the other through their negation of modern reality—the realm of wholeness where the subject was not yet divided from reality. In this context it must suffice to mention poems like "Osterinsel" and "Palau" that transcend the direct and sometimes fairly crude opposition of Benn's early poetry. At the same time Benn was more and more drawn into the heated intellectual debates of the Weimar Republic, where the progressive and the conservative forces fought over the meaning of human evolution and progress. Benn's essays are with rare exceptions occasional pieces, responses to specific political and social issues, or they are literary essays on favorite intellectual figures like Heinrich Mann. Their common thread is a very outspoken, sometimes rabid critique of the social and political conditions of the Weimar Republic. Like the dadaists and the surrealists Benn was convinced that capitalist society, overemphasizing competition, underscoring the technological use of the natural sciences, and privileging the logic of scientific positivism, marked the end of human history. To give an example of this kind of social criticism I quote from his essay "Saison" (1930):

Spiritually and socially the prototype of our time: without experience and existence; charged with the search for truth; truth is what can be demonstrated, a confirmed calculation that can be checked and used with a good profit margin. At home they possibly collect stamps, play the violin, and feel close to nature; perhaps they pose with a daring lock as creators, demigods, cosmic feelings in their narrow chests. (2:124 f.)

The vicious polemic bourgeois individualism is characteristic of Benn's extreme position during the 1920s. But unlike the left avant-garde

(Piscator and Brecht) or a working-class author like Willi Bredel, Benn refuses to believe in any form of social praxis. For him the modernization of society, whether carried out under the aegis of liberalism and capitalism or that of socialism, is pernicious as well as irreversible. European history has reached its ignominious final stage.

Some years ago Dieter Wellershoff correctly observed that this irrational response to modern society brought Benn, who was generally considered a member of the left, dangerously close to the theory and practice of fascism.[5] Indeed, Benn's short but important alliance with German National Socialism, which he incidentally confused with Italian fascism, was anything but an accident. There was more at stake than personal ambition or a misjudgment of the forces he was dealing with—although these elements must not be excluded. We have to understand the political implications of Benn's avant-gardist aestheticism. His aestheticism, which he laid open in exemplary fashion in his inaugural lecture at the Prussian Academy (Akademie-Rede) and his *laudatio* on the occasion of Heinrich Mann's sixtieth birthday, goes beyond the celebration of autonomous art and the redemption through the beautiful; rather, this project calls for extreme formal experiments. Form has to replace content because, according to Benn, the semantic basis of meaning has evaporated. In 1932 Benn pointed to the increasing "cerebration" of the mind and the growing loss of reality that his generation experienced. His answer to this dilemma was the formula: either we embrace rationalism in its extreme form or we valorize hallucination; these are the only acceptable solutions. Man's choice is pure thought or intoxication. Hence poems like "Osterinsel" or "Paulau" celebrate the other, the archaic age of humanity, the phase when subject and object were not yet divided. Obviously, these themes were not entirely new, being derived from the romantic tradition; still, they are central for the understanding of Benn's position, that is, the longing for a new kind of praxis, a form of communality that cannot be materialized in modern industrial societies.

This tension between cerebration and hallucination, between rational consciousness and prerational wholeness, found its release in Benn's commitment to German fascism. As a member of the literary avant-garde and a friend of Marinetti he argued in 1933 that the historically necessary destruction of middle-class values and traditional art must result in the praise of fascism. Benn publicly supported the German fascists. He vehemently castigated his old friends on the left and praised *Führer* and Party as the destiny of the German people.

This is not the place to analyze Benn's political adventure in detail. The point that has to be made, however, is this: Bürger's theory of the avant-garde overlooks the fact that the concept of the new social practice, developed out of an *abstract negation* of given social formations, can also be used by the political right. In other words, the *utopian element* of the avant-garde can be equally adopted by the radical forces of the left *and* the right. Yet this project does not necessarily cancel the concept of aesthetic autonomy. In the case of Benn the opposite is true. His decision to embrace National Socialism is ultimately no more than a shift of levels. His radical aesthetic project moves from literature to politics. This move, as Walter Benjamin shrewdly observed,[6] aestheticizes the political sphere. When by 1936 Gottfried Benn fully realized that his ideas and hopes had little to do with the political goals of the German fascists he withdrew from the political realm. Some of the poems written between 1934 and 1936 already expressed a critical stance; his prose of the 1940s, for instance *Der Roman des Phänotyp* (1944), went much further in critiquing the underlying assumptions of the avant-garde. The position that Benn defended during World War II (the so-called inner emigration) is very close to a stance that we would characterize today as postmodernist. Benn's critique underlines two aspects: he turns away from history and he reemphasizes the importance of the aesthetic project. Nietzsche's dictum that the world can only be justified through aesthetic categories again becomes central for Benn's thinking. Still, I would argue that the nature of the project has changed. The utopian moment of the avant-garde, that is, the hope, the expectation even, that the most radical use of art, the deconstruction of all traditional notions of culture, would eventually bring about a new organic life-world, is missing. The late Benn therefore affirms an anti-utopian, aesthetic nihilism, critiquing even Nietzsche for idealist notions of utopian communality. Benn insists on pure *Ausdruckswelt* and praises "the shift from content to expression, the cancellation of substance in favor of expression" (1:489) as the solution for post-history. This position favors a world without origins, without metaphysical truth, and without totality. For the late Benn the project of the avant-garde, his own project, had failed when the National Socialists, instead of supporting his radical claims for the rebuilding of the German nation, attacked him because of his early literary experiments. These radical formal experiments, as he realized in 1935, could subvert but not transform the social reality of his time.

Thus the conclusion of my argument would be that indeed we have to reexamine the theory of the avant-garde by deemphasizing the negation of aesthetic autonomy and stressing the ideologically charged continuation of this problematical category. The avant-garde movements did not fail, as Bürger claimed, because they did not achieve the projected reintegration; rather, they failed because they continued to uphold in theory and practice the aesthetic project of overcoming reality through art. They collapsed, in other words, not because they were too radical but because they were not radical enough.

A general theory of the avant-garde would have to include these findings and therefore offer a more differentiated view. Bürger's thesis that the European avant-garde movements of the early twentieth century aimed at the destruction of the institution of art, that is, the destruction of the aesthetic sphere, has to be modified. In its present form it generalizes certain tendencies, while omitting other trends. It has achieved its force and consistency by making surrealism the center of the European avant-garde and relegating other movements to the margin. This attempt to locate a center is not a mere matter of personal preference; rather, it relies on an evolutionary understanding of the total logic of history. Bürger works with the assumption that approximately by 1810 the category of aesthetic autonomy had been worked out in the writings of Kant, Schelling, and the romantics as well as institutionally accepted throughout Europe. Consequently, the institution of art had become identical with the concept of autonomy. However, this assumption is historically untenable for two reasons: first, older concepts of art were still very much alive during the nineteenth century and could be reformulated even in the twentieth century. The utilitarian concept of art, as it was developed by the enlightenment, remains a viable position within the institution of art throughout the nineteenth and the twentieth century. Second, the unfolding of the theory of the autonomous artwork already provokes its own critique during the nineteenth century. Heinrich Heine, for instance, realized as early as 1830 that the institutional quest for autonomy might well cancel the subversive force of aesthetic forms, the very critical force which romantic theory foregrounded. To put it differently, the self-critique of aesthetic autonomy, which according to Bürger is historically due only after we have gone through the phase of modernism (aestheticism), is already part of the stage that is dominated by the hegemonic concept of autonomy. In other words, this critique itself is part of the institution.

Hence the notion of a unified historical process with clearly marked phases (romanticism, modernism, avant-garde) has to be modified. Instead of pressing the various and often contradictory moments of the development into a model of linear evolution, we have to artic-ulate a theory that can account for the variety of different responses to the problem created through the rift between social reality and the aesthetic sphere. Autonomy of art has to be recognized as a *hege-monic ideology* that, because of its institutional power, marginalized other options. This hegemonic ideology, however, can articulate itself in a number of different ways within the institution of art. Still, what they have in common is the thrust toward social reality. As Odo Marquard puts it: "The legitimation of illusion turned, so to speak, around. It is no longer reality that wants to be an artwork; rather, the work of art wants to become reality."[7] Thus Wagner's project of the *Gesamtkunstwerk* means to prepare, even to create, an imme-diate *Lebensakt*. While Wagner affirms reality, though in the form of a new myth, dadaism and surrealism, as Bürger has shown, un-derscore the negative aspect. Here we find the explosion of tradi-tional boundaries and the forced approximation of art to the life-world that Bürger's theory ascribes to the avant-garde in general. Benn's project, on the other hand, would be closer to what Marquard calls the "indirekte extreme Gesamtkunstwerk,"[8] which in its most ex-treme articulation tends toward the aestheticization of political life (fascism). Artists like Benn (and here Ernst Jünger also comes to mind) favor the notion of an ultimate crisis that can be solved only through a violent revolution or war. Finally, even the opposite solution, that is, a reform of the social structure, owes its force to the ideology of aesthetic transformation. Social planning, as soon as it becomes a totalizing project, has its inherent aesthetic qualities. Again there is an attempt at closing the gap between the aesthetic sphere (blue-prints) and social reality. What these different models ultimately share is the valorization of the aesthetic sphere, the instistence that art is not only autonomous but can and will eventually change history.

Notes

1. Gottfried Benn, *Gesammelte Werke in vier Bänden,* ed. Dieter Wellershoff, 4 (Wiesbaden:Limes, 1961), 30. The following quotations in the text are taken from this edition.

2. Matei Calinescu, *Faces of Modernity: Avant-Garde, Decadence, Kitsch* (Bloomington and London: Indiana University Press, 1977).

3. Peter Bürger, *Theory of the Avant-Garde* (Minneapolis: University of Minnesota Press, 1984), 22. The following references in the text are to this edition.

4. Dorrit Cohn, *Transport Minds: Narrative Modes for Presenting Consciousness in Fiction* (Princeton: Princeton University Press, 1978).

5. Dieter Wellershoff, *Gottfried Benn: Phänotyp dieser Stunde* (Cologne and Berlin: Kiepenheuer & Witsch, 1958).

6. Walter Benjamin, "The Work of Art in the Age of Mechanical Reproduction," *Illuminations* (New York: Schocken, 1969), 241 f.

7. Odo Marquard, "Gesamtkunstwerk und Identitätssystem," in *Der Hang zum Gesamtkunstwerk: Europäische Utopien seit 1800,* Catalogue (Aurau and Frankfurt am Main, 1983), 40–49, quotation on p. 44.

8. *Ibid.,* 46.

Each One as She May:
Melanctha, Tonka, Nadja

Judith Ryan

Despite the proliferation of discussion immediately following the appearance of Peter Bürger's theories of the avant-garde in 1974,[1] our understanding of this phenomenon does not appear to have moved forward substantially in the last several years, precisely the time frame during which one might have expected a second phase in critical avant-garde theory. One problem arises no doubt as a result of the rapid transition from ideological criticism to deconstructionist and reader-oriented criticism. The newer methods, whose ideological implications are less overtly manifest, have been unable to engage effectively with the controversies unearthed by the techniques they supplant.

It is my hope to present a more differentiated picture of the avant-garde than that offered by Peter Bürger and his early critics—one that would take more explicit account of the relation between ideology and form. I shall fill out this picture by way of three moments in the avant-garde, two of which may be seen as a vanguard in the sense that they attempt to usher in a new epoch that has still not yet begun: the end of the age of psychoanalysis. To provide the context for my account of these three moments, I shall begin with a brief review of Bürger's theories and some of the objections that have been raised to them. Peter Bürger distinguishes between works of the avant-garde and other works written in the same general time frame by regarding the avant-garde as the "self-critical" phase of bourgeois art. Although the avant-garde does not, he says, in fact abolish the "institution of art," by means of which creative works are made to serve the end of stabilizing the social status quo, it does permit a critique of this conservationist function of art by making its essential premises evident. He shows how the avant-garde emerges from its predecessor, aestheticism, by breaking down its foundation in the concept of artistic autonomy and effecting a "transference of art into life praxis."[2]

Several criticisms of Bürger's theory have been put forward: Bürger bases his analysis too much on dada and surrealism, which may not be entirely typical of the avant-garde as a whole; he does not sufficiently account for the varying motivation of the "transference of art into life praxis" promulgated by the different avant-garde movements; and despite his emphasis on the critique of bourgeois life, the ideological component of his theory remains inadequately developed. One of Bürger's most cogent critics, Burkhardt Lindner (1976) claims that the movement from aestheticism to the avant-garde is really no more than a "dialectical reversal on the same plane."[3] In particular, he argues, the avant-garde still retains the same promise of resolution held out by romanticism and its successor, aestheticism. And he asks, finally, how an art form that expressly aims to abolish the distance between art and life can be capable of criticizing life.

For my own part, I should like to suggest that it is not so much the critique of bourgeois life that marks the avant-garde movements as such—this, after all, is undertaken quite decisively by the nineteenth-century novel and the naturalist drama—nor even the critique of the bourgeois institution of art—this, too, is performed quite effectively, by and large, in the nineteenth-century novel (e.g., *Madame Bovary*). Far more crucial to the avant-garde movements is, I believe, their explicit consciousness of their own ideologies, their awareness of the futile promise of resolution to which they stubbornly cling. By referring to this touchstone I intend not only to show the relation of my three literary moments to each other but also to question Bürger's assumption that dada and surrealism are the quintessential models for the radical avant-garde. In doing so, I shall attempt to reread the ruptures by means of which these texts accomplish the aims that Bürger sees as the principal ends of avant-garde art.

My first example is Gertrude Stein's story *Melanctha,* the middle tale of the tripartite *Three Lives,* written in 1905 and published in 1909.[4] By taking an early text of this type, I hope to be able to show more clearly than would be the case with a more experimental work like *Tender Buttons* how the transition from nineteenth-century models takes place.[5] In particular, we must ask how this story, which moves laboriously through the development and dissolution of a relationship between two people, differs from impressionistic writing or *Sekundenstil*. To establish this difference is to establish the boundary between the avant-garde and its literary predecessors.

Of *Melanctha* Gertrude Stein says:

> In that there was a constant recurring and beginning there was a marked direction in the direction of being in the present although naturally I had been accustomed to past present and future, and why, because the composition forming around me was a prolonged present.[6]

Here, in her characteristic iterative style, she suggests an underlying perception of reality that at first seems not too different from that of the impressionists: a moment-by-moment vision that cannot omit even the tiniest and subtlest change and that does greater justice to the immediacy and subjectivity of perception than even those foregroundings of subjectivity that had been introduced in prose fiction since at least the middle of the nineteenth century. But Gertrude Stein is not only interested in the surfaces of things; she is also concerned, as she herself states, with the insides of them:

> I had to find out inside every one what was in them that was intrinsically exciting and I had to find out not by what they said not by what they did not by how much or how little they resembled any other one but I had to find it out by the intensity of movement that there was inside in any one of them.[7]

The "intensity of movement" inside her characters is readily felt by the reader. We discover along with Melanctha, and in the same slow and painful process of gradual recognition, that her friend Jeff does not really care for her to the extent he claims and in the way she expects. Their excruciating circling around a small terrain of emotional differences is duplicated by the circling language through which Gertrude Stein puts to most remarkable effect her idiosyncratic invention of "insistence," those repetitions with minuscule variations that reflect her discovery, upon listening closely to actual speech, "how everybody said the same thing over and over again with infinite variations but over and over again until finally if you listened with great intensity you could hear it rise and fall and tell all that there was inside them, not so much by the actual words they said or the thoughts they had but the movement of their thoughts and words endlessly the same and endlessly different."[8] In *Melanctha* characterization depends on just such repetitions by a narrative voice that recognizes how very minimal the distinguishing features are by which we generally apprehend a person's inner nature. The notion of rounded characters familiar to readers of traditional fiction is explicitly rejected by this text: Melanctha's mother, for example, is described by no more than the two phrases "pale yellow" and "sweet-appearing," despite the fact that the mother's negative influence on Melanctha during her growing-up is an essential premise of the plot. Language, reduced to a narrow minimum, becomes in this text a medium that veils rather than reveals reality. This is especially true of Jeff, whose responses to Melanctha are depressingly slow and inadequate because they are always mediated by his attempts at rational reflection. The narrator attempts to approximate his troubled reactions by imitating the slowness and incoherence of his thinking in language very close to his, but not quite identical with it:

Now Melanctha, with her making him feel, always, how good she was and how very much she suffered in him, made him always go so fast then, he could not be strong then, to feel things out straight then inside him. Always now when he was with her, he was being more, than he could already yet, be feeling for her. Always now, with her, he had something inside him always holding in him, always now, with her, he was far ahead of his own feeling.[9]

Jeff's and Melanctha's awareness moves at different speeds. Melanctha is more straightforward, more aware of her desires:

It's because I am always knowing what it is that I am wanting, when I get it. I certainly don't never have to wait till I have it, and then throw away what I got in me, and then come back and say, that's a mistake I just been making, it ain't never at all like I understood it, I want to have, bad, what I didn't think it was that I wanted. It's that way of knowing right what I am wanting, makes me feel nobody can come right with me, when I am feeling things, Jeff Campbell.[10]

But the story is not just a detailed reproduction of the discrepancies in thought and feeling between two lovers, it also criticizes implicitly the traditional form of tales of tragic love. Such stories aim to induce forgetfulness of real life; but this one, with its deadening repetitions, weighs heavily on us:

And Jeff tried to begin again with his thinking, and he could not make it come clear to himself, with all his thinking, and he felt everything all thick and heavy and bad, now inside him, everything he could not understand right, with all the hard work he made, with all his thinking. And then he moved himself a little, and took a book to forget his thinking, and then as always, he loved it when he was reading, and then very soon he was deep in his reading, and so he forgot now for a little while that he never could seem to be very understanding.[11]

This paragraph suggests one way in which the tale *Melanctha* presents its critique of traditional art—the kind of reading that acts as an escape mechanism—but this idea is not too far removed from the critique of reading familiar to us from *Madame Bovary* and its successors. More important for Stein's critique of art are two other features of this text. The first and most obvious of these is the way in which it undermines our expectations of causality in plot. Once Melanctha finally breaks with Jeff, she helps another woman during pregnancy and childbirth, takes up and again breaks with another man. But the conclusion of the story does not follow from this, and for us as readers there is neither poetic justice nor its lack. Melanctha does not kill herself, as her friend Rose Johnson anticipates she will, nor does she live to enjoy the fruits of the new phase of her life in which she begins to "work and live regular."[12] Instead, she simply dies of consumption. Thoroughly in tune with the conventional nineteenth-century novel ending—we may think, for example, of *Effi Briest*—this conclusion is fundamentally discontinuous with the rest of the narrative, despite its emphasis on illness and despite the fact that Jeff Campbell is a doctor. Unlike Effi, Melanctha has always been the strong one, the one who flouts convention and takes her emotional suffering in a fighting spirit. In this sense—the story's undermining of the conventional love plot—*Melanctha* provides a fundamental critique of art and its familiar forms.

The second feature by means of which the tale undermines conventional forms is the situation of the narrator. The narrative voice moves constantly between Jeff's and Melanctha's positions; indeed, it is not always clear where it is situated at any given moment. We have here the beginning of Stein's attempt to adapt to prose fiction certain of William James's theories about consciousness. But the attempt succeeds less well in *Melanctha* than in such later works as *Tender Buttons* (1924), which dispenses with plot and characterization altogether. Nonetheless, we can observe in *Melanctha* an early stage of this development, which I believe is critical for an understanding of the avant-garde in general. Indeed, I should like to go beyond my opening definition of the radical avant-garde as that which is conscious of its own ideology to suggest that its most truly revolutionary forms are those that put empiricist, rather than psychoanalytical, theories of consciousness into literary shape. I will talk first about Jamesian theories as they are illustrated in *Melanctha* and return from there to the whole problem of ideology in this story. The interaction of the two will tell us a great deal about this kind of avant-garde text.

For William James the self was merely a label of convenience. It is something that must be continually constituted and reconstituted from moment to moment. He writes: "Resemblance among the parts of a continuum of feelings (especially body feelings) experienced along with things widely different in all other regards, thus constitutes the real and verifiable 'personal identity' which we feel."[13] Or again: "The same matters can be thought of in successive portions of the mental stream, and some of these portions can know that they mean the same matters which the other portions meant. . . . This sense of sameness is the very keel and backbone of our thinking."[14] The linguistic repetitions and the "insistence" of Gertrude Stein's *Melanctha* are an attempt to illustrate this sense of hypothesized continuity or sameness by means of which any individual consciousness constitutes its own identity. Jeff and Melanctha's speech and thought move constantly through such discoveries of sameness. At the same time, their two identities are not kept rigorously apart, as is the case with texts based on more conventional psychologies—Faulkner's *The Sound and the Fury*, for example, in which each character's consciousness stands separate and distinct. Jeff feels what Melanctha wants him to feel and yet at the same time he does not feel it. The phenomenon recalls William James's example of Peter and Paul who go to sleep in the same bed: how does Peter's consciousness know, upon awakening in the morning, to link back to Peter's consciousness of the previous evening rather than Paul's? Why don't the two consciousnesses become intertwined? What Gertrude Stein shows most forcefully in *Melanctha* is that consciousnesses do in fact intertwine. "Knowledge about a thing," writes William James, "is knowledge of its relations." In *Tender Buttons* Gertrude Stein was to show how consciousness of objects also includes the entire context of these objects, including whatever other thoughts and associations the experiencer may have on her mind while observing the objects. "When I was working with William James I completely learned one thing, that science is continuously busy with the complete description of something, with ultimately the complete description of anything with ultimately the complete description of everything," Gertrude Stein said in recalling her student days when she attended James's courses.[15] The complete description of Melanctha and Jeff's relation includes the terrifying, deadening, obstructing way in which the lovers' thoughts and feelings merge to the point where they feel their individual "identities" threatened. It is an empiricist experience of the first order—and such experiences are invariably frightening.

Now in the face of such terror and immobilization, how can the text perform its critique? In what sense can it be claimed that *Melanctha* is conscious of its own ideology? The clue, I think, lies in its dual structure. On one level, the story is about the failure of understanding in a relationship between two people; as such, it depends upon the notion that lovers should "understand" each other and that in the ideal course of things there should be some give and take between their different "ways of seeing" things. A certain ideology of social interaction, still popular today, underlies and motivates this assumption. On another level, the story demonstrates that individuals are not as separate and distinct as they conceive themselves to be and that, by extension, subjectivities are not discrete either from each other or from the object of their consciousness. On this level, the narrative "deconstructs" its readers' expectations that it will help us understand the psyches of two particular characters. Here is the "rupture" that produces a critique of popular psychology and that alerts us to the presence of this critique.

It is time to move ahead some nineteen years to my next example, Musil's story *Tonka* (1924).[16] Although this novella originated during the "prime time" of European modernism, it still bears in many ways the distinct marks of a transitional piece: once again, remnants of

literary impressionism turned to another purpose. Not entirely co-
incidentally, *Tonka* is the middle piece of a triptych, *Drei Frauen,*
just as *Melanctha* was the middle piece of *Three Lives.* It has been
suggested that Stein's *Three Lives* may have been influenced in its
conception by Picasso's *Three Women;*[17] be that as it may, it can
scarcely be claimed that Musil's *Drei Frauen* is similarly influenced.
More important for my thesis here, all three depictions of a triad of
female figures are the result of an understanding of reality as per-
ceivable only through multiple facets, facets that are triple rather than
binary, female rather than male (despite the presence of male figures
in them).

Tonka is the tale of a man who falls in love with a simple young
woman and allows her to come and live with him. When she becomes
pregnant, he calculates to his distress that the conception must have
taken place while he was away on a trip; and when Tonka dies it is
of a disease that must have originated with the baby's father and been
communicated to her through the fetus. The young man is not himself ill; and yet Tonka stubbornly maintains that the child is his. The
mystery is never resolved, and the literary power of the tale depends
in large measure on its irreducible ambiguity. This has its roots in
Musil's belief in empiricist principles not far different from Gertrude
Stein's, in his case derived from his study of Ernst Mach, on whom
he wrote his doctoral dissertation. Musil makes clear from the outset
that characters and context are not distinct: part of Tonka's charm
lies in the way she appears as a continuum with her surroundings:

On a fence. A bird sang. The sun suddenly went behind the bushes. The bird
was silent. It was evening. The farm girls came singing across the fields.
What details! Is it trivial when such details cling to a person? Like leeches?
That was Tonka. Eternity sometimes flows in drops.[18]

This remarkable passage shows very clearly the empiricist presuppositions underlying the story: the insoluble tangle of thoughts and
things, consciousness and its object. A later passage makes this even
more explicit.

He just had to look out the window and suddenly the world of the cab-
driver waiting below and that of a passing mailman overlapped and gave
rise to something cut up, a revolting confusion and coexistence on the street,
a chaotic net of intersecting lines, each surrounded by a halo of confidence

in world and self, and all these things were constructs to enable one to walk upright in a world without top and bottom. Knowledge, desire, and feeling are tangled in a knot; you don't notice it until you've lost the end of the thread; but perhaps the thread of truth is not the only path through the world?[19]

Tonka's function has been to illustrate to her friend this unravelable knot. There is no possibility, we reluctantly come to see, of solving the mystery: neither he nor the reader will ever know whether Tonka was really faithful, as she claims to have been.

The narrative technique of *Tonka* is more single-minded than that of *Melanctha:* now the narrator identifies essentially with the male protagonist and tells the story in what virtually amounts to a continuous reported monologue. The uncertain positioning of the narrator that characterized *Melanctha* has given way to what seems at first glance like a return to the single, limited subjectivity that had become a commonplace of modern literature since the late nineteenth century. If we see things this way, it is merely logical that we should never find out the paternity of the infant, since the young man never does so and we are never allowed to step beyond the sphere of his consciousness. But why is there no indication of where the young man's insufficiencies lie? After all, even Kafka, despite his rigorously limited third-person narration, lets us become aware that his dog-scientist cannot perceive human beings or that Gregor Samsa repeatedly half-forgets that he has been turned into an insect. In contrast, the protagonist's consciousness in *Tonka,* though limited, is not discrete: it constantly flows over into its surroundings just as Tonka herself is part of the world outside. The very moment of his greatest crisis and confusion in understanding the puzzle of Tonka's faithfulness is the time of his greatest professional success: he is able to resolve problems in chemistry with a sure-footedness that eludes him when he tries to think through the problem of Tonka. And while this contrast should alert him to the inadequacies of scientific or rational thinking, he refuses to see them, and "numbs himself with work."[20]

His difficulty lies in the extent to which Tonka is both the other and a part of the self. As someone outside his subjectivity, Tonka is incomprehensible to him, and hence potentially—indeed, quite probably—unfaithful. As a part of his own awareness, Tonka's truth is his own; some instinct inside himself seems to keep repeating that she was faithful after all. As she lies dying in the hospital, he experiences this vacillation of perception to an extreme degree: "At this moment, he saw her quite clearly. She was a snowflake falling, all alone, on a summer's day. But in the next instant this was no explanation at all."[21] The phenomenon is endemic to empiricism, in which there can be no objective point of view, and where imagined explanations are the only ones we can have.

If we now attempt to apply to *Tonka* the categories that distinguish, in Peter Bürger's view, the avant-garde work of art, we find that the narrative satisfies all the tests. In terms of the critique of "life," the narrator's inability to establish the paternity of the infant defies our ingrained notions that such things can and must be verified and that origins and inheritance are significant. In terms of the critique of "art," the tale defies our expectations of the mystery story, in which, even in cases where no solution is actually reached, an implied solution is present and simply awaits its discovery by the reader. "Art" is criticized, further, by virtue of the fact that the act of narration does not itself bring clarity. Here is a fundamental rupture in this work that alerts us to the fact that it functions on two levels. At the end, the young protagonist believes that he continues to "dream Tonka's dreams while yet awake." She lives on in him in the same vacillating way in which her guilt or innocence had lived in him while she was alive:

Memory cried out in him: Tonka! Tonka! He felt her from head to foot, he felt her whole life. All that he had never understood was present to him at this moment, the blindfold seemed to have fallen from his eyes; but just for a moment, for the very next he seemed merely to have had a fleeting thought.[22]

With this vacillating conclusion *Tonka* confounds all clichés that suggest that one learns something profound and lasting from experience. Yes, the protagonist *is* somehow permanently changed: "All this could help Tonka no longer. But it helped him. Even if human life passes so quickly for us to be able to catch every mood and find the answer to it." The underlying ideology of this text—the reason why it purports to be told—is that writing brings understanding and individual development. But if the protagonist is changed, this change is impossible to articulate. In this way, the narrative undermines a fundamental premise of all narratives: the ideas that putting experiences into words inevitably clarifies them. But if it doesn't, the function of art altogether is placed in question. Why write at all, if not to bring clarity? Musil's *Tonka* questions the nature of art in a more fundamental way than do other texts that present a "critique of the institution of art," since the ones Bürger is thinking of criticize not art the enlightener but art the reinforcer of the status quo. Here is a truly problematic use of art, and one that threatens to pull the rug out from underneath it in a way much more drastic than that of the usual self-critical artwork. Where *Melanctha* abolishes the notion of discrete subjectivity, *Tonka* goes one step further, and abolishes the notion of the therapeutic function of artistic self-reflection.

I will conclude with a few brief marks about *Nadja*, since in view of the special priority Bürger gives to dada and surrealism, this text is an important touchstone for his theory. Superficially, *Nadja* may seem to illustrate much better than *Melanctha* or *Tonka* the "transference of art into life praxis." In fact, however, it illustrates only the transference of life into art. Breton himself locates the origin of the text in a real place: "My point of departure will be the Hotel des Grands Hommes,"[23] and his claim to refer to something real is substantiated by his frequent references in the first part of the novel to real people, friends and acquaintances of his, his inclusion of photographs of real places, and the reproduction of what at least purports to be documentation concerning Nadja (her drawings, for example). Life carries over into art. But the text is less concerned, I would contend, with continuity than with the gap between events—a gap that illustrates again and again what Breton calls the "victory of the involuntary over the ravaged domain of conscious possibilities."[24] The photographs of places experienced and mentioned in the narrative fall short, he says, because of their inability to contain the "special angle [of vision] from which I myself had looked at them";[25] the metonymy for this phenomenon is the Porte St. Denis, which he describes as "useless"; another image for it is the photograph of Robert Desnos in his "Nap Period," that is, during a time when his consciousness is temporarily absent. Such lacunae, the narrator says, may "cast a shadow across my narrative, across what, taken as a whole, cannot be substantiated."[26] Nadja herself seems able to fill these gaps in a mysterious and inexplicable way: she stares into the vacant air, looks at a feather not on her hat, and is repeatedly described by images of absence: she is the "spirit of the air," "the soul in limbo," "like the heart of a heartless flower."[27] What most attracts the narrator is her simultaneous difference from him and identity with him: she is a mystery he cannot solve, yet she seems at the same time to pick up his thoughts: "Those are your thoughts and mine."[28] Nadja and the narrator relate to each other like the communicating vessels that Breton uses in his manifesto of surrealism as an image of the interaction between the real and the imaginary. Nadja illustrates for the narrator—though only for a limited time—the interpenetration between self and world characteristic of the avant-garde attempt to break down the sovereignty of the ego. For all its psychoanalytical implications, this work demonstrates very nicely the continuity of things and their context, consciousness and its objects, that is basic to this entire literary period. Freud recognized this aspect of surrealism when he criticized it for placing fantasy on the same level as reality; he preferred to decode the one to discover the other. In its acceptance of the equivalence of the real and the imaginary, surrealism undermines the hierarchical structuring of consciousness fundamental to Freudianism and its predecessor, romanticism.

Nadja is certainly, in Bürger's terms, a critique of the bourgeois institution of art. Life flows over into the text without any clear boundary; what begins as a personal memoir turns into something very like a work of fiction. Nadja mocks both the teleological view of reality and the genre of autobiography. The text foils all attempts to assign it to a conventional genre, even if it were to be an antiversion of that genre. I am not sure in what way the transference from art into life praxis is effected here, since Nadja's ultimate confinement in an asylum seems to be of little concern to the narrator, but Bürger does not seem, in his theory, to be speaking of the kind of carry-over we find in socialist avant-garde literature such as Döblin's Berlin Alexanderplatz or Brecht's dialectical dramas. On the ideological plane, indeed, the work appears to be highly problematic. The modern reader's indignation over the ending of Nadja is doubtless a function of the text's lack of consciousness of its own ideological weaknesses. Endlessly fascinating in other ways, Nadja seems numb in this regard. The lacunae it asks us to fill are not in any fundamental conflict with the parts it does narrate: they represent simply the other vessel with which the accessible world is (by the nature of the surrealist conception) in communication. Breton's gaps acquire shape and significance from the material that surrounds them: the text requires less to be deconstructed than to be filled in. Stein's and Musil's texts, by comparison, are marked by a fundamental rupture between the two conflicting views they contain. Their radical revision of institutionalized structures of belief and expectation can only be perceived by an act of deconstruction in which this rupture is revealed.

It should have become evident by now why these resisting texts take for their titles the names of their female protagonists. While names define, these women represent indeterminacy. While names imply identity, these women resist identification. Their opaqueness to male rationality is a function, not just of their otherness, but also of this very indeterminacy. It is a result of the way they flow over into the male awareness while also functioning as projections of their own troubling participation in that which is indeterminate. Gertrude Stein's subtitle to *Melanctha,* with its implications of the old opposition between individual and society ("each one" as opposed to the regulating "as she may"), is defied and undermined by the text itself.[29] These ruptures between work and title, naming and indeterminacy, are yet other signs of the works' revisionist tendencies. Whereas the figure of Nadja retreats and allows the male narrator to reconstitute his individual integrity and independence, Tonka and Melanctha come to mean much more than the person signified by these names: they expand to encompass the entirety of an experience elusive to any other kind of naming. These two works, *Tonka* and *Melanctha,* represent the most radical extreme of the avant-garde: texts that resist not only familiar notions of life and art but also familiar patterns of thought itself.

Notes

1. Peter Bürger, *Theorie der Avantgarde* (Frankfurt am Main: Suhrkamp, 1974); W. Martin Lüdke, ed., *"Theorie der Avantgarde." Antworten auf Peter Bürgers Bestimmung von Kunst und bürgerlicher Gesellschaft* (Frankfurt am Main: Suhrkamp, 1976). English translation of the former: Peter Bürger, *Theory of the Avant-Garde,* trans. Michael Shaw, foreword by Jochen Schulte-Sasse (Minneapolis: University of Minnesota Press, 1984).

2. Bürger, *Theorie,* 67 (my translation; Shaw renders this as "sublation of art into the praxis of life," p. 51).

3. See Lüdke, *"Theorie,"* 19.

4. In *Three Lives* (London: Peter Owen, 1909).

5. On *Tender Buttons,* see my forthcoming book, *The Vanishing Subject: Early Psychology and the Beginnings of Modernism.*

6. "Composition as Explanation," in Gertrude Stein, *Writings and Letters 1909—1945,* ed. Patricia Meyerowitz (Baltimore: Penguin, 1967), 25.

7. "Portraits and Repetition," *ibid.,* 183.

8. "The Gradual Making of the Making of Americans," in *Lectures in America* (New York: Random House, 1935, repr. 1975), 138.

9. *Melanctha,* 107–8.

10. *Ibid.,* 120.

11. *Ibid.,* 112.

12. *Ibid.,* 154.

13. *Principles of Psychology* (New York: Henry Holt and Co., 1890), 336.

14. *Ibid.,* 459.

15. "The Gradual Making of the Making of Americans," 156.

16. In *Drei Frauen: Prosa, Dramen, Späte Briefe,* ed. Adolf Frisé (Hamburg: Rowohlt, 1957). English translations given here are my own.

17. See Marianne Teuber, "Formvorstellung und Kubismus oder Pablo Picasso und William James," in *Kubismus,* Exhibition and Catalogue, arranged by S. Gohr, Kunsthalle, Cologne, 1982, p. 32.

18. *Prosa,* 264.

19. *Ibid.,* 291–92.

20. *Ibid.,* 292.

21. *Ibid.,* 298.

22. *Ibid.,* 299.

23. *Nadja* (Paris: Gallimard, 1928). English versions given here are taken from Richard Howard's translation (New York: Grove Press, 1960). Here p. 23.

24. *Ibid.,* 16.

25. *Ibid.,* 152.

26. *Ibid.,* 24.

27. *Ibid.,* 71, 111, 71 respectively.

28. *Ibid.,* 86.

29. In her response to this essay, Gabriele Schwab stressed particularly the working out of race, class, and gender problems in *Melanctha* and *Tonka.* In *Melanctha* all three play an important role; in *Tonka* only the last two. Schwab pointed out, furthermore, that both texts treat a number of other nineteenth-century themes besides those of the tragic love affair and the consumptive woman: both stories also continue (and subvert) the nineteenth-century motif of the simple woman (cf. Flaubert's *Un coeur simple,* which Stein was translating at that time; see Jayne Walker, *The Making of a Mod-*

ernist: Gertrude Stein from "Three Lives" to "Tender Buttons" [Amherst: University of Massachusetts Press, 1984], 19–25), and *Tonka* picks up the nineteenth-century male fantasy of the fallen angel punished by illness. These observations about the social ideologies underlying the texts provide an important additional dimension to the narrative ideologies discussed here.

PART II

Modernist Cities:
Paris—New York—Berlin

Paris/Childhood:
The Fragmented Body in Rilke's
Notebooks of Malte Laurids Brigge

Andreas Huyssen

La modernité, c'est le transitoire, le fugitif, le contingent, la moitié de l'art, dont l'autre est l'éternel et l'immuable.—Charles Baudelaire

The psychological basis of the metropolitan type of individuality consists in the *intensification of nervous stimulation* which results from the swift and uninterrupted change of outer and inner stimuli.—Georg Simmel

If ever there was a German poet said to embody the essence of high modernism, it surely must be Rainer Maria Rilke. And if literary modernism found its ultimate manifestation in lyric poetry, then Rilke's *Sonette an Orpheus* and his *Duineser Elegien* had to be full-fledged embodiments of this privileged art form of the twentieth century. The poetry of the mature Rilke certainly seemed to fulfill the stringent requirements traditionally made of modernist poetry, such as originality of voice, the work as hermetically closed to the outside world, self-sufficiency, and purity of vision and language, all of which would guarantee the work's timelessness and transcendence.

But in recent years such codifications of modernism have increasingly come under attack for being too narrow, and we have come to understand them as themselves historically contingent—related to the post-1945 revival of the autonomy aesthetic—rather than expressing some ultimate truth about modernism. In German literary criticism, this kind of codification of modernist literature first emerged in the mid-1950s in the work of Hugo Friedrich and Wilhelm Emrich, and it fast made its way into Rilke scholarship. Characteristic of this account of modernism and typical of German intellectual life at the time was the obliviousness to the major debates about modernism, expressionism, and realism that had taken place in the 1930s involving Brecht, Lukács and Bloch, Benjamin and Adorno. And yet, the periodization of this postwar account of modernism roughly corresponds to that of the earlier debate—like Benjamin or, very differently, Lukács, Hugo Friedrich posits a rupture with Baudelaire in the middle of the nineteenth century. The criteria for this periodization, however, are now intrinsically literary and structural, if not metaphysical, rather than historical, contextual, or sociopolitical. The separateness of the literary from the social and political was central to this theory of modernist literature, which used symbolist poetry as its paradigm. So was its claim that there is an unbridgeable gap between the feeling and experiencing *I* that expresses itself in romantic poetry and the modern poetic subject that operates analytically, cerebrally, constructively, and that ultimately succeeds in purifying itself and achieving a kind of poetic transcendence. Specifically Friedrich's account of the trajectory of poetry from Baudelaire to surrealism[1] revolves around the notion that modernist poetry can no longer be understood in terms of the experience or self-conception of the poet. Categories such as depersonalization, self-abandonment, or dehumanization provide the basis for the claim that the poetic subject is forever separate from the empirical, feeling, and experiencing subject of the author, or, for that matter, the reader. Already this account of modernism was a discourse of loss and absence, loss of subjectivity as well as loss of authorship in the traditional sense. It was a discourse of negativity that aimed at salvaging the transcendence of poetic word and vision by jettisoning traditional romantic concepts of poetic subjectivity, expression, and authorial intention that the experience of modernity itself had vaporized.

Rilke scholarship shifted easily into this kind of discourse. It seemed more appropriately modern and literary after the preceding hagiographic Rilke cult or the existentialist readings that continued to co-exist in uneasy tension with what I am calling in shorthand the high modernist readings.[2] With the emphasis increasingly on Rilke's hermetic late poetry, rather than on his more accessible early verse or on the popular *Geschichten vom lieben Gott* or the *Cornet*, a Rilke image took hold that valorized Rilke primarily as a representative of what I would call the cold stream of modernism, a modernism of disembodied subjectivity, metaphysical negativity, and textual closure, the classicism of the twentieth century.

How, then, does Rilke's novel, *The Notebooks of Malte Laurids Brigge,* fit into all of this? It hardly comes as a surprise that the high modernist readings of Rilke pay scant attention to *Malte,* an unabashedly personal and experiential, though carefully constructed text, whereas existentialist critics[3] see the novel as a breakthrough to Rilke's most mature work, as an existentially necessary text in which Rilke laid the foundations for his late poetry. It is easy to see how *Malte* had to cause the high modernist critic considerable theoretical embarrassment, since nowhere are the autobiographic and psychological roots of Rilke's writing more evident than in this novel, key passages of which are lifted almost without alteration from the poet's correspondence. Indeed, the closeness of the empirical subject Rainer Maria Rilke to his fictional protagonist Malte Laurids Brigge has been amply documented,[4] and Rilke's letters show how what one might call his "Malte complex" never ceased to play a major role in his life and writings, even after the novel was published. But the dialectic of blindness and insight prevented high modernist critics from actually reading this constellation. Even the existentialist critics who did focus on the pivotal role of *Malte* in Rilke's writing life often lost sight of the text by subjecting their reading to one or another version of existentialist metaphysics. And yet, as the construction of high modernism took hold in criticism, some readers have attempted to pull the text into the orbit of the high modernist canon. Thus critics have read *Malte* as a kind of modernist *Künstlerroman*—the portrait of the alienated artist in crisis, who eventually learns to overcome alienation in his writing[5] and moves from a merely subjective to a more properly objective narrative;[6] or they have argued for some level of fundamental coherence of this extremely fragmented text, a coherence, even closure, that was said to result from the "law of complementarity"[7] structuring the text or from the "closed world of a limited subjectivity" determining the text via the three interweaving clusters of Malte's learning how to see, his remembrances, and his attempts to narrate.[8]

While many of those readings are quite insightful and compelling in their attempts to secure a place for Rilke's text in the canon of the modernist novel, they almost invariably lack an interest in reading Malte's experiences and remembrances psychoanalytically, let alone historically. Given the methodological premises of high modernist criticism, or, for that matter, of existentialist criticism, it comes as no surprise that psychoanalytic readings of Rilke stand almost totally apart from the rest of Rilke scholarship and that the insights of psychoanalysis have by and large been shunned by Rilke scholars as irrelevant for the literary and aesthetic assessment of the novel.[9] Such methodological abstinence is no longer plausible since the theoretical turn in recent literary criticism has radically changed the ways in which we conceptualize the relationship of psychoanalysis to writing and reading. Once we begin to understand subjectivity as social construct, mediated through language, family structure, gender positioning, and historical experience, we can attempt to develop alternative forms of psychoanalytic readings, readings that are no longer divorced—as psychoanalytic interpretations often used to be—either from aesthetic considerations or from historical-political questions.

II

Thus the aim of this essay is not to provide a more updated psychoanalytic reading of *Malte* in the narrow sense, nor simply to recouple Malte with his author whose symptoms the text would display and displace in narrative form. The aim of the essay is a larger one. By focusing on the overwhelmingly powerful, even haunting imagery of the fragmented body in *Malte*, I want to inquire into the relationship between Malte's childhood experiences, so vividly remembered during his stay in Paris, and his perceptions of the modern city that recent research has shown to be quite representative for the literature of the early twentieth century.[10] My hypothesis is that the relevance of Rilke's novel for an expanded understanding of literary modernism has something to do with the way in which the text suggests connections between aspects of early childhood experience and the disrupting, fragmenting experience of the modern city. If such a reading can be sustained, then it should also be possible to map *Malte* onto a discourse that, from Baudelaire via Georg Simmel to Walter Benjamin, has attempted to define the parameters of the experience of modernity as rendered by the literary text via a theory of perceptions of city life, perceptions as much determined by outside stimuli as they are dependent on psychic processes. But before we get to the larger issue of how to read in *Malte* the dialectic of what Simmel described as the tragic split between objective and subjective culture, let me first focus on the nature of Malte's experiences as Rilke renders them in the text.

Critics have always emphasized that the basic experience of Malte, the 28-year-old aristocratic Dane who comes to Paris with artistic and intellectual aspirations and begins to record his life crisis in his notebooks, is one of ego-loss, deindividualization, and alienation. Often this disintegration of the ego is attributed to Malte's city experiences alone, and his childhood, which also features dissolutions of self, is said merely to foreshadow, to anticipate the later experiences. Not only is such a narra-teleological account not tenable, oblivious as it is to the much more complex narrative structure of the novel and to the always problematic "inmixture" of past and present in narration, but the very thesis of disintegration of self, of *Ent-ichung*,[11] actually presupposes a stable self, a structured ego, a personality in the sense of bourgeois culture and ego psychology that could then show symptoms of disintegration under the impact of the experience of the modern city. What if Malte had never fully developed such a stable ego? What if, to put it in Freudian terms, the id/ego/superego structure, which after all is not a natural given but contingent on historical change, had never fully taken hold in Malte so that all the talk of its disintegration was simply beside the point? What if the fixation on the ego, which the late Freud has in common with traditional non-psychoanalytic notions of self, identity, and subjectivity, was simply not applicable to *Malte*? What if Malte represented a figuration of subjectivity that eludes Freud's theory of the structure of the psychic apparatus and that cannot be subsumed under Freud's account of the oedipal? Perhaps we need an entirely different psychoanalytic account for what has usually been described as disintegration of self and loss of ego in Rilke's novel.

It is particularly the haunting imagery of the body—Malte's own body and the bodies of the *Fortgeworfenen,* the members of the Paris underclass as they collide with Malte in the streets—that can give us a clue here. The text is obsessively littered with descriptions of body parts (the hand, the abscess, the torn-off face of the poor woman, the second head, the big thing) and of bodily sensations. Such images of threatening body fragments, which take on a life of their own, are paralleled by descriptions of people (the patients at the Salpetrière hospital, the woman on the streetcar) that focus almost fetishistically on separate body organs. In every case the imaginary unity of the body surface is disrupted: from his glance at the rash on the baby's forehead on the first page to his close-up perceptions of the Salpetrière patients' eyes, legs, throats, hands, Malte does not see holistically. Rather he perceives fragments, and this bodily fragmentation causes his anxieties, anxieties of bodily organs growing out of bounds, exploding inside the body, swelling the body beyond recognition and altering or destroying its surface unity. Clearly, these are not primarily anxieties of loss in the sense of the Freudian account of castration anxiety; they are rather anxieties of excess, of flowing over, of unstable bodily boundaries. Significantly, these anxieties are often followed by a sensation of a total dissolution of boundaries, a merging of inside and outside that is also experienced by Malte as threatening and invasive.

Indeed, it is important to insist that these experiences of excess are not to be misread as positive expansions of self, as a dynamic of liberated flows of desire in the mode of Deleuze and Guattari's schizo body, or as a pleasurable symbiotic merger of self and other, along the lines, say, of Freud's notion of the oceanic self. Rilke's constant use of the imagery of disease and filth, aggression and death clearly points in a different direction. Indeed, we face the paradox that these visions of bodily excess are simultaneously experiences of loss. But it is not the localizable loss of the Freudian account that is at stake here; it is a more totalizing loss, a wiping out of identity, a voiding of a sense of self, as in the often-quoted passage:

How ridiculous. I sit here in my little room, I, Brigge, who am twenty-eight years old and completely unknown. I sit here and am nothing. And yet this nothing begins to think . . .[12]

Or, perhaps less abstractly, after his experience with the epileptic on the Pont Neuf:

What sense would there have been in going anywhere now; I was empty. Like a blank piece of paper, I drifted along past the houses, up the boulevard again. (71)

The nothing that begins to think, the blank piece of paper that, it seems, is waiting to be written on—obviously a connection is suggested here between the voiding of self and writing, and I will come back to that later.

But first let me stay with the way in which Rilke presents such dissolutions of the boundaries of the self. Already at the beginning of the novel there is a description of such a crisis of boundaries, limited here, it seems, to the specifics of auditory perception. Malte describes his sensations while lying in bed with the window open:

Electric trolleys speed clattering through my room. Cars drive over me. A door slams. Somewhere a window pane shatters on the pavement; I can hear its large fragments laugh and its small ones giggle. (4)

But the breakdown of the inside/outside boundary is not limited to auditory perception. In the famous passage in which Malte describes the horrifying, almost hallucinatory recognition of the residual inside wall of a demolished house as outside wall of the adjacent building, revealing an inside that is no longer there, the loss of boundary is clearly described in a visual dimension. And the wall of the apartments thus exposed is described in a language that again approximates the human body, just as throughout the novel the dissolution of boundaries affects the boundary between the body and things, the animate and the inanimate:

It was, so to speak, not the first wall of the existing houses, . . . but the last of the ones that were no longer there. You could see its inside. You could see, at its various stories, bedroom walls with wallpaper still sticking to them; and here and there a piece of floor or ceiling. Near these bedroom walls there remained, along the entire length of the outer wall, a dirty-white space through which, in unspeakably nauseating, worm-soft digestive movements, the open, rust-spotted channel of the toilet pipe crawled. The gaslight jets had left dusty gray traces at the edges of the ceiling; they bent here and there, abruptly, ran along the walls, and plunged into a black, gaping hole that had been torn there. (46, translation modified)

And the passage ends with Malte's terror:

I swear I began to run as soon as I recognized this wall. For that's what is horrible—that I did recognize it. I recognize everything here, and that's why it passes right into me: it is at home inside me.

Indeed, the experience of horror cannot be attributed to the city alone, which, as it were, would overwhelm an overly sensitive but, deep-down, authentic subject. True, the horror passes right into him, outside to inside, but it also is already at home in him. Thus even if Malte may initially hope to get some relief by remembering his childhood, it very soon becomes clear that his childhood itself is packed with very similar experiences of the horrifying and the uncanny: the experience of being voided in the dinner hall at Urnekloster ("it sucked all images out of you," 26); the terror of the appearances of the ghosts of Christine Brahe and Maman's sister Ingeborg; the experience of the fragmented body with the hand coming out of the wall toward Malte while he is groping for a pencil in the dark under the table; the childhood diseases and hallucinatory anxieties; and, above all, the mirror scene. It is true that his first reflections about his childhood suggest a fundamental difference between now and then, the city and the country, the factory-produced death in the big city hospital as opposed to the individual death of the old days: "When I think back to my home, where there is no one left now, it always seems to me that things must have been different back then" (10). But already here the reader should get suspicious. For despite its ostensible gesture as statement of fact, this phrasing rather expresses desire ("must have been") and hesitation ("it seems to me"). And while the following reminiscences of grandfather Brigge's death at the estate may indeed be a good example of what Malte means by a death of one's own, the description of the chamberlain's body growing larger and larger and swelling out of the dark blue uniform as a result of his deadly disease already contains the same images of uncontrollable body growth and violent deformation that haunt Malte in his various Paris encounters with the man in the crémerie, the epileptic, the patients in the hospital. Malte's loneliness in Paris makes him want to escape into the past: "If at least you had your memories. But who has them? If childhood were there: it is as though it had been buried. Perhaps you must be old before you can reach all that. I think it must be good to be old" (17). But then Malte's childhood resurfaces with a vengeance, and soon enough he recognizes that rather than providing relief his memories compound the crisis of his life in Paris: "I prayed to rediscover my childhood, and it has come back, and I feel that it is just as heavy as it used to be, and that growing older has served no purpose at all" (64, translation modified).

In a first attempt to read the basic similarities between Malte's childhood and his Paris experiences, one might suggest, following Freud, that we are facing here a kind of repetition compulsion. In *Das Unheimliche,* Freud argues that the uncanny is "that class of the terrifying which leads back to something long known to us, once very familiar."[13] Freud also points out that the uncanny experience comes about "when repressed infantile complexes have been revived by some impression or when the primitive beliefs we have surmounted seem once more to be confirmed."[14] Of course, there is a difference. Malte does not just "experience" the uncanny in Paris. He also describes it, writes about it, tries to work through it, and in yet another register, of course, it is Rilke himself who is engaged in working through his Paris/childhood experiences by having Malte write about them in a fictional voice. Since the publication of Lou Andreas-Salomé's book about Rilke (1928)[15] and the publication of the first volumes of Rilke's letters (1929 ff.), a rigorous separation of Malte from his author, as if we could have Malte without Rilke's childhood anxieties, is as ludicrous as a total identification of Malte with Rilke would be.[16] Rilke himself put it succinctly enough: "Er [Malte] war mein Ich und war ein anderer."[17]

But my primary interest at this stage of the argument does not concern the relationship between Malte and Rilke, which has been documented fairly well. It rather concerns the question to what extent the "impression" of the city triggers the repetition compulsion. Is this a mere coincidence? Could Malte's childhood memories have broken loose with equal force in any other circumstances? Is the external stimulus even necessary for the repetition compulsion to surface? Freud after all goes so far as to claim that "where the uncanny comes from infantile complexes the question of material reality is quite irrelevant; its place is taken by psychical reality."[18] But in opposition to Freud, I want to suggest that it is actually Malte's particular experience of the city that triggers the resurfacing of childhood disturbances and confronts Rilke/Malte with the necessity of working through them: the city, as it were, functioning, in a very unProustian spirit, as the Proustian madeleine for all the childhood anxieties related to the phantasm of the fragmented body. But before broaching the relationship between modernization and figurations of subjectivity directly, we must still try to understand the origins of Malte's phantasms of the fragmented body, a task that the text itself does not engage in, but rather complicates through a constant shifting between authorial subject and fictional subject.

At this juncture it should be noted that Freud's text also draws our attention to the uncanniness of severed limbs as they appear in literary texts such as E. T. A. Hoffmann's *Der Sandmann* or Wilhelm Hauff's *Die Geschichte von der abgehauenen Hand*. Of course, Freud interprets these phenomena in terms of his theory of castration anxiety, which, as I shall argue, is not really applicable in the case of Malte. Only as an afterthought, which is not further elaborated, does Freud mention the uncanny fear of, and fascination with, the idea of being buried alive, a "phantasy of inter-uterine existence."[19] Here indeed Freud comes very close to the problematic that is articulated in the novel, and it is interesting to note that we know from Lou Andreas-Salomé's accounts that Rilke himself did have one such dream.[20] Ultimately, however, Freud's interpretation of the uncanny is only pertinent to a reading of Rilke's novel in that it emphasizes the phenomenon of repetition compulsion in uncanny experiences. In order to understand the specifics of this repetition compulsion, however, one needs a different framework, one that is not locked into the oedipal mode.

III

Such an expanded account of the uncanny in phantasy life, I think, is present in the work of post-Freudian psychoanalysts such as Melanie Klein, Margaret Mahler, Michael Balint, and others, all of whom have focused on what commonly is called the "preoedipal" phase of child development, the phase of symbiotic unity of child and mother and the painful process of separation of the child from the mother.[21] It is no news to Rilke readers that Malte's relationship to his mother, and later to his mother's youngest sister Abelone, is far more important in the narrative than his relation to his father. Malte's key childhood experiences revolve around the realm of the Brahes, his mother's family, rather than the Brigges, the family of his father. Ghosts in Malte's Denmark, which one would expect to be male and mouthpieces for the law of the father, are invariably female in this novel: Christine Brahe and Ingeborg, both of whom furthermore belong to the mother's side of the family. And then there is Malte's powerful and deeply problematic identification with femininity, first as a little boy when he pretends to be his own sister Sophie and dresses up in girl's clothes in order to relish his emotional identification with his mother in scenes of secret intimacy that one might read as attempts at a secondary symbiosis; later as an adult and a fledgling writer in Paris when his anxiety-ridden identification with the *Fortgeworfenen,* the Paris street people, is displaced by his joyful identification with *die grossen Liebenden,* the abandoned women in love, from Sappho via Gaspara Stampa, Mariana Alcoforado, and Louise Labé to Bettina Brentano. Significantly, in both cases the autobiographic parallels of these identifications with the feminine are well documented.[22] Once again Malte serves as a screen for Rilke's projections.

The dominance of the mother's sphere in Rilke's novel is so overwhelming that even Freudian readers like Erich Simenauer have had to concede that there is remarkably little oedipal repression going on here. Indeed, I would claim that the *Notebooks* have to be read primarily in terms of the dyadic relationship between Malte and Maman rather than in terms of the oedipal triangle, not to be sure in the sense of an either/or, but certainly in the sense emphasized by post-Freudian psychoanalysis that the dyadic relationship with the mother that precedes the oedipal triangle can produce psychic disturbances of its own when the transition from symbiosis to object relations is not made successfully. Among these disturbances, murderous phantasies of the violent, fragmented body, anxieties of fragmentation, of objects that enter the body or grow inside it, fear of merger and dissolution are paramount, as Melanie Klein and others have shown in their work with very small children and in analyses of psychotics. In such patients hallucinatory, ecstasylike states abound, intensities of affect that are not worked over by consciousness, and that even in analysis remain impenetrable to narrative articulation. The conclusion researchers have drawn is that such patients either lack the Freudian instance of the ego or that its development has been fundamentally disturbed in the transition from the symbiotic to the postsymbiotic phase.

It seems evident that Malte's hallucinatory perceptions of dissolution and his phantasms of the fragmented body, either in childhood or in Paris, can be well accounted for by such psychoanalytic work. The puzzling question, however, remains why the adult Malte should suffer at all from such early childhood traumas. After all, his relationship with Maman is presented as successfully "symbiotic" throughout, as thoroughly nurturing, so that the typical roots of later disturbances do not seem to pertain. In other words, neither is Maman the harsh and unnurturing mother who rejects her child too early or never really accepts it; nor is she the overprotective mother who does not allow the child to perceive himself as object separate from the mother. One answer to this question, I would suggest, can emerge if we superimpose what we know of Rilke's childhood onto the childhood of the novel's protagonist. As has been amply documented, Phia Rilke was the harsh mother who was both unaccepting of her son ("guilty" of being second-born to a girl who had lived only a few weeks after birth) *and* overprotective and all-embracing. Or, rather, she alternated between these two states either by withdrawing from baby René, who, in his first year of life, had twenty-four different wetnurses and caretakers,[23] or by showering him with attention when she paraded him in little girl's clothes in front of her friends. The anger and hatred that Rilke harbored for his mother is well known, but it is not matched by anything in the novel. It is as if Rilke, by writing the novel, created an ideal mother image for himself, the mother he always desired, but could not have. The psychic necessity of this fictional creation becomes evident if one considers the guilt feelings that accompanied his relationship to Phia all his life: guilt feelings not of an oedipal kind of desiring union with the mother but rather of hating the person he most desired and who, given her character and psychic dispositions, continually withdrew from that desire. The results of that powerful and never resolved double bind in Rilke's life are Malte's phantasms of the fragmented body, his anxieties of dissolution of boundaries, and a fundamental lack in ego development and object relations as they appear in the novel. The contradiction constitutive of the narrative, then, is that Rilke creates the figure of an ideal mother (Malte's), but that the real mother (Rilke's) is inscribed into the text via Malte's psychic disturbances, which have to be read as narratively displaced from the real subject to the fictional subject.

IV

Once we have read the hallucinatory perceptions of Malte as being rooted in the phantasm of the fragmented body rather than simply as susceptibility to Scandinavian spiritism, his fear of fragmentation, of breaking to pieces, and of shattering stands out even more starkly. Here, another dimension of fragmentation comes into focus: his fearful identification with shattering objects, a displacement of traumatic symptoms from subject to objects unsurprising in someone who is fundamentally unsure of the boundaries of his body, the boundaries between himself and the world.

From the very beginning the theme of fragmentation is related to the fear of death. Thus when the dying chamberlain Brigge desires to be carried into the room in which his mother had died a long time ago and people and dogs burst into this room nobody had set foot in for twenty-three years, the breaking of things is described with emotional sympathy, as if they were animate:

Yes, it was a terrible time for these drowsy, absentminded things. Down out of books which some careless hand had clumsily opened, rose leaves fluttered to the floor and were trampled underfoot; small, fragile objects were seized and, instantly broken, were quickly put back in place; others, dented or bent out of shape, were thrust beneath the curtains or even thrown behind the golden net of the fire-screen. And from time to time something fell, fell with a muffled sound onto the rug, fell with a clear sound onto the hard parquet floor, but breaking here and there, with a sharp crack or almost soundlessly; for these things, pampered as they were, could not endure a fall. (11 f.)

Later on in the novel, when Malte falls sick in Paris, the lost fears of his childhood resurface, impressing on the reader that the fear of going to pieces is nothing experientially new in his life:

All the lost fears are here again. The fear that a small woolen thread sticking out of the hem of my blanket may be hard, hard and sharp as a steel needle; the fear that this little button on my night-shirt may be bigger than my head, bigger and heavier; the fear that the breadcrumb which just dropped off my bed may turn into glass, and shatter when it hits the floor, and the sickening worry that when it does, everything will be broken, forever. (64)

The imagery of shattering objects is finally woven back into that of the fragmented body in a crucial passage where Malte describes his anxiety of separation as fear of death and then conjures up an image of apocalypse in writing and language that might bring his pains to an end:

But the day will come when my hand will be distant, and if I tell it to write, it will write words that are not mine. The time of that other interpretation will dawn, when there shall not be left one word upon another, and every meaning will dissolve like a cloud and fall down like rain. . . . this time, I will be written. I am the impression that will transform itself. (52 f.)

This of course would be the moment of the modernist epiphany, the transcendence into a realm of writing that would leave all contingency behind and achieve some ultimate truth and coherence. However, Malte recognizes that he cannot take the step "to understand all this and assent to it" because "I have fallen and I can't pick myself up because I am shattered to pieces" (53).[24] Prerequisite for taking that step, for turning misery into bliss, as Malte puts it, seems to be some notion of a self that remains outside of Malte's reach, a nonshattered, even nondifferentiated self that would be symbiotically all-encompassing and whose writing would achieve transcendence in that other "glorious language" (257). What Malte expresses here is the intense modernist longing for another kind of language that would, in psychoanalytic and ontogenetic terms, correspond to a phase preceding the development of language, which is after all constituted quintessentially as differentiation. But the desire for such a fluid language before differentiation is accompanied by Malte's equally strong acknowledgment (at least at this point in the novel, though perhaps not at its very end) that such a language cannot be attained, that the desire for it is an impossible, even dangerous desire. Consequently he turns back to writing another's, not *the* other, language. He copies others' texts into his novel, texts that serve him as prayers. A Baudelairean prose poem and a passage from the Bible are collaged here into the narrative, proving how distant Malte is from the "time of that other interpretation." Malte's discourse, indeed, is not the authentic, transcendent discourse of modernism that provides, in Wilhelm Emrich's phrasing, "unendliche Sinnfülle," an unlimited plenitude of meaning; his discourse remains rather the discourse of various others: that of Baudelaire and the bible as well as that of Rilke's letters and a variety of other historical texts. Most important, though, it is Rilke's unconscious that speaks with a vengeance in this novel. I am tempted to say that it is Rilke who is being written already while Malte is still waiting for this to happen, but if that is so then it must also be said that Rilke's being written is an entirely different kind from the one Malte imagines and prophesies.

Finally, the fear of shattering, when tied to the lack of an imaginary unity of self, ego, or identity, as well as to the desire and fear of symbiotic fusion, culminates in the famous mirror scene, that childhood experience which, as Lou Andreas-Salomé has pointed out,[25] Rilke transplanted from his own life into Malte's. Malte's mirror scene, however, produces the exact opposite of what Lacan has described in his seminal work on the mirror stage.[26] Where in Lacan an anticipatory sense of identity and unity of the subject is first constituted when the toddler jubilantly discovers his or her full bodily reflection in the mirror, precisely the failure of such imaginary unity to come about via the mirror image characterizes Malte's experience.[27] Important for my argument here is not the fact that Lacan analyzes this anticipatory self-recognition as a misrecognition, in the sense that the mirror image *is not* the self, but remains outside the self, serves as its reflection, is in the position of the other to the self. What is important for a reading of Rilke's novel is the fact that Malte never even reaches the stage of imaginary identification of self with the mirror image, which functions like a visual representation of the unitary, fully differentiated, and fortified ego. On the contrary, the mirror experience in the novel is not one of pleasurable confirmation of an identity, even an imaginary one, but an experience of total shattering, of being overwhelmed and wiped out. Of course, another difference between Lacan's and Rilke's mirror scene is that Malte is not just looking at his plain self but is actually playing dress-up in front of the mirror, which adds yet another level of complication, the conscious play with identity.[28]

Let us now take a closer look at how the mirror stage is symbolically reenacted and remembered in the novel. First of all, it is important to note that the horrors of the scene, which resurface with full force in Malte's account, cannot be attributed to feverish hallucinations. Traumatic anxiety is not brought forth here by disease and "the world of these fevers" (100), but it emerges when Malte inadvertently oversteps the boundaries of the world of normal, taken-for-granted identities:

But when you played by yourself, as always, it could happen that you inadvertently stepped out of this agreed-upon, generally harmless world, and found yourself in circumstances that were completely different, and unimaginable (*gar nicht abzusehen*). (101)

Malte plays dress-up in the out-of-the-way attic guest-rooms at Ulsgaard, puts on old costumes and ancestral clothes, and then takes pleasure at seeing himself in the mirror. He loves these disguises because they heighten his contradictory feelings about himself, but as a result of his ego-weakness they can also become quite overpowering:

It was then that I first came to know the influence that can emanate from a particular costume. Hardly had I put on one of them when I had to admit that it had me in its power; that it dictated my movements, my facial expression, even my thoughts. (103)

But Malte maintains conscious and playful control of the *mise-en-scène*. He remains aware of the fact that he is both subject and object of the look, and he maintains a sense of identity through all of his disguises:

These disguises, though, never went so far as to make me feel a stranger to myself; on the contrary, the more complete my transformation, the more convinced I was of my own identity. I grew bolder and bolder; flung myself higher and higher; for my skill at catching myself again was beyond all doubt. (103 f.)

That security of playing with images of self in disguise, the pleasure of seeing himself seeing himself—as Lacan puts it with reference to Valéry's *La Jeune Parque*—is disrupted when Malte discovers an armoire full of paraphernalia for masquerades, gets transported into a kind of intoxication in which he randomly dresses himself in scarves, shawls, veils, and spacious cloaks, and then steps in front of the mirror in order to seek his magnificent image. While turning around in front of the mirror in order "to find out what I actually was" (106), he knocks over, owing to his limited vision behind the mask, a small table carrying a number of fragile objects that now shatter and break on the floor. The aesthetic play with mirror images and identities turns into existential disaster:

The two useless, green-violet porcelain parrots were of course shattered, each in a different, malign way. A small bowl had spilled out its pieces of candy, which looked like insects in their silk cocoons, and had tossed its cover far away—only half of it was visible, the other half had completely disappeared. But the most annoying sight of all was a perfume bottle that had broken into a thousand tiny fragments, from which the remnant of some ancient essence had spurted out, that now formed a stain with a very repulsive physiognomy on the light rug. (106)

Malte quickly tries to clean up the mess, but, hampered both in vision and in movement, he is unsuccessful and is caught by a violent rage against his "absurd situation." Desperately he tries to free himself from his costume in front of the mirror, but he only succeeds in entangling himself further. And then something happens to Malte that cannot be accounted for by the theory of the mirror stage at all. His desire to see and to learn how to see—later in life his stated Paris project—is stopped cold; the gaze becomes fundamentally problematic, split, as it were, between seeing and being seen:

Hot and furious, I rushed to the mirror and with difficulty watched, through my mask, the frantic movements of my hands. But the mirror had been waiting for just this. Its moment of revenge had come. While I, with a boundlessly growing anguish, kept trying to somehow squeeze out of my disguise, it forced me, I don't know how, to look up, and dictated to me an image, no, a reality, a strange, incomprehensible, monstrous reality that permeated me against my will: for now it was the stronger one, and I was the mirror. I stared at this large, terrifying stranger in front of me, and felt appalled to be alone with him. But at the very moment I thought this, the worst thing happened: I lost all sense of myself, I simply ceased to exist. For one second, I felt an indescribable, piercing, futile longing for myself, then only *he* remained: there was nothing except him. (107)

It is clear that Malte's traumatic fear about the image turning into a real *Doppelgänger* and reducing the real self to an illusion explodes not at the sight of the strange creature in the mirror alone but rather at the point when he knocks over the table and breaks the perfume bottle. The experience of shattering objects, combined with the heavy and pervasive vapor of the spilled perfume, suddenly ruptures his ability to play at disguise and masquerades. A total loss of self, abandonment to an absurd and unrecognizable mirror image, is the result. But the conjunction of mirror image and fragmentation is even further emphasized by the text. Even the mirror surface isn't whole, nor does it have the usual transparency of reflection:

I . . . ran to the nearest guest-room, in front of the tall, narrow mirror, which was made up of irregular pieces of green glass. Ah, how I trembled to be there, and how thrilling when I was: when something approached out of the cloudy depths, more slowly than myself, for the mirror hardly believed it and, sleepy as it was, didn't want to promptly repeat what I had recited to it. But in the end it had to, of course. (103)

Given its peculiar makeup, this mirror itself is incapable of providing the imaginary identity and unity of the body. It conspires, as it were, in Malte's fragmentation. The mirror voids him, sucks all images of self out of him, and leaves him, at the end of the scene, lying on the floor "just like a piece of cloth" (108), reduced to a stage of infantile motor incoordination (Lacan).

This variant of the Lacanian mirror scene is so crucial for an understanding of the *Notebooks* not just because it confirms Malte's ego deficiency but because it opens up the problematic of seeing and being seen. We must remember here, first, that vision is central for Rilke's experience of the city and for the construction of his aesthetic, and, second, that Malte describes his own life crisis with the words: "I am learning to see" (5 and 6). But as the mirror scene shows, there is no seeing without being seen. This basic split in the organization of the scopic field of course played a major role in Sartre's *Being and Nothingness,* and it also appears in Lacan's later essay "The Split Between the Eye and the Gaze." In this essay Lacan goes beyond the argument of the mirror stage and distinguishes the narcissistic *méconnaissance* of the specular image—Malte seeing himself seeing himself—from a scopic situation marked by what Lacan calls the "pre-existence to the seen of a given-to-be-seen."[29] The gaze is always deeply implicated in processes of desire, and for Rilke this fact cannot appear as anything but a basic contamination of vision. The passage in *Malte* could then be read as a breaking open of the initial narcissistic identification with the specular image, a disruption of narcissistic satisfaction by the recognition that there is no purity, no oneness of vision, but that the scopic field is always already split. Malte's childhood experience with the mirror thus contains already his relationship to the Paris outcasts whose gaze pursues him everywhere in his wanderings through the city. His learning to see is consistently disrupted and spoilt by the fact that he is being seen, an object of the gaze rather than its privileged subject. It is here, then, that Malte's childhood experiences mesh with his experiences of the modern city for which Simmel and Benjamin have emphasized the prevalence of vision over hearing.[30] It is perhaps primarily this concern with the problematics of vision that places Rilke's novel squarely within the culture of early twentieth-century modernism.

But this is also the place where a fundamental contradiction emerges, a contradiction that may well be paradigmatic for a certain constellation in modernism in general. Just as Rilke's modernism successfully articulates the problematics of vision as a central experience of metropolitan modernity, it also constructs an aesthetic designed to evade the very problem that gave rise to it in the first place. Thus Malte's whole project in the second part of the novel can be read as an attempt to elude the gaze, to undo the split between the eye and the gaze, and to restore some imaginary purity of vision and of writing via the myth of the "women in love" and the parable of the prodigal son with which the novel ends. It is difficult to think that Malte's project was not close to Rilke's own heart, even though Rilke has Malte fail in his attempt to learn how to see and to create that other language. That failure, I think, is all but inevitable. The text itself shows why the desire to get out of the structures of desire and temporality and to enter into a realm of purity of language and vision is a dead end, both theoretically and aesthetically. Rilke may still identify with Malte's project, but, as I will argue, by the end of the novel that project reveals itself to be hopelessly vitiated.

V

Let me turn now to the broader question of metropolitan experience and the mechanisms of perception. I have shown how, in the process of writing his Paris diary, Malte himself becomes increasingly aware that his country childhood was actually haunted by the same kinds of phantasms that make life miserable for him in the big city, and he senses that it is the city itself that makes his childhood resurface. As I am not satisfied with a mechanical Freudian reading of this repetition compulsion, which would put all the emphasis on the early childhood experience alone, I still want to explore further why it is the city that not only triggers the repetition compulsion but also compels the effort to work it through, to displace it into fictional discourse. The question is whether there is not some more substantial link between Malte's psychological constitution and the experience of modernity as produced by urban life in the late nineteenth and early twentieth centuries. Perhaps the constellation of city experience and the early childhood trauma of the fragmented body can tell us something about modernist subjectivity that may not only be paradigmatic for a certain kind of modernist male artist but also have broader implications.

One of the major accounts of perceptions of modern city life and their psychic implications since the mid-nineteenth century was elaborated aesthetically by Baudelaire, critically by Georg Simmel and Walter Benjamin.[31] At first sight, Malte seems quite distant from the central concerns of these writers. As an artist, he certainly has nothing much in common with Baudelaire's painter of modern life, except perhaps that vision is as central to Baudelaire's work as it is to Rilke's. If the experience of modernity, as described by Baudelaire, Simmel, and Benjamin, has centrally to do with the relationship of the artist to the metropolitan crowd, then Rilke's Malte seems a rather atypical protagonist. Sure, the crowd is there in *Malte,* as "a hidden figure" (Benjamin's term for the crowd in Baudelaire's poetry) rather than as a described reality, something like a screen onto which Malte projects his phantasms of the fragmented body and from which he then escapes into the solitude of his rented room. But moving through the crowds does not energize Malte as it energizes Baudelaire. Baudelaire describes the crowd as an "immense source of enjoyment," as "an enormous reservoir of electricity" in which the man of genius finds inspiration, even ecstasy.[32] In this sense Malte clearly is not a man of the crowd, nor is he a flaneur or dandy, nor is he ever concerned with fashion as a key element of modernity. The issues of exchange, commodification, and emerging consumerism, which are so powerfully worked out by Simmel and Benjamin, are all but absent from Rilke's novel. And Benjamin's concern with the impact of a newspaper and information culture on the structure of experience appears in Rilke at best as part of a vague and fairly unoriginal critique of the superficiality of modern civilization against which he posits the project of modernist writing.

The point of comparison is elsewhere. It is in the theory of perception, shock, and shock defenses that, according to Simmel and Benjamin, transformed the basic structures of human experience in the nineteenth century. In his essay "The Metropolis and Mental Life," Simmel has argued that the metropolis creates psychological conditions having to do with the "rapid crowding of changing images, the sharp discontinuity in the grasp of a single glance, and the unexpectedness of onrushing impressions."[33] Against the threats of an everchanging environment metropolitan man develops a protective organ that Simmel describes thus:

The reaction to metropolitan phenomena is shifted to that organ which is least sensitive and quite remote from the depth of the personality. Intellectuality is thus seen to preserve subjective life against the overwhelming power of metropolitan life.[34]

Simmel then goes on to link that protective intellectuality with the matter-of-factness of the money economy and describes blaséness, reserve, indifference, and a general blunting of discrimination as key features of metropolitan psychic life. The same pattern of interpretation appears in Benjamin's 1939 essay "Some Motifs in Baudelaire." Simmel's binary opposition of subjective versus objective culture reappears in Benjamin in the psychoanalytically more complex opposition between *Erfahrung* and *Erlebnis, Erinnerung* and *Gedächtnis*. Benjamin uses Freud's thesis from *Beyond the Pleasure Principle* that consciousness plays a major role in the protection against stimuli (*Reizschutz*) and that becoming conscious and the inscription of memory traces are mutually exclusive. What Simmel and Benjamin have in common is the notion that consciousness neutralizes the shock experiences of metropolitan life and that this neutralization is essential for self-preservation, even if the price for such self-preservation is an impoverishment of experience in the emphatic sense, an atrophy of subjectivity.

At this point, we run up against a problem we had encountered earlier in a different context. In relying on the strength of consciousness to provide *Reizschutz* against a traumatic breakdown, protection against the stimuli, shocks, and accidents of street life in the city, Benjamin and Simmel implicitly assume a psychic instance in control, the conscious ego. What else is this consciousness but part of the armor of the fortified ego, which, in Lacan's account, achieves its first imaginary shape during the mirror stage, and which proves itself in fending off the shocks and assaults of city life on human perception. That, for Benjamin, was the essence of Baudelaire's "heroism of modern life." Here it becomes clear that the Simmel-Freud-Benjamin account of the psychic processes triggered by the modern city experience does not apply to Malte. The main problem Malte has in his encounters with the city is precisely his *inability* to protect himself against the chaos of stimuli and shocks. This inability is of course rooted in his psychic constitution, in his childhood past. By juxtaposing past and present, Rilke actually focuses on a dimension of experience that neither Simmel nor Benjamin incorporates into his reflections.[35] Therefore Malte experiences the city very differently from, say, Benjamin's Baudelaire. Rather than parrying the shocks of modern life with his poetic imagination—an image that Benjamin took from Baudelaire's "Le Soleil"—Malte is totally defenseless against the shocks of the city, which penetrate right down to the deepest layers of unconscious memory traces, hurling themselves, as it were, like shells into the quarry of Malte's unconscious childhood memories, breaking loose large chunks that then float up to the surface as fragments in the narrative. Ironically, the effect the city has on Malte is precisely the effect Rilke feared from psychoanalytic treatment. Rilke's statement about psychoanalysis—"Es ist furchtbar, die Kindheit so in Brocken von sich zu geben"[36]—has often been used by critics to keep psychoanalysis at bay in their readings. Little did they notice that spitting out his childhood in bits and pieces is precisely what Rilke does in his novel, even though he does so in an aesthetically highly controlled way. Forced by his experience with the shocks and assaults of the modern city, Malte reproduces fragment upon fragment of his past, fragments that lack, to be sure, the unifying intervention of the analyst or, for that matter, of the traditional narrator who would impose a linear order of representation and perspective onto the seemingly chaotic material. In Rilke's case, the modernist narrative with its tortured subjectivity, its experimental ruptures and discontinuities, emerges out of the constellation of a childhood trauma of the fragmented body with the shattering and unavoidably fragmentary experience of the metropolis. The absence of an adequate *Reizschutz*, resulting from a deficiently developed ego, characterizes Malte Laurids Brigge and determines the course of the narrative, thus making the Paris/childhood constellation central to any reading of the novel.

The broader question remains as to what extent Malte may be a paradigmatic case of male subjectivity within modernity. If the ways in which Malte reacts to city experience cannot be grasped with Simmel's or Benjamin's account of the experience of modernity, perhaps these accounts are deficient, or at least not generalizable. Malte might be quite representative for another psychic disposition produced, or at least exacerbated, by modernization, and characterized by ego deficiency, phantasms of fragmentation anxiety, and lack of defensive mechanisms against the assault of modernization on the senses and the psyche. Already in Freud's days this disposition must have been much more common among men than the disposition Freud theorized, with its emphasis on ego, consciousness, and sublimation. At least that is strongly suggested by the investigations of Klaus Theweleit in *Male Phantasies,* which constructs the imagination of the fascist male in ways very different from Freud or, for that matter, the Frankfurt School.[37] It is indeed striking to see—and one is at first reluctant to admit it—that Malte shares quite a number of traits with the "fascist male" as analyzed by Theweleit: basic psychic disturbances going back to an unsuccessful separation from the symbiotic stage, vacillations between paranoia (Malte's constant fear of being seen) and phantasms of omnipotence (the creation of the new language), narcissistic disturbances, idealization of the mother combined with an inability to form lasting relationships with women, fears of being overwhelmed, engulfed, reduced to nothingness. This said, we must immediately backtrack. Of course, Malte is anything but the fascist male. Where Theweleit's Freikorps men, out of "unresolved" symbiosis, develop fantasies of violence and destructive rage and direct this aggression outward against anything that connotes femininity, Malte actually identifies with the feminine and his violent phantasies are invariably and masochistically directed against himself only. Where the Freikorps man forges his male identity out of a fear of the feminine and develops an image of the male body as armored terror machine, simultaneously longing and fearing to explode on the battlefield, Malte deals with the ambivalence between desire for fusion and the fear of it in a nonaggressive way. Rather than turning to violent action against the feminine, he appropriates the feminine and uses it to create the modernist aesthetic, the phantasmagoria of a magnificent new language that will speak him, but that has never yet been heard, a language that would transcend, or rather precede, language as we know it, precede the mirror phase, as it were, and fulfill the narcissistic desires of omnipotence and fusion.

It is easy enough to interpret Malte's reflections on the divine, on transcendent love, on the necessity of loving rather than being loved, on the prodigal son's relation to God as Malte's way of overcoming fragmentation and working toward fusion, symbiosis, reconciliation of everything that is split or shattered. There is also no need to elaborate how his concern with narrative and temporality, his attempt to create a narrative in which time would be suspended, his projective identifications with figures of the distant historical past all aim in the same direction. It is also easy to see that Malte's identification with femininity, his praise of intransitive love, a love without object, is in itself highly problematic, a paradigmatic case of a male-imagined femininity. While this aspect of the novel, strongly foregrounded only in the second part, may be read as a critique of the property inscriptions and the violence of male possessiveness in the bourgeois institutions of love and marriage, Malte's reflections on Gaspara Stampa, Mariana Alcoforado, Louise Labé, Bettina Brentano, and finally Sappho also reproduce typical bourgeois idealizations of female selflessness and renunciation. Any ambivalence is lost, however, when the identification with the feminine is narratively retracted at the very end of the novel. The woman writer as *die große Liebende* no longer provides the model for Malte. After all, it was commonly held at the turn of the century that the male artist can appropriate femininity while the woman with artistic aspirations does violence to her nature.[38] With his rewriting of the biblical parable of the prodigal son as the one who loves but does not want to be loved, the one who will be written and is longing for the modernist epiphany of that other language, Rilke redelivers the project of writing back to a male authorial voice. The novel ends with a retraction of that breaking of the patriarchal chain—"Today Brigge and nevermore" (159)—that seemed so central to Malte's life and writing project. The identification with femininity has fulfilled its function: it has allowed Malte to escape from city terror and childhood trauma into reconciliation. But this reconciliation is achieved on the basis of a problematic male appropriation of the feminine that ultimately serves only to solve the crisis of male creativity, to help Malte move closer to that ever elusive purity of vision and of language.

Rather than providing a solution, the ending of *Malte* strikes me as the culmination of a series of evasions of the splits and tensions that tear the protagonist apart, evasions also of the reality of the experiences of modern city life. Rather than read the second part of the novel as an achievement of narrative coherence, I see it as obsessive evasion in every sense, existential as well as aesthetic. I also cannot read the ending as tragic failure; the novel just comes to the end of a dead end. Despite this failure, Rilke's greatness perhaps lies in the fact that he does not attempt to transform Malte's failure into an epiphany, not even into a negative epiphany. Rilke had great difficulty with the ending of the novel, and he knew it. What Rilke had to offer modernist prose, I would argue, is all in the first part, which focuses radically and uncompromisingly on the truth of an unreconciled and antagonistic present. One only needs to follow the trajectory of Malte's identificatory strategies from his pained and paranoid identification with the Paris street people, to an imaginary and bodiless femininity of the "women in love," to the mystificatory use of the biblical story of the prodigal son to note the progressive dematerialization, the flight from the reality of his experiences and his subjectivity. The city recedes as the novel goes on and the concrete memories of childhood are soon overtaken by mere phantasms of wish-fulfillment. It is no coincidence that the new glorious language will speak *through* Malte rather than being spoken *by* him. The modernist aesthetic of transcendence and epiphany constructs itself here as a simultaneous voiding of subjectivity, which is more an avoiding of an unanchored and threatening subjectivity that has become too hard to bear. In Rilke's novel, the dream of another language, central to the modernist aesthetic at the turn of the century, is just another projection, another imaginary, another mirror image in which the trauma of the fragmented body and that of an unavoidably fragmentary and multiply split language is finally dissolved, the experience of modernity transcended. The best that can be said about the end of *Malte* is that reconciliation is only anticipated, not realized. But reconciliation is nevertheless false, just as delusory in its promise of an anticipated narcissistic fusion in and with a kind of fluid, non-

differentiated language as the Lacanian mirror image is delusory in
its anticipation of the unity of the subject. Rilke's *Notebooks of Malte
Laurids Brigge* is both a powerful articulation of a crisis of subjectivity under the pressures of modernization and an equally powerful
evasion of the problem. It projects the very real and yet impossible
desire for fusion and symbiosis into the aesthetic realm, the realm of
language where it cannot be fulfilled any more easily than in reality.
If Rilke's work embodies one of the most persuasive instances of high
modernism, then the *Notebooks* represents that moment in his work
in which he himself calls that project into question in the very process
of articulating it. The novel is a case of high modernism against itself.
That is what makes it such fascinating reading in a postmodern age.

Notes

1. Hugo Friedrich, *Die Struktur der modernen Lyrik* (Reinbek: Rowohlt,
1956).
2. Of course the criteria of negativity, dominant in the high modernist
readings, could be seen as parallel to the existentialist emphasis on alienation
and *Geworfenheit*, except that existentialism put a stronger emphasis on a
notion of self that the high modernist readings, and justifiably so, had begun
to put in doubt.
3. E.g., Otto Friedrich Bollnow, *Rilke* (Stuttgart: Kohlhammer, 1951).
4. Most recently, Judith Ryan has again emphasized this point in her
essay "Rainer Maria Rilke: *Die Aufzeichnungen des Malte Laurids Brigge*
(1910)," in *Deutsche Romane des 20. Jahrhunderts,* ed. Paul Michael Lützeler
(Königstein: Athenäum, 1983).
5. Theodore Ziolkowski, *Dimensions of the Modern Novel* (Princeton:
Princeton University Press, 1969), 3–36.
6. Ernst Fedor Hoffmann, "Zum dichterischen Verfahren in Rilkes
Aufzeichnungen des Malte Laurids Brigge," in *Rilke's "Aufzeichnungen des
Malte Laurids Brigge,"* ed. Hartmut Engelhardt (Frankfurt am Main: Suhrkamp), 214–44.
7. Ulrich Fülleborn, "Form und Sinn der Aufzeichnungen des Malte Laurids
Brigge: Rilkes Prosabuch und der moderne Roman," *ibid.,* 175–97.
8. Judith Ryan, " 'Hypothetisches Erzählen': Zur Funktion von Phantasie und Einbildung in Rilkes 'Malte Laurids Brigge,' " *ibid.,* 244–79. In a
certain register, Ryan's approach is not that different from Fülleborn's, except that she emphasizes subjectivity rather than the objectivity of narrative
form.
9. The major exception still is Erich Simenauer's *Rainer Maria Rilke:*

Legende und Mythos (Bern: Verlag Paul Haupt, 1953). The rejection of a psychoanalytic approach was often simply based on the observation that Rilke himself refused explicitly to subject himself to analysis.

10. Thomas Anz, *Literatur der Existenz: Literarische Psychopathographie und ihre soziale Bedeutung im Frühexpressionismus* (Stuttgart: Metzler, 1977). Anz explains Malte's anxieties and insecurities primarily as those of the artist outsider whose social position is increasingly devalued and who therefore begins to question the validity of traditional norms and meanings. In this account, Malte's problems with perception and with himself result only from the changing social position of the artist under the onslaught of modernization and the traumatic experience of the city. The fact that all of Malte's problems have their roots in his childhood, which is precisely not "die heilere Welt der Vergangenheit" (84), falls through the cracks of Anz's approach.—For a critique of Anz's treatment of *Malte* and a more complex focus on Malte's reflections on the social function of writing in bourgeois society, see Brigitte L. Bradley, *Zu Rilke's Malte Laurids Brigge* (Bern and Munich: Francke, 1980), esp. 36 ff.

11. Paradigmatically analyzed by Walter Sokel, "Zwischen Existenz und Weltinnenraum: Zum Prozess der Ent-Ichung im Malte Laurids Brigge," in *Probleme des Erzählens: Festschrift für Käte Hamburger,* ed. Fritz Martini (Stuttgart: Klett, 1971), 212–33.

12. Rainer Maria Rilke, *The Notebooks of Malte Laurids Brigge,* trans. Stephen Mitchell (New York: Random House, 1985), 22. All further page references will be given in the text.

13. Sigmund Freud, "The Uncanny," *Collected Papers,* 4 (New York: Basic Books, 1959), 369.

14. *Ibid.,* 403.

15. Lou Andreas-Salomé, *Rainer Maria Rilke* (Leipzig: Insel Verlag, 1928). Andreas-Salomé is one of the few critics who emphasized the importance of Rilke's fractured and ambivalent relationship to his own body and to gender for a reading of the *Notebooks*.

16. Many of the relevant letters are now easily available in *Rilke's "Aufzeichnungen des Malte Laurids Brigge,"* ed. Hartmut Engelhardt.

17. Maurice Betz, *Rilke in Frankreich* (Vienna, Leipzig, Zurich: Herbert Reichner Verlag, 1938), 114. Translation: "He was my self and was an other."

18. Freud, "The Uncanny," 403. Translation modified.

19. *Ibid.,* 397.

20. Lou Andreas-Salomé, *Aus der Schule bei Freud,* ed. Ernst Pfeiffer (Zurich: M. Niehans Verlag, 1958), 213.

21. Michael Balint, *Therapeutische Aspekte der Regression: Die Theorie der Grundstörung* (Stuttgart: Klett-Cotta, 1970); Margaret S. Mahler, *Symbiose und Individuation,* 1 (Stuttgart: Klett-Cotta, 1972); Melanie Klein, *Das Seelenleben des Kleinkindes und andere Beiträge zur Psychoanalyse* (Reinbek: Rowohlt, 1972).

22. Both Lou Andreas-Salomé and Erich Simenauer have provided the relevant facts and interpretations.

23. Carl Sieber, *René Rilke: Die Jugend Rainer Maria Rilkes* (Leipzig: Insel Verlag, 1932), 69. Also mentioned in Simenauer, *Rilke*, 245.

24. Translation modified. The crucial phrase "weil ich zerbrochen bin" is inexplicably missing in the English translation.

25. Andreas-Salomé, *Rilke*, 48.

26. Jacques Lacan, "The Mirror Stage," *Ecrits: A Selection*, trans. Alan Sheridan (New York: Norton, 1977).

27. Whether Lacan is right or wrong with his analysis of the mirror stage as pivotal in development is not my concern here. There are indeed good reasons to believe that the mirroring process is already under way at a much earlier stage and does not need to be interpreted as thoroughly pessimistically as Lacan does. What is at stake in the novel is at any rate not the clinical event but rather its metaphoric reenactment. In this context, however, Lacan's account allows me to reread the scene in support of my general argument about Malte's ego-weakness.

28. I want to mention at least two more instances that make the reading of this scene in relation to Lacan's account so appealing. First, Lacan himself theorizes the relationship between the phantasm of identity as linked to an image of the fortified body and the developmentally earlier, but complementary phantasm of the fragmented body, thus permitting us to read this mirror scene in relation to Malte's persistent anxiety of body fragmentation. Second, it must be more than coincidence that both Rilke and Lacan make explicit references at crucial junctures of their texts to that perhaps paradigmatic painter of the fragmented body, Hieronymous Bosch. See Rilke, *Malte*, 184 f.; Lacan, *Ecrits*, 4–5.

29. Jacques Lacan, "The Split Between the Eye and the Gaze," *Four Fundamental Concepts of Psychoanalysis*, trans. Alan Sheridan (New York: Norton, 1978), 74.

30. Thus Benjamin quotes Simmel's reflections approvingly in his essay "Das Paris des Second Empire bei Baudelaire," *Gesammelte Schriften*, 1:2 (Frankfurt am Main: Suhrkamp, 1974), 540.

31. Rilke actually heard some of Simmel's famous lectures on modernity in Berlin, and Baudelaire's poetic prose clearly provided a model for Rilke's own prose in the *Notebooks*, especially in the fragmentary segments of the first part. Benjamin in turn not only made Baudelaire the centerpiece of his writings on the prehistory of the nineteenth century, but he also was very familiar with Simmel's work. As to Benjamin's relationship to Rilke, it seems clear that he never thought much of Rilke's poetry, which to him was fatally vitiated by its origins in Jugendstil. In the only text where he deals with Rilke, he does not mention the *Notebooks*. Walter Benjamin, "Rainer Maria Rilke und Franz Blei," *Gesammelte Schriften*, 4:1 (Frankfurt am Main: Suhrkamp, 1972), 453 f.

32. Charles Baudelaire, "The Painter of Modern Life," in *Baudelaire: Selected Writings on Art and Artists* (London, New York: Cambridge University Press, 1981), 399 f.

33. Georg Simmel, "The Metropolis and Mental Life," *The Sociology of Georg Simmel*, trans. and ed. Kurt H. Wolff (New York: The Free Press, 1964), 410.

34. *Ibid.*, 410 f.

35. However, Benjamin does deal with this dimension of experience in his more autobiographic texts such as *Berlin Childhood*.

36. Translation: "It is terrifying to spit out one's childhood like that in bits and pieces." Quoted in Ernst Pfeiffer, "Rilke und die Psychoanalyse," *Literaturwissenschaftliches Jahrbuch*, Neue Folge 17 (1976): 296.

37. Klaus Theweleit, *Male Phantasies*, vol. 1 (Minneapolis: University of Minnesota Press, 1987). Vol. 2 forthcoming. Theweleit shows that is is not the desire for the authority of the father that is at stake, but rather a desire for fusion.

38. That Rilke shared this view was pointed out by Simenauer, *Rilke*, 634.

Kafka and New York: Notes on a Traveling Narrative

Mark Anderson

But Socrates, I have no way of telling you what I have in mind, for whatever proposition we put forward goes around and refuses to stay put where we establish it.—Plato, *Euthyphro*

Le moral, c'est le travelling.—Jean-Luc Godard

No, Kafka never went to New York. But he did imagine it and, as we know, gave an astounding presentation of the city—though perhaps not the city we commonly mean when we say "New York"— in his first novel, *Der Verschollene*, which Max Brod later published under the title of *Amerika*. Why did Kafka choose New York as a subject of representation for his first sustained literary project? What did this city represent to him? And what bearing did the notion of "America" or "New York" have on the literary texts he had already written?

The key to these questions is the notion of *Verkehr*, a complex word that, for the time being, I will translate simply as "traffic."[1] Kafka was fascinated by traffic patterns in the modern city and, more important, by the aesthetic spectacle and metaphysical dilemmas these patterns implied. Here we should keep in mind the general shift in art, philosophy, and science that was taking place in Kafka's society at the turn of the century: a shift away from the representation of people and things securely rooted in a stable, constant environment, and toward a relativized perception of things in motion, of subtle or unconscious displacements of energy, fluctuating or ephemeral patterns of circulation and exchange. Increasingly, modern artists, philosophers, and scientists were turning to the analysis of phenomena that their nineteenth-century predecessors would have avoided as too unstable, transitory, intangible, or illogical to capture in a stable representation, be it artistic or scientific. What French painters had achieved and made into a cliché as early as the 1880s continued to dominate other fields of thought throughout the *Jahrhundertwende*. As cursory, almost random examples of this tendencey—in which Kafka's beginning work is also implicated—one might single out Simmel's *Lebensphilosophie* essays on fashion and the circulation of money; or Freud's charting of the logic of "error" in everyday life and the displacements of unconscious psychic energies; or Ernst Mach's use of statistical analysis to account for sense impressions and to refute the idea of a stable, unifying "ego."

For Kafka the word *Verkehr*—which in German means not only traffic but commerce, exchange, circulation, social and sexual intercourse, even, in composite forms, tourism and epistolary correspondence—subsumes precisely this order of transitory phenomena. Thus his early interest in the literal forms of "traffic" must be seen as part of a more general concern with the problem of appearances, with the place of the subject in a merely apparent or *scheinbaren* world, and with the grounding of discourse in such an unstable terrain. In these early texts "traffic" merges into a larger network of signification that includes fashion, clothing, masks, theatrical façades, the obscure but codified rituals of social intercourse, the fetishization of desire, and finally the fragmentary, illusory quality of perception in general. To put it most simply and abstractly: in his early work Kafka is always concerned with the apparent groundlessness of material reality, that is, with *things in motion*.

A rare insight into Kafka's epistemological and aesthetic theories of this period can be gleaned from his fragmentary essay "On Perception" ("Über Apperzeption"), which Max Brod first published in his history of the Prague Circle in 1966, but which has been strangely neglected by subsequent research. A polemic response to Max Brod's articles on aesthetics in *Die Gegenwart* of February 17 and 24, 1906, the five philosophical propositions in this essay insist that perceptions are always "new": "for given that all objects are located in a continuously changing time and illumination, and we spectators no less so, we always encounter these objects in a different place." Hence perception is not a state but a movement ("Apperzeption ist kein Zustand, sondern eine Bewegung"). Kafka then attempts to illustrate this proposition with the example of a person without any sense of place ("ganz ohne Ortsgefühl") who comes to Prague as if it were a foreign, unknown city and who therefore cannot perceive it.[2]

An important work for Kafka in this early period is Oscar Bie's *Der gesellschaftliche Verkehr* (Social Intercourse), which was first published in 1905.[3] Kafka's critics have long been under the mistaken impression that Bie's book is a manual of social etiquette, a kind of Emily Post for the German world at the turn of the century.[4] In fact, it is an artfully written philosophical essay patterned after works by Simmel, Burckhardt, Castiglione, and della Casa. In this impressionistic essay Bie attempts to describe the aestheticizing effect of big-city traffic on modern society, an effect he claims is comparable to that of dance, religion, and courtly ritual in earlier cultures. Bie writes:

The spectacle of human traffic . . . is an artwork endowed with such strong and various charms that it can never fully be explained. Each second on city streets and in apartments, the rhythmic patterns of people in social motion (*verkehrende Menschen*) are carried out. . . . The noise that rises up from the street, the symphony of the first alarm clocks in the morning to the last stragglers at night . . . the hundred variations of comings and goings in an apartment building, the confusing *tempi* of life. . . . Even here the masses stylize life. . . . Trains travel across countries, ships voyage across the oceans, streetcars crisscross the city—they all represent the summation of individual rhythms and their timetable is the book of their artfully stylized motion, the product of an infinitely complex codification of mass traffic. (3–4)

Kafka's first extant work, *Description of a Struggle* (written in 1904–7), reveals traces of his reading of Bie's essay. But Kafka "misreads" Bie, emphasizing not only the aesthetic stylization of urban traffic but also its contingent violence. In Kafka's text, modern traffic is perceived as a theatrical spectacle, but this spectacle is incongruous, shocking, aggressively artificial. A brief quote in which the Supplicant imagines life in Paris will make clear Kafka's debt to Bie as well as the gap between them:

But it might happen that, suddenly, two carriages stop in an elegant neighborhood on some busy boulevard. Servants open the doors. Eight elegant Siberian wolfhounds come dancing out and race up the street, barking and jumping. And it's said that they are young Parisian dandies in disguise.[5]

In the imagination of the naïve Supplicant, the people in Paris are made of "decorative clothing"; society ladies stand on high, illuminated terraces while their liveried servants lift giant painted canvases to create the illusion of a foggy morning. But this Paris of masks, theatrical façades, pink clouds, and artful illusion is also a labyrinth of accident, disorder, uncertainty, rootlessness, and death. The Supplicant asks:

Isn't it true that these Paris streets suddenly fork out in different directions? They're turbulent (*unruhig*), aren't they? Not everything is in order there—how could it be? Sometimes there's an accident, people gather together from side streets with that big-city stride that hardly touches the pavement . . . they breathe fast and crane their tiny heads forward. (43)

Confronted with this accidental victim of *Verkehr*, the Parisian crowd reacts with conventional, lightly grotesque excuses: " 'I'm so sorry . . . it wasn't intentional, it's so crowded, please excuse me.' That's the way they talk," comments the narrator, "while the street lies numb and chimney smoke falls between the buildings."

The big city as a theatrical space marked by its "traffic" and hence by the problem of "accident"—of *Unfall*, but also of contingency (*Zufall*), chance, and death—this, roughly speaking, is the double optic through which Kafka's text views the modern world. With its ornate traffic, the modern city offers its inhabitants a giant stage for theatrical performance, quotidian mini-spectacles, street "happenings." But accident and randomness break into this stylized, mechanized realm, unmasking its disordered temporality, violence, and falsehood. Chimney smoke "falls" between the buildings, pedestrians are run over by machines, the decorative Parisians themselves turn out to be automatonlike prisoners of conventional language much like the trees in the Paris wax-figure museum that bear the names of famous criminals, heroes, and lovers inscribed on tiny signboards. Metaphysically, this street theater is ungrounded: the "big-city stride" barely touches the pavement, the strollers in a city park in the verse epigraph sway, off balance, beneath a vertiginously empty sky,[6] and finally all the inhabitants of this text are compared to mutilated tree trunks lying like corpses in the snow, whose rootedness in a ground beneath the white surface is denounced as merely apparent.[7]

II

This aggressive, uneasy fascination with the spectacle of modern traffic marks all Kafka's early writings, from the short prose pieces in *Meditations* such as "On the Streetcar," "Children on a Country Road," and "The Sudden Walk," to the aborted novel fragment *Wedding Preparations in the Country,* to the travel diaries Kafka kept during his visits to Milan and Paris (which contain a detailed description of a traffic accident Kafka witnessed in front of the Opéra), and finally to the "breakthrough" story of 1912, "The Judgment," which concludes with the words "unendlicher Verkehr" and the image of an infinite city traffic streaming across a bridge. In all these writings, which in another context would merit detailed individual treatment, "traffic" defines the world around the Kafkan protagonist; it defines the moving space of the other, the other *as* movement. Before turning to Kafka's rearticulation of this theme in his American novel, we should note briefly that this attention to things in motion tends to problematize, destabilize, or even efface the objects of representation. A good example of this tendency is Kafka's difficult early text, "The Wish to Be a Red Indian," which consists of the following hypothetical, unfinished sentence:

If one were only an Indian, instantly alert, and on a racing horse, leaning against the wind, kept on quivering jerkily over the quivering ground, until one shed one's spurs, for there needed no spurs, threw away the reins, for there needed no reins, and hardly saw that the land before one was smoothly shorn heath when horse's neck and head would be already gone. (390)

The peculiar traffic of this text results in a "deterritorialization" of the writing subject, a process that operates as much on the level of images—the progressive disappearance of rider, horse, and American plain—as on the grammatical/syntactical level of subjunctive verbs, unfinished hypothetical clauses, etc. The text proposes itself as the possibility of an image that its own subsequent movement then retracts or suspends. The reader is left with no rider, no horse, and certainly no specific, geographically situated image of "America."

The same is true on a larger, more complex scale of Kafka's first novel, which, as we know from his letter of November 11, 1912, to Felice Bauer, he intended to call not *Amerika* but *Der Verschollene*. The difference between these two titles merits some reflection. Very few of Kafka's texts are located in a geographically or temporally specific landscape, and it is an indication of Max Brod's failure to understand this aspect of his friend's break with nineteenth-century conventions of writing that he chose to publish the novel with the title that has since become famous. Everything in this text—and in a sense still to be defined, especially the novel's *Verkehr*—argues against this nominal localization. The actual title "Der Verschollene" defies any simple English translation: in German it indicates an un-named person who has gotten lost in obscure circumstances and whose existence hangs in doubt. This loss is often the result of an accident (ship passengers lost at sea are *verschollen*) and can refer to manu-scripts as well as persons (like the first version of Kafka's novel). Etymologically, the title suggests a progressive silencing (from the verb *verschallen*, "to die out").

Critics have overlooked the fact that Kafka probably derived this title from Arthur Holitscher's book *Amerika: Heute und morgen,* a series of travel reports that were first published in the *Neue Rund-schau* shortly before Kafka began work on the second version of his novel.[8] Holitscher's work also begins with the journey by ship to New York; shortly before docking, he receives a telegram that prompts him to make the following observation:

Up above on the sun deck, in this bizarre yellow city of smokestacks, wind-breakers with gaping jaws, ventilators, swaying lifeboats and humming ca-bles, sits the little brown house [the ship's telegraph office] that establishes the bond between us, the missing ones (*uns Verschollenen*) and the secure world.[9]

But whereas Holitscher confidently asserts the stability of this con-nection, Kafka undermines it, seizing on the notion of a sustained "Verschollen-Werden"—an effacing and silencing of the subject of representation—that becomes the actual subject of his novel, its starting point but also its destination. Holitscher's book names and describes America, tours the famous landmarks and buildings, repeatedly seeks to situate both writing subject and reader in the new world. Kafka's novel works instead to undermine Karl Rossmann's position in the world, to deterritorialize and disfigure America's identifying signs, to unname and silence the named. Thus, as in the text "The Wish to Be a Red Indian," the reader is confronted with an image of America that presents itself with uncommon force and vividness, only to erase itself in a series of ambiguous, contradictory, antimimetic gestures.

In *Der Verschollene*, Kafka accomplishes this erasure primarily through the thematic and structural device of *Verkehr*. The novel presents itself as a text in motion, as a traveling narrative. Each chapter offers a new form of "traffic" that propels the protagonist relentlessly into new circumstances: the steamship in the opening chapter gives way to the complex traffic patterns of New York City, to automobile and pedestrian movement along the highway, to the vertical *Verkehr* of the thirty elevators in the Hotel Occidental, to the sexual traffic in Brunelda's apartment, and finally to the subway and train that lead to the Oklahoma "Nature Theater" (described as a "wandering circus"). Kafka's narrative is literally *unterwegs*, "on the road," as a new mode of transport supplants the previous one in projecting the novel into an endless and in a certain sense timeless space of the "American" continent.

A few examples of how this traveling text works to destabilize and defamiliarize Karl Rossmann's perception of the world may prove useful. The novel begins of course with Karl's sudden expulsion from his own family for having fathered the illegitimate child of the family's maid; that is, the novel begins by *severing* its protagonist from the network of familial, social, and linguistic relations that in more traditional novels—novels one might call "narratives of property"—customarily serves to situate characters and events. Almost no reference is made throughout the novel to this past life, and the few tangible remains Karl has of it (notably his father's army suitcase and a photograph of his parents) are lost along the way. Thus severed from his past, Karl is free to experience a kind of rebirth in new, unfamiliar surroundings. But before he has time to adjust to these surroundings, to establish himself in a net of personal and professional ties, the initial gesture of expulsion that sets Karl's voyage and the text into motion is repeated: the stoker, the uncle, Mr. Pollunder and Klara, Robinson and Delamarche, the head cook and Theresa at the Hotel Occidental—all these characters in successive chapters momentarily allow Karl into their world only to expel him from it into another set of foreign circumstances. Throughout the text, Karl remains outside, *unterwegs*, in motion.

The law of this type of narrative thus initially seems to be that characters do not return or, if they do, that their reappearance will not add up to any final effect or resolution of plot. Banished from one circle of relations to the next, Karl encounters in random fashion the aptly named vagabonds Delamarche and Robinson who, like himself, have been truncated from their past and forced to wander the streets. Karl and the reader never learn about their past in a way that would make their present situation, actions, and character intelligible. The novel does not project them into the future, but into an endless present, a temporal mode unorganized by any stable origin, endgoal, destination, or plan. As a result, the reader is placed in the position of having to judge the characters in this text on the basis of extremely vivid but fragmented descriptions that never add up to a cumulative history or story. In this sense, the reader is in Karl's position vis-à-vis his uncle's unintroduced guests: "For Uncle Jacob hardly ever said even a passing word about any of his acquaintances and always left it to Karl to figure out by his own observation whatever was interesting or important about them."[10]

The curious flattening of character that results from this narrative technique is of course part of the peculiarity of Kafka's fictions as a whole and marks the distance between them and the psychological realism of nineteenth-century works. Kafka's characters emerge in vivid, sharp details—often "present" like photographic likenesses as they execute some characteristic gesture—but they exist only as partial, flat surfaces without the depth of a past history or nuanced individual psychology. This technique might be likened to portraits by Gustav Klimt in which a particular anatomical detail, usually the face, is isolated against a two-dimensional decorative surface. Kafka's characters are temporally flat—cut out of a historical continuum and presented to us as isolated, tantalizingly vivid, but finally opaque objects of interpretation.

The same destabilization of character in Kafka's novel also undermines his depiction of America as an identifiable, geographically defined location. Here the first disorienting image of Kafka's novel— the Statue of Liberty holding a sword rather than a torch—stands as a warning against those readers who would enter Kafka's "America" as if it were a garden of mimesis. For after referring to this disfigured but still recognizable monument, Kafka's text stubbornly refuses to name any famous street, building, tourist sight, etc., that would allow its readers to recognize and find themselves in the space Karl Rossmann traverses. The Hotel Occidental, Butterford and Rameses, Clayton and the Nature Theater of "Oklahama" (as Kafka spelled it in the manuscript)—the few places marked with a proper name are so improbable, contradictory, or imaginary that they seem to constitute a mythical rather than a referentially verisimilar landscape. Indeed, in this improbable landscape even Kafka's apparent mistakes seem to take on a bizarre, "postmodern" logic:[11] a bridge leads from Manhattan to Boston (rather than Brooklyn) and hangs over the Hudson (rather than the East) River; Karl pays for a meal with pounds rather than dollars; a hotel only five stories high has thirty elevators and thousands of employees; a modern country house outside New York is slowly revealed to contain a gothic labyrinth of unlit corridors, a marble chapel, and bedrooms guarded by liveried servants bearing candelabra.

Unmarked or deliberately obscure transitions between scenes and chapters heighten this fundamental sense of disorientation. Although Karl's journey begins in New York, we are never told where his uncle's apartment is situated. During the two months of his stay he lives in a confined, unidentifiable space that has nothing to do with "New York." Thus, when Karl looks at the city from a distance with Delamarche and Robinson during their "March to Rameses" in chapter four, his vision is oddly abstract, empty. His companions, we are told (in a passage unambiguously indicating the restricted nature of Karl's perception),

clearly saw much more; they pointed to right and to left and their outstretched hands gestured over squares and gardens *which they named by their names.* They could not understand how Karl could stay for two months in New York and yet see hardly anything of the city but one street. And they promised, when they had made enough money in Butterford, to take him to New York with them and show him all the sights worth seeing. (112, my emphasis)

Similarly, when Karl leaves New York for Mr. Pollunder's country house, he falls asleep during the ride and hence cannot tell how far or in what direction he has traveled. The dark, endless corridors of this house prevent him from finding his way in it, and when he finally escapes he chooses a "chance direction" (*eine beliebige Richtung*) and sets out on his way. His random encounter with Delamarche and Robinson results in their march to Butterford, which is unexpectedly interrupted when Karl finds refuge in the Hotel Occidental. Banished from the hotel, Karl is driven to what he infers to be a distant street outside the city that, against the recommendations of his friend the head cook, he has refused to visit.

The cumulative result of Karl's movement, which he experiences passively as a series of "accidents," is to drive him further and further from any known point of origin and reference. Again, Karl's predicament is largely akin to that of the reader as the narrative moves implacably ahead, abandoning unnamed places and inscrutable characters for new ones, apparently following a random, unpredictable course and without posting identifiable spatial and temporal signboards.[12] Karl never engages in introspection, rarely thinks back over the course of his adventures in order to give them some coherence or meaning, passively endures the accidents and adventures that befall him and propel him forward. Thus he never learns from his experiences, but reexperiences the same events in a timeless, deterritorialized present. Even the few exceptions to this rule confirm its general validity. For instance, when Karl suddenly reveals his identity as a German from Prague in the fifth chapter, the head cook introduces herself as Grete Mitzelbach from Vienna, claiming to have worked in the "Golden Goose" restaurant in Karl's hometown. But this brief moment of recognition, of a shared past and "territorialization" of the narrative, is immediately retracted: " 'The old Golden Goose,' Karl said, 'was torn down two years ago' " (134). The cook's name is never repeated, and the fact of their shared past has no further bearing on subsequent events.

The unfinished state of Kafka's manuscript makes any speculation problematic about the conclusion of Karl Rossmann's adventures and the absolute linearity of the narrative.[13] What should be noted, however, is that in the fragmentary ending Kafka wrote, Karl Rossmann takes a job as a technical worker, under the pseudonym of "Negro," in a traveling theater or "Wandercircus." With this artistic *Aufhebung* of his protagonist's identity—"Negro" seems less a pseudonym than the lack of a name—Kafka apparently has effaced the last identifying marks of property that defined Karl Rossmann with respect to the "secure world." Without a name, without material possessions (he spends his last dollar for train fare to Clayton), "Karl" is now truly *verschollen*.

One can of course read this effacement of the writing subject in political terms. In writing *Der Verschollene,* Kafka was clearly interested in portraying the situation of the poor, the unemployed, the homeless, as the basic feature of immigrant life in America. As studies by Jahn, Loose, and Binder have shown, Kafka drew on František Soukup's socialist lectures in Prague for the description of striking workers, political demonstrations, and general living conditions for foreigners who had been brutally displaced from their homeland.[14] But this sociopolitical rootlessness (the *Lumpenproletariat* exemplified by Delamarche and Robinson) merges with the problem of a metaphysical *Bodenlosigkeit,* with the groundlessness of Karl's existence in a world of changing appearances, unstable impressions, accident, and death: a world of "traffic." It is at this point that the novel's political content intersects with its aesthetic and epistemological structures.

III

What I have been trying to describe is the distance separating Kafka's text from traditional novels of the nineteenth century—whether written by Jane Austen, Balzac, Fontane, or the young Thomas Mann—that are organized according to the notion of property. By property narrative I mean any text that works to establish the identity of its main protagonist as well as the stability of those narrative structures through which that identity is apprehended by encircling the protagonist in a network of property relations. Property is not just land or economic wealth but all the advantages and attributes that generally accompany either: a proper name, first of all; a house, perhaps an aristocratic residence bearing the same name or some bourgeois imitation of it; a wife and children also marked with this name; a line of ancestors and descendants that makes the protagonist's identity accessible as a form of historical, psychological, or epistemological property. Situated in a precise historical and geographical space, the property narrative is obsessed with determining the origins of its protagonists, the motives for their behavior, the consequences of their decisions. The persons and places it represents are offered to the reader as stable, ultimately knowable objects of perception; are offered to us as a form of narrative property that we can acquire and make our own.

The modernist traveling narrative denies this form of consumptive reading because it is always in motion, is always one step ahead of its reader, never turns around to question its own origins or motives and allow the reader to catch up with it. The pleasure it offers is random, vicarious, shifting. A traveling text works to destabilize the identity of the protagonist as well as the genealogical structures through which this identity is normally presented. The protagonist has no property, is always on the road, never knows what is about to happen, and never asks why he is there at all. The proper name is tenuous, thin, disguised, or unimportant, for its bearer is continually forsaking the place where it is recognized. Desire is not fixed to a specific object, intent on possessing this subject or amassing with it various forms of property, but is itself on the road, merging with the crowd, getting lost in traffic, moving on.[15]

Linked to the development of the big city, late capitalism, and increasingly fluid, shifting forms of property, the traveling narrative has become a privileged mode of narration in twentieth-century literature. In German, the conflict between property and traveling narratives can be illustrated in the difference between Thomas Mann's *Buddenbrooks* and Robert Musil's *Man without Qualities*. Mann's novel turns obsessively around the family name, house, property, and ancestral line, even though it ultimately is concerned with the breakdown and *Verfall* of this tradition. Musil's novel begins with the description of random atmospheric conditions and a traffic accident in a modern city, two mathematical "figures" that serve to introduce a protagonist defined negatively—as the absence of "qualities" (or "properties"), as a life suspended in the "subjunctive" mode. The montage novels of Alfred Döblin and John Dos Passos, Michel Butor's *La Modification,* or Peter Handke's *The Wrong Move (Falsche Bewegung)* provide further examples of a widespread modernist tendency to use the theme of "traffic" to create a destabilized, shifting mode of narration opposed to the nineteenth-century novel's insistence on narrative "property." This tendency in modern literature inevitably merges (and in some cases collaborates) with similar efforts in cinema. Perhaps the most radical use of traveling narratives has been made by filmmakers such as Jean-Luc Godard, Werner Herzog, and Wim Wenders, whose films repeatedly thematize mechanized forms of travel as a self-reflexive gesture toward the moving, unstable nature of cinematic representation. The Godard quotation with which this essay began its itinerary—"Le moral, c'est le travelling"—provides the most succinct definition of this kind of wandering text. Subject, camera, and projected image are all implicated in the traffic of traveling images.

IV

At this point, and by way of conclusion, I would like to return to Kafka's text and discuss two specific instances of his presentation of New York traffic. This will have two functions: first, it will provide an illustration of the destabilizing, antimimetic effects of *Verkehr* that I have attempted to describe generally; and second, it will introduce an additional element to Kafka's use of a "traveling" narrative, one that I feel marks it as a peculiarly modern text.

The first chapter of *Der Verschollene* takes place on board the ship that has brought Karl Rossmann to America. Our first view of New York occurs midway through the chapter when the novel's young protagonist looks through the windows of the captain's office at the harbor traffic.

Meanwhile outside the windows the life of the harbour went on; a flat barge laden with a mountain of barrels, which must have been wonderfully well packed, since they did not roll off, went past, almost completely obscuring the daylight; little motor-boats, which Karl would have liked to examine thoroughly if he had had time, shot straight past in obedience to the slightest touch (*Zuckungen,* jerky movements, twitches) of the man standing erect at the wheel. Here and there curious objects (*eigentümliche Schwimmkörper*) bobbed independently out of the restless water, were immediately submerged again and sank before his astonished eyes; boats belonging to the ocean liners were rowed past by sweating sailors; they were filled with passengers sitting silent and expectant as if they had been stowed there, except that some of them could not refrain from turning their heads to gaze at the changing scene. A movement without end, a restlessnes transmitted from the restless element to helpless human beings and their works! (17)

In this passage, which seems to be the reworking of a dream Kafka noted in his diary shortly before beginning the novel,[16] everything is movement, flux, appearance and effacement. Various moving vehicles and floating objects come into Karl's view and then disappear.

The reasons for their movement, their origins and destination, remain hidden. Karl perceives only a fragment of their trajectory, which has been cropped randomly by the position he happens to occupy at that moment. These objects hence appear opaque to him: the logic behind the arrangement of the mountain of barrels, the identity of the strange *Schwimmkörper* bobbing in and out of sight, the thoughts of the expectant passengers—everything in this scene is silent, unexplained, distant, and obscurely indifferent to his presence. The traffic unfolds without Karl's participation, he experiences it passively. And yet Karl is also on water, is himself a part of the "movement without end" that transmits its own restlessness (*Unruhe*) to "helpless human beings and their works."

At the same time, the unstable, inscrutable motion of this harbor traffic provides a highly vivid, illuminated scene. Framed by the windows of the captain's office, the traffic offers itself as an image momentarily isolated from Karl's immediate surroundings. But this image is not frozen: it passes by, is succeeded by another, which in turn also disappears and is replaced. What Karl sees, in other words, is a succession of moving images that is strikingly cinematic. The autonomous, disembodied movement of these images, their indifference to any spectators, even the passing shadow cast by the barge that momentarily darkens the office and makes it like a movie theater—all these elements contribute to Karl's cinematic perception of the harbor.

The same cinematographic quality—cinematographic in the sense of a tension between intensely vivid, framed images and their self-canceling movement—marks the description of the New York street traffic that Karl perceives from the sixth-floor balcony of his uncle's apartment:

A narrow balcony ran along the entire front wall of Karl's bedroom. But what would probably have been the highest vantage point in Karl's home town here offered little more than the view of one street which ran perfectly straight between two rows of squarely chopped buildings and therefore seemed to be fleeing into a great distance where the massive outlines of a cathedral loomed up in a dense haze. And mornings and evenings and in the dreams of the night a never ending traffic (*Verkehr*) pulsed along this street which, seen from above, looked like an inextricable confusion, forever newly improvised, of distorted human figures and the tops of moving vehicles of all types, and from which arose a new, variegated, wilder confusion of noises, dust and smells, all of which was seized and penetrated by an intense light that was dispersed, carried off and then reflected back again by the multiplicity of objects, a light that appeared so palpable to the mesmerized eye that it seemed as if every instant a huge plate of glass covering the entire street were being shattered with tremendous force again and again. (38–39)

This image of "New York"—the only detailed image the reader ever perceives—again presents the spectacle of an infinite, ceaseless, mechanical traffic. The syntactical structure of this last, monstrously long sentence is, I think, intentionally complex. The proliferation of dependent clauses, the doubling of the word "confusion," the shifting focus of attention as one subject replaces the next, all lead to a linguistic confusion that reinforces the impression of an infinitely complex, vital, unchartable traffic pattern that is perhaps meant to convey the bewilderment of Kafka's young, naïve protagonist in observing New York for the first time. Seen from such a height, the pedestrians seem disembodied, distorted. The moving vehicles exist only synecdochically, as flat rectangles without human agents to control their motion. Haze, noises, dust, smells assault Karl's senses; even the New York light[17]—the same element that illuminates the image Karl is observing—is so intense that it actually disrupts a focused, accurate perception of the street. But most of all the movement of this spectacle—the constantly shifting, discontinuous, self-improvising quality of images that flee into a hazy distance outside Karl's field of vision—undermines and deterritorializes this vision of "America." Karl's eyes are *betört*, confused, deluded.

We should also note the unusual spatial organization of this scene. Kafka does not situate his protagonist high enough above New York to perceive what is after all one of the most formally ordered cities in the world. In this respect Kafka does not follow Holitscher who, in his American tourist book, climbs from the confusion of a busy street to the top of a skyscraper where he surveys an ordered, Cartesian grid of named streets, buildings, parks, and monuments. To Holitscher, the city presents itself as a map in which he can retrace his steps, read and relive the brief history of his visit, in short, situate himself spatially and temporally in a foreign world (57–61). Karl Rossmann is given only the perception of a single, unnamed street whose relation to the rest of New York is never disclosed.[18] What would have provided the "highest vantage point" at home, a panorama of a totality to be observed, studied, measured, represented, here offers a fragmented image without relation to a surrounding whole. As a result, the city remains foreign, unintelligible to him.

And yet, despite the elusive, fragmented nature of its contents, the image of this traffic is marked by its visuality. The image is again framed: at the front edge by Karl's balcony, to the left and right by the buildings that have been "squarely chopped" off, at the top edge, less emphatically, by the outlines of the cathedral. The traffic flows in a "perfectly straight" line away from Karl not unlike a ribbon of celluloid images passing before the eye of the projector. The context for vision and representation is also affirmed by the curious metaphorical appearance of a giant plate of glass. But the intensity of the light, the violent energies of *Verkehr* cannot be contained in a stable representation: as in a painting by Magritte, the glass of representation shatters, leaving Karl and the reader figuratively blinded.

Whether or not Kafka was aware of the cinematographic quality of these passages is unimportant. Edgar Allan Poe, in describing the flow of a London crowd perceived from a café window in his short story "The Man of the Crowd," presented an equally cinematographic image some forty years before the invention of film. What is striking, however, is the similarity between these images of American traffic and Kafka's own comments on cinema in his diaries and letters. The common element is *Unruhe*, the restless, rapid movement of images that "blind" the spectator by preventing any stable, controlled act of perception. In reference to his visit to the "Emperor's Panorama" in Friedland in 1911, the year before he began his American novel, Kafka noted in his diary: "The images [of the panorama] are more lifelike than in the cinema because they offer the eye all the stability (*Ruhe*) of reality. The cinema imposes on perceived objects the instability of its own motion."[19]

Kafka's ambivalence toward the cinema—on the one hand, his undeniable fascination with its photographic realism, on the other hand his discomfort with the speed of these images' succession on the screen—may well explain why he chose "the most modern New York"[20] as the site for Karl Rossmann's exile. For if New York is defined by its "traffic," by the relentless movement of its framed images, then the city offers itself as an eminently cinematic space. The fitting metaphor for Paris and Prague (in *Description of a Struggle*) is theater; New York, with its highly developed technology, requires the cinema. Kafka imagines New York through the grid of film, as if the only adequate mode of transmitting its unstable, complex *Verkehr* were through an artistic medium itself in motion, traveling. But to thrust Karl Rossmann into such a cinematic world is to condemn him to the nightmarish observation of a life that won't stand still and is profoundly indifferent to his presence—as indifferent as film and projector are to the spectators in a moviehouse. Karl comes to America thinking he will observe, learn, understand, *see* it. Instead, the images move too quickly, peripheral phenomena distract him, and when he looks again the images have left the screen. Karl sees everything in America as if for the first time, which is to say that he sees nothing at all.

Other critics, notably Wolfgang Jahn in the first book-length study of *Der Verschollene,* have noted the cinematographic quality of Kafka's first novel.[21] The montage-like narrative, the openness and freedom of movement distinguish it from the enclosing topographies of *The Trial* and *The Castle.* In the above remarks I have tried to show that the cinematic aspect of *Der Verschollene* extends beyond the montage arrangement of specific scenes to the general problematic of *Verkehr,* indeed, that these scenes are themselves inscribed in the logic of a "traveling narrative." This logic permeates the novel's structure, making each individual scene, image, and detail part of a phenomenological description of the act of seeing,[22] or rather, of the ultimately impossible act of viewing a world in self-canceling, "forever newly improvised," motion. Image, frame, light, movement— these are the constitutive ingredients for Kafka's presentation of "America," as we can now see in rereading the novel's opening sentence:

As Karl Rossmann . . . stood on the liner slowly entering the harbor of New York, a sudden burst of sunshine seemed to illumine the Statue of Liberty, so that he saw it in a new light, although he had sighted it long before. The arm with the sword rose up as if newly stretched aloft. (3)

Karl, the ship, the light, even the statue are moving in this (moving) image. Kafka did not have to travel to New York to write this passage. As he is said to have remarked to Gustav Janouch: "I didn't draw any people [in "The Stoker"], I told a story. Those are pictures, only pictures. . . . One takes a photograph of things in order to forget them. My stories are a way of closing my eyes."²³

Notes

1. *Verkehr* is a central term in Kafka's own vocabulary and has been heavily interpreted. Much of this interpretation focuses on "The Judgment" and Kafka's remark, related by Max Brod, that in writing the last sentence of this story ("At this moment an unending stream of traffic was going over the bridge") he was thinking of a "giant orgasm." Although the sexual connotations of *Verkehr* are implicit in the following remarks, I have attempted to shift the discussion toward a literal reading of this term as well as point out the relationship between writing and mechanized traffic patterns (rather than sexuality). Finally, although the notion of "traffic" is central to all three works written in the fall of 1912 ("The Judgment," "The Metamorphosis," and *Amerika*), it also informs all of Kafka's earlier texts. Malcolm Pasley's intriguing contention that Kafka's 1912 "breakthrough" was preceded by three years of an intense interest in *Reisebeschreibungen* and travel literature can be seen as part of the more general and earlier problematic of *Verkehr* ("Kafka als Reisender," in *Was Bleibt von Franz Kafka?* [Vienna: Braumöller, 1983], 1–15).

2. *Der Prager Kreis* (Stuttgart: Kohlhammer, 1966), 94–95, my translation.

3. Published by Cornelius Gurlitt as part of a bibliophile series entitled "Die Kultur," Bard Marquardt and Co., Berlin.

4. Wagenbach mentions Kafka's acquisition of Bie's work in connection with his frequenting of Prague's upper classes (*Franz Kafka: Eine Biographie seiner Jugend* [Bern: Francke, 1958], 134). Ernst Pawel reproduces and amplifies Wagenbach's mistake, describing Bie's essay as "the standard work on proper manners . . . the Emily Post of his day" (*The Nightmare of Reason* [New York: Farrar, Straus and Giroux, 1984], 135).

5. *The Complete Stories* (New York: Schocken, 1976), 43. Translation slightly altered (as in subsequent passages). In general, once an edition has been cited, all further quotes will be noted within parentheses.

6. "Und die Menschen gehn in Kleidern/ schwankend auf dem Kies spazieren/ unter diesem grossen Himmel/ der von Hügeln in der Ferne/ sich zu fernen Hügeln breitet." Marked by the Hofmannsthalian cadence typical of Kafka's early period of self-conscious aestheticism, this verse epigraph introduces the problem of stylized but unstable movement in an urban context. The lines also suggest a relation between this instability and the empty sky or heaven ("Himmel"), that is, the precariousness of human existence in a world ungrounded by a divine order. What should be noted, however, is Kafka's technique of taking this "existential" question literally by de-

picting the protagonists in his text as off-balance, dizzy, or falling—the victims of "accident."

7. The passage begins "For we are like tree trunks in the snow" (45) and was later published as an independent fragment in 1912 in the collection *Meditations*.

8. Kafka's first draft of the novel was destroyed or lost; most of the second version was written in late September, October, and early November of 1912. Holitscher's America travelogue first appeared in installments in the *Neue Rundschau* in 1911 and 1912, in book form by the S. Fischer Verlag, Berlin, in 1912. Kafka later acquired the second edition of this book (1913), which is the edition used here.

9. The German text reads: "Oben auf Sonnendeck . . . steht das kleine braune Haus, das die Verbindung herstellt zwischen uns Verschollenen und der sicheren Welt" (26).

10. *Amerika* (New York: Schocken, 1962), 49.

11. Postmodern in the sense of Robert Venturi's *Complexity and Contradiction in Architecture* (New York: Museum of Modern Art, 1966), in which he argues for the deliberate juxtaposition of conflicting styles.

12. This movement appears to have something in common with the "random" or at least unprogrammed mode in which Kafka wrote his longer narrative. As Malcolm Pasley has suggested in an important article, "Kafkas Erzählungen, einschliesslich der Romane, wären im Grunde *planlos,* ohne jegliche Vorentscheidung über den Handlungsverlauf oder gar über die Figurenausstattung einfach *ambulando* entstanden." See his "Der Schreibakt und das Geschriebene: Zur Frage der Entstehung von Kafkas Texten," in *Franz Kafka: Themen und Probleme,* ed. Claude David (Göttingen: Vandenhoeck and Ruprecht, 1980), 14.

13. In an afterword to the novel, Max Brod suggests that Kafka intended to conclude the work on a note of reconciliation, allowing Karl "to find again a profession, a stand-by, his freedom, even his old home and his parents, as if by some celestial witchery" (299). Even if this is true, one can see how the logic of Kafka's linear, traveling text would conflict with such a magical (not to say conventional) conclusion, a conflict that may well have contributed to Kafka's inability to close his text.

14. Kafka apparently drew heavily from Soukup's *Amerika: Rada obrazu americkeho zivota* (America: A Series of Pictures of American Life), which is unfortunately unavailable in English or German translation. From the few passages Binder quotes in his *Kommentar zu den Romanen* (Munich: Winkler, 1976), however, we can see that Soukup's class portrait of American life also stresses the element of "traffic"; consider, for instance, the following description of New York light: "One, two, a hundred, a thousand—suddenly all the streets start burning and New York is swimming in a sea of light waves . . . from the roofs to the sidewalks everything is a single giant orgy of electric light rays. And everything is in constant motion and flux" (as quoted in Binder, 100). Kafka attended Soukup's lecture and slide pre-

sentation of "America and Its Civil Servants" on June 1, 1912, in Prague. See also G. Loose's *Franz Kafka und Amerika* (Frankfurt an Main: Klostermann, 1968).

15. See Leo Bersani's notion of "wandering desire" in his study *Baudelaire and Freud* (Berkeley and Los Angeles: University of California Press, 1977).

16. See the entry for Sept. 11, 1912; there Kafka labels the New York harbor traffic an "ungeheuer fremdländischer Verkehr," claiming it to be more interesting than the traffic on a busy Paris boulevard.

17. See Soukup's description of the New York light in note 14.

18. In establishing Kafka's use of Holitscher's book, Hartmut Binder makes the naïve claim that the street Karl sees is Broadway (*Kommentar*, 99). Not only does Kafka's description not match the picture of Broadway on page 49 in Holitscher's book (the cathedral is missing, the street is open on one side, etc.), but it deliberately denies a perception of the street as a named, situated locale. Binder's general project of anchoring Kafka's text in a biographical, referential context frequently goes against the grain of the text's will toward "namelessness," and in this respect he repeats Brod's emblematic error of naming the novel *Amerika*.

19. *The Diaries 1910–1924* (New York: Schocken, 1948, repr. 1967), 241.

20. The phrase is Kafka's from his letter to Kurt Wolff of May 25, 1913.

21. *Kafkas Roman "Der Verschollene" (Amerika)* (Stuttgart: Germanistische Abhandlungen, 1965); see also his "Kafka und die Anfänge des Kinos," *Jahrbuch der Deutschen Schillergesellschaft* 6 (1962): 353–68. Hanns Zischler documents Kafka's early interest in film as well as his gradual ambivalence for the medium in "Masslose Unterhaltung: Franz Kafka geht ins Kino," *Freibeuter* 16 (1983): 33–47.

22. I am indebted to Herbert Blau for stressing the "act of seeing" in Kafka's novel. Cf. also Anne Hollander's excellent discussion of the cinematic quality of Flemish painting in "Moving Pictures," *Raritan* 3 (Winter 1986): 82–102.

23. The full passage in German is: "Ich zeichnete keine Menschen [im "Heizer"]. Ich erzählte eine Geschichte. Das sind Bilder, nur Bilder. . . . Man photographiert Dinge, um sie aus dem Sinn zu verscheuchen. Meine Geschichten sind eine Art von Augenschliessen" (*Gespräche mit Kafka* [Frankfurt am Main: Fischer Tachenbuch, 1961], 45; my translation).

The City as Narrator:
The Modern Text in Alfred Döblin's
Berlin Alexanderplatz

Klaus R. Scherpe

In question here is the narratability of the city. Even as Alfred Döblin sends his hero Franz Biberkopf into the city, to test him, as it were, and supplies him with a dramatic narrative text meant to demonstrate his identity—"I have something to do, something will happen, I won't stir from here, I am Franz Biberkopf"[1]—he deprives Biberkopf of his "own" narrative terrain. Franz Biberkopf wanders through the city like all the others: as an average passerby, by no means a flaneur to whom things bend meaningfully as he turns an astute glance their way.

The faces of the eastward wanderers are in no way different from those of the wanderers to the west, south, and north; moreover they exchange their roles, those who are now crossing the square towards Aschinger's may be seen an hour later in front of the empty Hahn Department Store. Just as those who come from Brunnenstrasse on their way to Jannowitz Brücke mingle with those coming from the reverse direction. Yes, and many of them turn off to the side, from south to east, from south to west, from north to west, from north to east. They have the same equanimity as passengers in an omnibus or in street-cars. The latter all sit in different postures, making the weight of the car, as indicated outside, heavier still. Who could find out what is happening inside them, a tremendous chapter. And if anyone did write it, to whose advantage would it be? New books? Even the old ones don't sell, and in the year '27 book-sales as compared with '26 have declined so and so much per cent (221).

In Döblin's novel the dominant force is this emptiness of profusion, this disqualification of factual events, this accumulation and inflation of events to the point of uneventfulness. Precise topographical elements in the narrative are introduced in such a compacted, rushed fashion that they start spinning dizzily. As the traffic-hub and nucleus of all human relationships and transactions, the city radiates beyond its limits and is dispersed in all directions: "The wind scatters chaff over all of them alike" (220–21).

It is well known that Döblin willingly confessed to being a *Zivilisationsliterat*. He resolutely opposed the *völkisch* motto "Away from Berlin" (*Los von Berlin*), adopting as his motto "Away from the book" because "the book is the death of real language."[2] With these words Döblin dismisses a mode of literary representation that had presumed to use psychological and sociological analyses in order to capture the world on paper with more precise knowledge and greater narrative reliability. In his "Berliner Programm" (1913), an essay inspired by futurism, and his later *Bau des epischen Werkes* (1929), which bears the stamp of an elementalism indebted to natural philosophy, Döblin breaks with nineteenth-century narrative positivism and historicism. His polemic demolishes the traditional narrative edifice in order to create a site for the construction of the modern epic.

For now, let me call attention only to the sum and substance of this dismantling of traditional fiction, insofar as it leads to a new narratability, a narratability of the reality of the modern metropolis in all its complexity. In place of a "house of fiction" (Henry James) that is constructed from a blueprint of causal elements, personal correspondences, and integrated plot lines, Döblin envisions a construction site. Rather than explain "how" and "why," he simply registers movements and durations. Instead of a merely—for Döblin—"pseudorational," constructed plot, he describes the "transformations of actions and effects."[3] In opposition to the deceptive authenticity of unmediated expression Döblin proposes a "fanaticism of self-suppression" (*Entäußerung*): "The author's hegemony must be broken."[4] Among his favorite images are the "language body" and the stage of speaking and writing, into which every preconceived notion of narrative is "destructively integrated."[5] Under the signature of "depersonalization" narration becomes reflexive: "one thinks one is speaking and one is spoken, or one thinks that one is writing, and one is written."[6] It follows then that Döblin's motto "Away from the book" accompanies the equally necessary and painful exhortation "Away from humanism"[7]—albeit not in the sense of the joyful deconstruction of human obligations fashionably advocated today, but in order to uncover a deeper reality beneath a "soulless reality" (*entseelte Realität*).

Although this summary of Döblin's theory of the modern novel may have suggested otherwise, my intention is not to examine his epic craft from a postmodernist perspective, such as the one suggested by Thomas Pynchon's novels. Rather, I would like to provide a historical account of the status and structure of the narrative praxis of the 1920s, which did in fact break with an aesthetics of representation that thought it could reproduce the "giant system of mediations" (Hegel's *ungeheuren Vermittlungszusammenhang*) of bourgeois society in aesthetic artifacts, that is, through literary symbolism and an oppositional aesthetics of subjective expression.[8] And this is the point where the traditional notion of a "narrated city" becomes questionable, a notion I believe Döblin undermines in the experimental writing of his metropolis-text. The story of the metropolis itself—the text of the city *as* an all-encompassing, functional sign system of languages and discourses—appropriates the territory previously occupied by the book *about* the city, the image of the city and its residents. Ernst Bloch had already reached this same critical conception—critical of capitalism, that is—in the formula: "Berlin, Functions in the Void."[9]

Döblin's notion of Berlin as narrator-city is by no means the mere opposite of the narrated city, but rather a challenge to this older notion that is present in *Berlin Alexanderplatz*, notably in the narrative intention behind Franz Biberkopf's struggle with the city as "Whore of Babylon." In order to demonstrate that Döblin's city-text is a modern text we must recognize the problem of the *narratability of the city* historically. In the important book *Die erzählte Stadt* (The Narrated City),[10] Volker Klotz establishes a relation between urban content and the form of the novel more or less as the ultimate "prose of social relations and conditions." Here the city, as a concentrated center for the social, political, and cultural conflicts of a developing bourgeois society, is a historical given. The novel of the metropolis as *represented* reality traditionally focuses on the sights and symbols within the walls, the limits of the city (Victor Hugo's *Notre-Dame de Paris*); it thematizes the opposition between subjective desires and objective forces in the urban environment (Wilhelm Raabe's *Die Chronik der Sperlingsgasse*); it dramatizes the fate of individuals, classes, and institutions as criminal case-studies and as socioromantic or sociocritical history; it contemplates and illuminates excerpts from the great and fascinating panorama of a more or less "good society" (from Sue and Dickens to Zola, Heinrich Mann, and even Marcel Proust). The question is whether, as in Volker Klotz's study, the novels of Döblin and Dos Passos can still be explained by this representational model of the "narrated city," which relies on symbolization, subject-centeredness, and the dramatization of opposites. In his attempt to make Döblin's *Alexanderplatz* fit the concept of an "agonistic city" or Dos Passos's *Manhattan Transfer* that of "urban tides," Klotz employs the same narrative metaphors with which the ever-increasing diversity and complexity of the modern city was to be contained within the precisely defined and centered field of the "narrated city." What remains to be demonstrated is that in his novel Döblin substitutes a structural and discursive method of narrating the city for the older mythic narrative representations.

Historically, several modes of representing the city can be distinguished. The first mode would derive from that traumatic opposition in German eighteenth- and nineteenth-century novels between a "rural utopia" and an "urban nightmare."[11] In this example an earlier, allegedly peaceful subjective identity is threatened by advancing industrial civilization. Even Georg Simmel, in his remarkable essay "Die Großstädte und das Geistesleben" (1903, The Metropolis and Mental Life), passionately deplores the erosion of individual interiority and strength of feeling (*Innerlichkeit und Gemütskraft*) under the "merciless objectivity" of the marketplace and technology in the modern metropolis.[12]

In the socially critical, naturalistic novel of the nineteenth century the country-city opposition gives way to class conflict. This mode of representing the city achieves narrative coherence through its incorporation of major tenets of the dialectical philosophy of history or of natural scientific theory (Hegel, Marx, Comte, Taine). Here the negative consequences of industrialization and urbanization are represented. Especially in German naturalism, a restlessly subjective urban experience predominates as young writers from the provinces move to the metropolises of Munich and Berlin.[13] Urban life and experience are reduced here to an opposition between the individual and the masses, and dramatized as existential adventure and inferno. As in the later city lyrics of expressionism, the representation of the city withdraws into subjective expression, the symbolization of terror, and fascination with the city.

This mode of representing urban life and experience, which was initially socially progressive and later became merely expressive and aestheticized, is far removed from the contemplative gesture of the Parisian flaneur. Its reconstruction as the symptomatic constellation of modernity, undertaken by Benjamin in his study of Baudelaire,[14] is based on the imaginative potential of urban experience. Aesthetic opposition to the metropolis, understood as the operational center and nucleus of economic and political energy, takes shape on the periphery, in the ephemeral zone of isolated individual perceptions. The "reckless activity" of the modern metropolis—in the words of Max Weber—is countered by an aesthetic subject that apprehends objects spontaneously, fixing and securing them in its gaze. Apprehended in this way, the city is no longer the object of a narrative reconstruction and representation; rather, the city is represented selectively and partially through the intensity of perception of the aesthetic subject.[15] For the surrealist flaneurs Breton and Aragon, capitalist reification, contingency, and isolation, which are crystallized in urban existence, represented that precise condition for liberating the imagination, for releasing libidinal energy and an imagistic delirium. Benjamin's nostalgic retrospection on nineteenth-century Paris and his skeptical view of the aesthetic and political ecstasies of the French surrealists[16] may well indicate the limitations of deriving this specific aesthetic modernity from metropolitan existence.

Even as Benjamin was insisting on the return of the flaneur in Franz Hessel's *Spazieren in Berlin*[17] (Walk Through Berlin), an entirely different aesthetic strategy, involving neither the activist nor the contemplative subject-object opposition, had taken over the traditional means of representing the metropolis. In the 1920s, in an atmosphere of urban overload and loss of subject identity through a surplus of communication, commodity exchange, and productivity so particularized as to defy comprehension, a type of aesthetic representation of the city is introduced that takes pure functionality, the pure abstraction of metropolitan complexity, as its non-objective object. The attraction of the metropolis is experienced summarily, so to speak. The oppositions between country/nature and the city, between the individual and the masses, are leveled, even annihilated. The "city" is newly constructed as a "second nature" in terms of the dynamic flow of its commodities and human movements, which appear to take place according to self-sufficient and complementary patterns in space and time. Hints and suggestions for this modern means of representing the city can be found in the work of Ernst Jünger (e.g., in his aestheticizing arrangement of a worker demonstration in Berlin) and—in a different and critical form—in Siegfried Kracauer's "geometrically" designed analyses of the "ornament of the masses." This type of functional and structural narration, which breaks with traditional modes of representation, is most visible in the films of the period. The opening segments of Walter Ruttmann's *Berlin, Die Sinfonie der Großstadt* (1927),[18] in their dynamics of linear progression and in their rigidly systematic montage technique, resemble an agitated painting by Kandinsky from his "architectonic" phase. As a whole, the film integrates the different social, political, and cultural objects and discourses in the daily rhythm of metropolitan Berlin to form a truly non-objective image of the city. What is fascinating is less the city itself than its perfectly organized aesthetic *mise-en-scène*.

My thesis is that in Döblin's *Berlin Alexanderplatz* an aesthetics of modernism manifests itself precisely in the narrative impossibility of representing and narrating the city. The once virulent city-country opposition has entirely vanished from the narrative; Döblin's novel no longer uses the antagonistic technique of projecting an ideal image against an urban nightmare. Franz Biberkopf's "other place" is not nature but prison and the insane asylum. These, then, are the sites for this ever-present personal regression within the city, the sites of an *imaginary* "life of his own." Socially critical tendencies in a naturalist sense (stemming either from a historical, philosophical utopia or the evolutionary belief of positivist science) are reduced in the *Alexanderplatz* novel to rhetorical commonplaces or to parodic quotation. Franz Biberkopf plays his (language) game with the fanatical anarchist and syndicalist; excerpts from social law and from the book of sexual enlightenment are recited in the novel in a way that undercuts any feeling of pity.

Döblin's text also resists the aesthetics of perception as *epiphany*, that moment of aesthetic rupture and shock that is so rich in significance for life in the metropolis and by which the aesthetics of modernity as such is sometimes defined.[19] Döblin's city-text is produced by a constant being-under-way, a *rendez-vous-en-masse* as it were of primarily fortuitous and exchangeable meeting points: occasions for innumerable stories, out of which the *one* story of Franz Biberkopf is supposed to take shape. But this flaneur and occasional worker does not undergo the repeated and therefore renarrated *éducation sentimentale* of the petty thief,[20] as Benjamin suspects, nor is he a suitable medium for the aesthetic perception of, once again, the specific individual. Without question, Döblin's text has its greatest affinity with the kind of representation that apprehends the experiential space of the city as a "functional void," although without the effects of an aesthetically brilliant or even intoxicating formalism.

The assertion that the representationality of the city—the "narrated city"—is replaced in Döblin's novel by a structural and discursive method of city narration (city as narrator) must be demonstrated textually by a few examples and references. One question must concern the energy with which the various discourses are held together, for the text is more significant than a "gripping story" of individual characters that takes place in the city.[21] One can also question the opposition between the narrative text and the montage-text, which literary criticism continues to read as confirming the old subject-object dualism between threatened individual and threatening metropolis. Döblin's text must be credited with doing more than perpetuating the mythification and demonization of the menacingly complex, anonymous city. The imaginative potential released by the text is decidedly something different from that which the author gives to his hero as utopian fare to march off with in order to bring his metropolis-text to a happy end.

If we first consider the "pure" city passages produced by Döblin's montage technique—for example, "Rosenthaler Square is talking" (53); "A Handful of Men around Alex Square" (154); the tenement cross-section with its collection of professions, human fates, and small tragedies—we inevitably have the same impression of a dedramatization of actions and a radical elimination of qualifying motivations or causes. Döblin says, "Forward is never the motto of the novel. . . . In the novel, it's stack, collect, roll out, shift."[22] If Döblin describes here the idea of montage technique (he never used the term itself), it is clear that he does not dismantle narrative forms in order to reconstruct an organized or dialectical synthesis of meaning. Instead, he generates those effects that produce the impression of a virtually unlimited homogeneous field of meanings. A "panic of simultaneity"[23] is generated in which the drama of urban events implodes, suppressing itself rather than struggling for expression. The thousands of possible stories in the city—whether a love affair, a business on the rise, or perhaps the AEG conglomerate's increasing economic power—are stripped of their "own" narrative significance. For example, in one of the street scenes with the passersby ("the busstop Lothringer Street . . . a boy with earmuffs . . . Mrs. Plück and Mrs. Krause"), the story of a boy's later life and suffering is told in the future tense, and is thereby dissolved within the present tense of the narrated scene. In other words, the private story is deprived of its temporal dimension and consequently dedramatized. Simultaneously the public affairs of the city—its politics and economics—become increasingly abstract and spatialized in their representation. The currents of information that flow through the city, the text of shop signs, advertisements, and newspaper headlines, can be situated and understood here and there, but by virtue of their sheer number they are interchangeable and correspondingly without distinct boundaries and contours. The AEG is called a "monstrous enterprise" (54). Döblin would never have committed the error that Brecht pointed out of attempting to photograph the tremendous concentration of capital in the AEG conglomerate in a naturalistic fashion. He hits instead upon the technique of listing topographically a huge number of factories and subsidiaries, with their addresses (54).

That which Döblin presents as the text of the city in its network of traffic, commerce, information, and variegated flow of commodities is always a highly mediated, reproduced public sphere. The informed city dominates the "narrated city." When Rosenthaler Square "talks," the actions and conversations of the crowd are in fact the language of public information that has been inscribed onto individual destinies: political propaganda ("German comrades, never has a people been more shamefully deceived"), social policy ("Rent control is a scrap of paper"), justice ("I humbly request the privilege of taking the floor"), sexuality ("One may think more tolerantly of the mores regarding sexual intercourse among unmarried men"), religion ("We note especially the new version of 'St. Paul'"), business ("I

advise you against cattle. Cattle are down. Go with small live-stock"),
of culture (*"coeur-Bube* is a charming comedy. Whom does it charm,
what does it charm, with what does it charm, how do they contrive
to charm me"), and education ("Now, O Immortality, thou art entirely mine," Kleist or Goethe as dramatic quotation). About the people on Alexander Square it is said: "Each specimen sends a connoisseur's glance in both directions, and knows the traffic rules by heart"
(220). The text of the city, the city narration, can be exemplarily sum-
marized as a multifaceted grammar of discourses in which every individual discourse loses the core of its meaning, its *intentional* meaning. In the narrative text of the city individual discourses are, so to
speak, "hollowed out." What remains in the verbal activity of the
city are isolated functional effects of meaning, incidental signs of an
already prestructured world of images and signifiers. This structural
given is an inalterable element of Döblin's narrative craft, a kind of
petrified autonomy of the city that, in principle, structures and also
"mortifies" all experiences and events as well as their narration. The
transformation of an organic realm into an inorganic one is de-
monstrably the figurative principle organizing Döblin's novel, and in
this sense it verifies his own notion of the "petrified style."[24]

If, then, the structurally homogenized text of the city in Döblin's
metropolis novel cannot be "seen through" to the author's intentions, so that author and reader must "enter" the text together, the
question arises as to what extent all narrative texts have to be determined by this kind of "modern text" of the city. An aporia is at
work here that must likewise be regarded as a given—the "crisis of
the novel," which Benjamin describes in his "Storyteller" essay and
in his review of Döblin as the dilemma of narration in the age of new
"forms of communicating information."[25]

It is immediately clear that Döblin cannot "resolve" this aporia in
his novel *Alexanderplatz,* as he desired to do in his theory of the
"modern epic." But he is indeed able to *dissolve* it: the heterogeneity
of the narrative experiment works against the deadly uniformity and
homogeneity of the city as a "void." This experiment can also make
manifest the social logic of this homogeneity. Attempts at *rescuing*
narration must be distinguished from the narrative experiment itself,
which does not evade the web of systems and functions of the given
city-text, but rather works with and within that web. One example
of a "rescue" would be the narrative therapy that the two Jews per-

form on the recently released Franz Biberkopf in order to "strengthen" him against the city's overwhelming power. Another attempt can be heard throughout the novel in the narrative voice that accompanies the hero like a benevolent spirit as he wanders purposelessly through the city. This voice, to be sure, breaks down into a kind of role-playing prose: at times it is the helpless hero's internal partner in dialogue, at others a reporter of city news. Its particular cadence often evokes the traditional balladeer as a relic and a parodic quotation from the good old days of the omniscient narrator. Finally, of course, there is an attempted "rescue" in the overall narrative intention: namely, the attempt to identify the story of Franz Biberkopf within the city-text and direct it toward a goal, albeit one with an added, higher sense. Franz Biberkopf's rescue would therefore be equivalent to the rescue of narration itself, of his narratable story.

That this attempt does not succeed, that the novel, typically for Döblin, does not come to an aesthetically satisfying conclusion, has often been labeled a "failure." However, if we not only attribute this "failure" to the rapacious hand of the "Moloch" city, to the insurmountable opposition between "subject" and "World," but also focus on the functional system of narration in the novel, present in the city-text, we thereby alter our methodological point of view. The discursive and narrative style of *Berlin Alexanderplatz* certainly does not reproduce merely an indefinable chaos, conjured from the "spirit of narration." For one thing, Döblin stages the vertigo produced by the dynamics of the metropolis as the hero's vertigo (as in the image of "sliding roofs" [7]) and, what is more, as a frenzy of signifiers that overpowers the narrator's voice:

The Private Protective Agencies watch over everything . . . Automatic Alarms, Watch and Safeguard Service for Greater Berlin . . . Germania Protective Agency . . . Watch and Ward Division of the Café Proprietors' Association of the Society of Berlin House-Owners . . . West Side Central Watchmen's Service, Watch and Protection Company, Sherlock Company, collected works on Sherlock Holmes by Conan Doyle, Watch and Protection Company for Berlin . . . Apollo Linen Renting Agency, Adler's Wet-Wash Service . . . . (155–56)

However, the "frenzy" produced by the floating signifiers of the city remains firmly attached to a logic binding the apparently indiscriminate flow of information and commodities. The permanent dynamic in the interminable chain of discourses employed in the city narrative is indicative here of the dominant principle of *separation* as well as that of *exchange* among the activities, interests, and intentions already referred to. The montage-text does not work with contrasting effects in order to intensify the social antagonisms contained in the various discourses and, in this way, give "expression" to them. Rather, it pursues the trail of the logic of ever-increasing differentiation in the modern capitalist exchange society that, preeminently in the city, incessantly produces this *specific* anonymity, this *remarkable* emptiness. That which is no longer representable becomes recognizable nevertheless: the anonymity of the carriers of meaning, the exchangeability of meanings. That which cannot be represented thematically becomes the theme: commodity exchange and its anonymity.

With endless variety and in many voices, the text narrates really only one thing: the loss of identifiable meanings, orientations, and relationships. It speaks of the devastating effectiveness of an increasingly anonymous, amorphous violence. The logic of the principle of social violence surfaces in language. After suffering yet another heavy blow of fate, Franz faces up to the "Reencounter on Alex Square" (216) by simply being there again: "our man stands again where he stood before" (215). And the narrator comments: "he has not understood anything, nor learned anything more." Franz's perception, which he claims as his "own," creates the familiar picture of the Alexander Square for him, with its traffic, shops, advertisements, and pedestrians, the sound amplified by the noise of the subway construction ripping up the Square. Franz Biberkopf sees it all and understands nothing. And yet out of the mix of discourses, without any effort on his part, something is gradually articulated. It is this imperceptible principle of violence that dominates the scene. The city narration is held together here by a kind of grammar of violence: Franz Biberkopf begins to conjugate the phenomena, which strike him violently, as his "own" violent compulsion: "I beat everything, you beat everything, he beats everything with boxes of 50 and cardboard packages of 10, can be mailed to every country on earth, Boyero 25 pfennigs, this novelty has won us many friends, I beat everything, and then you're beaten to the ground" (217–18).

There can be no doubt that Döblin consciously conceived of his story of Franz Biberkopf in the metropolis as a narrative power play, a major battle, and as the minor skirmish of one isolated individual trying to remain "decent" in spite of all the hostility he encounters in the terrible normality of the city. Considered structurally, the narrative text—the story of Franz Biberkopf—struggles with the montage-text of the city,[26] which from the very beginning destroys the narrative text as a learning process. The hero in Döblin's novel is once again expected to search for his identity, to be tested and purified; and in the end the story grants him a transformation—"access into the heaven of literary characters," as Benjamin ironically puts it. Franz Biberkopf is reborn because he eventually ceases his willful, destructive self-assertion. At this point, as in his *Wallenstein* and the novel *Wang-lun,* the author introduces a *Weltanschauung* based on the philosophy of nature and Oriental wisdom. It proposes that the natural individuality trapped within Western rationalism must escape its bonds and be regenerated into a higher form of the self, beyond the destructive social logic of capitalism. One can read *Berlin Alexanderplatz* "intentionally" in this sense,[27] of course, but one should bear in mind that just such attempts to rescue the Western notion of the self were part of a trend in the 1920s and that the mystical habit of denying the subject problematic had its roots in the very social principle so radically manifest in the text of the city. At any rate, Franz Biberkopf's story is too thoroughly structured within the text of the city to allow for any miraculous narrative redemption, and certainly not in a single stroke. The text applies to its hero that principle of separation and exchange that betrays his claim to fictional identity.

To establish this thesis, one must not necessarily restage the primal scene of Franz Biberkopf, in which the imaginary misreading of one's own self has its origin. At least on the narrative level Biberkopf's story is remarkably without prehistory. The power of the various discourses, visible on the surface of the city, creates by itself an adequate basis for the permanent disintegration of alleged identity. When Biberkopf defends himself against the city's order of discourses, he can do so only through those very discourses.[28] As a necktie salesman and would-be competitor of the large department stores, he speaks assertively, but with a blend of discourses that undercuts that very braggadocio of the "little guy."

Why does the smart man in the West End wear a bow tie when the proletarian doesn't? Ladies and gents, right up here, you too, Fräulein, with your husband, minors allowed, it costs no more for minors. Why doesn't the proletarian wear bow ties? Because he can't tie 'em. Then he has to buy a tie-holder, and after he's bought it, it's no good and he can't tie the tie with it. That's swindling, it makes the people bitter; it pushes Germany still deeper into poverty than she is already. (76–77)

When Biberkopf finds his own voice by simply bellowing against the real walls, he can only sing an old chauvinistic song, "The Watch on the Rhine." Hence the role of outsider, which could provide him with a story of his "own," is just another delusion. Since Döblin does not narrate in a logical, causal manner, he presents his protagonist's actions and character traits in a structural and serial manner, that is, without endowing him with any individual peculiarities. Franz Biberkopf is a victim of society not only as an alienated and reified individual but also as a victim of the divisions and separations between the city's various discourses. His misfortune is that he does not identify with any one of the alternatives made available by such division. In love he is a ladies' man, but his true love goes to the lady-killer Reinhold, whom he needs as a witness to his own love for Mieze, and who in turn murders her. Just as Biberkopf stands here between heterosexuality and homosexuality, politically he stands between the Nazis and the Communists, legally between "respectability" and criminality, economically between employment and unemployment. When Franz Biberkopf does something on his own he always provokes its opposite. His fruitless attempt to become "respectable" could also be reconstructed according to the dominant principle of *exchange* relations, as in the model of *differentiation,* of *division* and *isolation* as a social principle. The "brisk trade in girls" that Franz and Reinhold stage follows the pattern of substituting one "love" for another. The women, for their part, behave no differently. Mieze loves Franz, but must put her love on the love market. Her love for Franz carries over to Eva ("you're gay, sister") when she insists that Eva have a love child by her dear Franz. It is not difficult—apart from the sexual pathology of this case—to recognize the principle of exchangeability in this kind of plot, which is dominant in the text of the city where unique events and experiences are becoming increasingly infrequent. Certainly, we can "identify" Franz Biberkopf only as a "keeper" or "deputy" of a self lost in the traffic of urban discourses.

I said above that Döblin's experimental novel mobilizes heterogeneous elements against the deadly homogeneity in the text of the city. It must be added now, however, that this obviously does not and cannot happen in the movement of the text toward a specific "other," toward a perspective or position from which the text of the city, which overwhelms Franz Biberkopf's story, could be seen in its limitations.[29] Of course the reader might naïvely follow the carefully planted markers pointing to a solution. In order to unify his city novel conceptually, Döblin invokes recognized symbols of the bestial city (slaughter yard, wilderness, whore) and positions Old Testament figures here and there in his text (Job, Jeremiah, Isaac, and Jacob); he also employs a mythical elementalism of events (wind and forest), and always, moreover, at the point where the rationally descriptive text of the city and the narrative text of Franz Biberkopf (which allows him to act rationally) come close to breaking down. At the end of the novel, in the insane asylum of Berlin-Buch, the apocalyptic drama of the city is finally staged, and the hero emerges as a new person, purged and purified.

But again, if we do not simply follow the author's intention, if instead we doubt his metaphysical prescriptions, we can recognize in the functional, systematically structured narrative text of the city a liberated potential for meaning that is not necessarily synonymous with the forced symbolic order of the text. Here the text touches upon an imaginary surplus of meanings that calls for closer reading. Not in the progressive transfiguration and sublation of the self, but rather in Biberkopf's linguistic regression—in his babbling, groaning, panting, and screaming, and in his hallucinations—here in the reservoir of prelinguistic utterances, a residue of resistance manifests itself against the symbolic power of the discourses. Similarly, on the level of exchange and exchangeability there are signs indicating a residue of productive resistance. Specifically, Franz Biberkopf gives, whereas everyone else only exchanges. What the blows of fate take from him, he surrenders with a naïve, superior smile; he surrenders even his body—first his arm and then, in the hospital, his whole physical existence. Rainer Werner Fassbinder's film captured this irrational and unconscious surrender in the constant smile on Franz Biberkopf's face. Franz even smiles as Reinhold pushes him out of the car. There is something about him that disturbs others profoundly. In giving, and in giving himself up, he behaves entirely without principle, dysfunctionally and idiosyncratically. He shuns common models of action embodied in the flowing and continual exchange of traffic, commerce, and information. Franz can escape his imagined identity as self-sustainer and "self-provider" only by interrupting that circulation.

In one of his chapter titles Döblin speaks of the "Defensive War against Bourgeois Society" (361). I do not intend to conclude my review of Döblin's narrative by emphatically imputing to it the same new, redemptive utopia of productive irrationality and sovereign prodigality to which the poststructuralist critique of reason resorts so often today. Unlike the aesthetic consciousness of the avant-garde, which predicates all hope on an aesthetic and political explosiveness within the "homogeneous and empty time" of commodity capitalism, Döblin's city narrative remains locked in the trench warfare of bourgeois society. His city narrative is "modern" not only because it retraces that "terrible normality of the modern period" but also because its artfully constructed system of signs points specifically to that which cannot be narrated or demonstrated, to the abstract complexity and anonymity of modern society. It is in *this* insight—rather than in social marginality or aesthetic transcendence—that a rereading of Döblin's novel should try to make visible its ineradicable will to resist, despite all obstacles. In the web of discourses in *Berlin Alexanderplatz,* certain passages such as the following stand out like neon signs: "Surely, that must be an error, a mistake, those terrible numbers with all the zeros" (289).

Translated by Max Reinhart and Mark Anderson

Notes

1. Quotations from *Berlin Alexanderplatz: The Story of Franz Biberkopf,* trans. Eugene Jolas (New York: Frederick Ungar Pub. Co., 1983). All quotations are taken from this edition except where otherwise noted.
2. Alfred Döblin, *Aufsätze zur Literatur* (Freiburg: Walter-Verlag, 1962), 132.
3. *Ibid.,* 16.
4. *Ibid.,* 18.
5. *Ibid.,* 128.

6. *Ibid.*, 131.

7. *Ibid.*, 18.

8. See Dietmar Voss, "Metamorphosen des Imaginären: Nachmoderne Blicke auf Ästhetik, Poesie und Gesellschaft," in Andreas Huyssen and Klaus R. Scherpe, eds., *Postmoderne: Zeichen eines kulturellen Wandels* (Reinbek: Rowohlt, 1986), 219–50.

9. Ernst Bloch, *Erbschaft dieser Zeit* (Frankfurt am Main: Suhrkamp, 1973), 212.

10. Volker Klotz, *Die erzählte Stadt: Ein Sujet als Herausforderung des Romans von Lesage bis Döblin* (Munich: Hanser, 1969). Meanwhile, numerous works have appeared on the theme of the literary representation of the city: e.g., Silvio Vietta, "Großstadtwahrnehmung und ihre literarische Darstellung," in *DVjs. für Literaturwissenschaft und Geistesgeschichte* 48 (1974): 354–73; Andreas Feisfeld, *Das Leiden an der Stadt: Spuren der Verstädterung in deutschen Romanen des 20. Jahrhunderts* (Cologne and Vienna: Böhlau, 1982); C. Meckseper and E. Schraut, eds., *Die Großstadt in der Literatur* (Göttingen: Vandenhoeck and Ruprecht, 1983); Jörg Hienger, "Großstadt Masse Maschine in der Literatur," in *Neues Handbuch der Literaturwissenschaft*, vol. 20: *Zwischen den Weltkriegen*, ed. Thomas Koebner (Wiesbaden: Athenaion, 1983), 239–68; Gerhart Kapner, *Architektur als Psychotherapie: Über die Rezeption von Stadtbildern in Romanen des 20. Jahrhunderts* (Vienna: Böhlau, 1984); Hans-Josef Ortheil, "Der lange Abschied vom Flaneur," in *Merkur* 443:40 (1986): 30–42.

11. See the standard essay of Friedrich Sengle, "Wunschbild Land und Schreckbild Stadt," in *Studium generale* 16 (1963): 619–30.

12. Georg Simmel, "Die Großstädte und das Geistesleben," in *Die Großstadt: Jahrbuch der Gehe-Stiftung*, 9 (Dresden, 1903): 187–206.

13. See Klaus R. Scherpe, "Die Literaturrevolution der Naturalisten: Der Fall Arno Holz," in Scherpe, *Poesie der Demokratie: Literarische Widersprüche zur deutschen Wirklichkeit vom 18 zum 20 Jahrhundert* (Cologne: Pahl-Rugenstein, 1980), 177–226.

14. Walter Benjamin, "Das Paris des Second Empire bei Baudelaire," in Benjamin, *Gesammelte Schriften*, 1, 2 (Frankfurt am Main: Suhrkamp, 1980), 511–604; Benjamin, *Das Passagenwerk*, 2 vols. (Frankfurt am Main: Suhrkamp, 1983); Wolfgang Fietkau, *Schwanengesang auf 1848. Ein Rendezvous am Louvre: Baudelaire, Marx, Proudhon und Victor Hugo* (Reinbek: Rowohlt, 1978).

15. For further information see Klaus R. Scherpe, "Ausdruck, Funktion, Medium: Transformationen der Großstadterzählung in der deutschen Literatur der Moderne," in Götz Großklaus and Eberhard Lämmert, eds., *Literatur in einer industriellen Kultur* (Stuttgart: Klett-Cotta, 1988), and Klaus R. Scherpe, "Nonstop nach Nowhere City? Wandlungen der Symbolisierung, Wahrnehmung und Lesbarkeit der Stadt in der Literatur der Moderne," in Scherpe, ed., *Die Unwirklichkeit der Städte* (Reinbek: Rowohlt, 1988).

16. Walter Benjamin, "Der Surrealismus: Die letzte Momentaufnahme der europäischen Intelligenz," in Benjamin, *Gesammelte Schriften*, 2, 1: 295–310.

17. Walter Benjamin, "Die Widerkehr des Flaneurs," in Benjamin, *Gesammelte Schriften*, 3: 194–98.

18. See William Uricchio, "Ruttman's Berlin and the City Film to 1930" (Diss., Philadelphia, 1982).

19. Similarly in Karl Heinz Bohrer, *Plötzlichkeit: Zum Augenblick des ästhetischen Scheins* (Frankfurt am Main: Suhrkamp, 1981).

20. Walter Benjamin, "Krisis des Romans: Zu Döblins Berlin Alexanderplatz," in Benjamin, *Gesammelte Schriften*, 3: 236. See also Ulf Zimmermann, "Benjamin and Berlin Alexanderplatz: Some Notes Towards a View of Literature and the City," in *Coll. Germ.* 12 (1979):256–72.

21. The secondary literature on *Berlin Alexanderplatz* as a rule deals with this question by focusing on either the hero Franz Biberkopf—and therefore also on the tradition of the novel of education or the quasi-theological novel of purification—or on the other "hero," the city. E.g., Fritz Martini, "Alfred Döblins Berlin Alexanderplatz," in Martini, *Das Wagnis der Sprache*, 7th ed. (Stuttgart: Klett, 1984), 336–72; Susanne Ledanff, "Bildungsroman versus Großstadtroman," in *Sprache im technischen Zeitalter* 78 (1981): 85–112; Theodor Ziolkowski, "Berlin Alexanderplatz," in Ingrid Schuster, ed., *Zu Alfred Döblin* (Stuttgart: Klett, 1980), 128–48; in similar form also in the standard monographs: Leo Kreutzer, *Alfred Döblin: Sein Werk bis 1933* (Stuttgart: Kohlhammer, 1970); Roland Links, *Alfred Döblin* (Berlin: Volk and Wissen, 1979); Klaus Müller-Salget, *Alfred Döblin: Werk und Entwicklung* (Bonn: Bouvier, 1972).

22. Döblin, *Aufsätze zur Literatur*, 20.

23. Similar to Bloch. See Günther Anders, "Der verwüstete Mensch: Über Welt- und Sprachlosigkeit in Döblins Berlin Alexanderplatz," in *Festschrift zum achtzigsten Geburtstag von Georg Lukács*, ed. Frank Benseler (Neuwied: Luchterhand, 1965), 435. Anders's essay, which he says was written as early as Hitler's assumption of power, is the most astonishing piece in the secondary literature on Döblin's novel. This precise textual study already contains all the elements of a later text-theoretical, psychoanalytic, and discourse-theoretical "deconstructive" methodology.

24. Döblin, *Aufsätze zur Literatur*, 18.

25. Walter Benjamin, "Der Erzähler," in Benjamin, *Gesammelte Schriften*, 1, 2: 444.

26. See the Berlin dissertation of Harald Jähner, "Erzählter, montierter, soufflierter Text: Zur Konstruktion des Romans Berlin Alexanderplatz von Alfred Döblin" (Frankfurt am Main, 1984), to which I owe some essential ideas. A work that likewise goes beyond a traditionally hermeneutic Germanist approach is Ulrike Scholvin's *Döblins Metropole: Über reale and imaginäre Städte und die Travestie der Wünsche.* (Weinheim/Berlin:Beltz, 1985).

27. Recently, Helmut Koopmann, *Der klassisch-moderne Roman in Deutschland: Thomas Mann—Döblin—Broch* (Stuttgart: Kohlhammer, 1983). Koopmann's concept of a "classical modern" derives from the notion of a new myth created within the epic work, which can be reconstructed from the author's *Weltanschauung* in the text.

28. Suggested by Thomas Elsaesser's Berlin lecture that analyzes Rainer Werner Fassbinder's film version of Döblin's novel.

29. It has been determined that Döblin crossed out many city passages in his manuscript in order to profile more clearly the story of Franz Biberkopf as conceived originally (Manfred Beyer, "Die Entstehungsgeschichte von Alfred Döblins Roman Berlin Alexanderplatz," in *Wiss. Zeitschr. d. Friedrich-Schiller-Universität Jena* 20 [1971]: 391–423).

PART III

Writing and Modernist Thought

Woman and Modernity:
The [Life]Styles of Lou Andreas-Salomé

Biddy Martin

Alice Jardine begins her study of the "Configurations of Woman and Modernity," or *Gynesis,* by staging an encounter between American feminism and contemporary French thought. Cognizant of the inevitable risks of homogenizing both actors in her standoff, Jardine outlines the tension between the two in terms that have an uncanny familiarity—in terms of a conflict between feminism, "a concept inherited from the humanist and rationalist eighteenth century about a group of human beings in history whose identity is defined by that history's representation of sexual decidability, *and* contemporary French thought which has put every term of that definition into question."[1] It is, of course, a profound reduction to imagine that feminist theory and politics are so neatly caught between a political feminism that seems to assume and hence reproduce the very representations of difference it wants to subvert, and a theoretical modernity that has itself been accused of subordinating the discontinuities of the social to the totalizing self-referentiality of philosophical deconstruction. However, for the sake of argument, let us acknowledge that the tensions in feminist practices between empiricism and its philosophical/theoretical critique not only exist but could operate productively. It was my own interest in those tensions and reciprocal interruptions that led to my preoccupation with Lou Andreas-Salomé, whose figurations of self and woman refuse the alternatives masculine/feminine, rational/irrational, life/style, who cannot be turned into an advocate for one or the other side of those hierarchical divides.

Salomé has survived the exclusionary practices of conventional literary historiography on the basis of her liaison with famous male modernists, her appeal for, and her putative power over, such master stylists of the feminine as Nietzsche, Rilke, and Freud, in short, on the basis of what is both fetishized and trivialized as her "lifestyle." We are alert to the ways in which women and "deviance" are made safe by being turned into issues of lifestyle that demand no more of those upholding the norm than fascination and tolerance. What fascinates biographers and critics most in the case of Salomé's lack of conventionality are the marriage she refused to consummate with the Orientalist Friedrich Carl Andreas and the friendships and/or affairs with such masters of the modern as Rée, Nietzsche, Rilke, Beer-Hofmann, Ledebour, Wedekind, Hauptmann, Tausk, and Freud.[2] What fascinates them less are the scores of women she is said to have "unsettled." The sustained fascination is in large part a consequence of her failure, as the biographers see it, to have left a clear record of those relations and of herself, the failure to demarcate clearly the line among friendship, intellectual exchange, and sexual liaison; she continues to fascinate because of the difficulties she creates in all attempts to separate out the intellecutal from the erotic, scenes of pedagogy from scenes of seduction, norms from their transgression.

One response to the bases of her fame would be to suppress the fascination with what is called lifestyle and elevate her as male moderns have most recently been elevated, on the basis of her texts and the isolation of those texts from biographical, not to mention biological, contingency. But to suppress biographical contingency in favor of textuality has done little to undo the traditional biographical monumentalization of male heroes, or anti-heroes, and tends in any case simply to perpetuate a reduction of modernism to a question of language and form. The alternative is not to reprivilege the biographical but to renegotiate the relations between empirical and textual, without falling back on naive referentiality, or onto claims to an unspecific politics of language. It seems to me crucial that discussions of the modernist project address that which was and continues to be central to its provocations and its limits, its participation in what might be called a politics of subjectivity, of sexuality and gender, which is inextricably linked to questions of language and literary form, but involves different forms of social practice and institutional supports.[3] It is in this context that I address the significance of Salomé as figure, and the importance of her own work. What has made her both object and fetish is precisely that which makes her important for us to take seriously, her resistance to various forms of institutional legitimacy, her refusal to occupy the positions held out for her within a number of discursive orders, that is to say, to occupy any One position in those orders, from the family, religion, and moral convention, to philosophical, literary, or psychiatric schools. It is, of course, a question not simply of exclusion from these institutions but of the tension between forms of legitimacy and illegitimacy, between the privileges that underwrote her access to male cultural elites and the strategies with which she negotiated her relations to them. It is within a context of shared privilege that her stated differences from her male colleagues/lovers/friends must be considered; the difference that will be most pertinent here is her insistence on the negotiation of social constraints and boundaries, as opposed to their emphasis on transgression and negativity.

Let me proceed with Salomé's performative defiance of the split between life and writing, on the one hand, and their reduction to one another, on the other. Salomé claimed over and over that all of her writing was autobiographical. She wrote fiction, "scholarly" studies of Ibsen, Nietzsche, Rilke, and Freud, numerous reviews, theoretical essays on the psychology of religion, eroticism, and femininity, and psychoanalytic treatments of all of the above; she also kept journals, and corresponded widely. What gives her writing its autobiographical quality and appeal is not self-representation but the continual repetition and recasting of certain themes and questions that invite but also frustrate attempts to get at the real Lou Andreas-Salomé. Salomé's fiction is inevitably read as thinly veiled autobiography in part because her novels and stories are expositions of questions that are posed by way of biographical anecdote in her theoretical work. Certainly, the most explicitly autobiographical of all her publications, her memoirs, works to turn her into her own figuration of the narcissistic woman, a Nietzschean *Freigeist*, free from the prejudices of habit and moral convention, absolutely at home in exile, autotelic and impregnable, but without anxiety or the compulsion to self-overcoming. Salomé seems to have endlessly displayed but never represented herself, to have always been her own object of analysis without ever having made an object of herself even in explicitly autobiographical writings—writings that have a strangely anonymous and universal quality. Salomé revised and rewrote not only manuscripts meant for immediate publication but her diaries and journals as well. This constant remaking of herself in writing, that which she and Nietzsche celebrated as the importance of style, has confounded her biographers who cannot get at the origin, the truth behind what comes to be seen as deceptive mask or masquerades. Certainly, Salomé refused to subject herself to the kinds of truth in representation required of the complicit confessor. It would seem that she saw the relation between her life and her writing in terms of the attempt to produce cultural forms in spite of convention, not for the sake of transgression, but in the service of style, of life/style. Nietzsche once remarked that he had never known anyone who could match Salomé's brilliance in turning her experience, her psychic life, into speculation and analysis. I would like to take a brief look at how that compulsion, if not that brilliance, is borne out in Salomé's memoirs.

Certainly, her memoirs, *Lebensrückblick,* written in the twenties and early thirties, demonstrate an interesting relation between self-display and anonymity.[4] The memoirs conceive her life as an enactment of the epistemological and experiential challenges of modernity. The first chapter of her memoirs, entitled "My Experience of God," begins with her conception of her own birth as a disappearance, a coercion into *human* being, and it continues with the narration of her, as any subject's, difficulties with the sacrifices demanded of every human subject. The result of her own resistance to those sacrifices was what she called her *Zurückrutsch,* a sliding back, and the regressive narcissistic production of a God of infinite generosity, one who authorized her desire to have and be all. The death of this god, as well as the confrontation with the incommensurability of life and its forms, of desire and its representatives, of fantasy and its marriage to reality, had as a consequence, according to Salomé, both a profound demystification of a moral and social order robbed of self-evidence and a profound reverence for, and gratitude toward, the life that lived through but was not encompassed, mastered, or exhausted by the conscious self. According to Salomé, her childhood *Zurückrutsch* left her with an at least fantasized relation to an original indeterminate unity, without God, but equally without danger of falling out of the world. Precisely because of her relation to a pre-subject/pre-object indeterminate All, she, that is, woman, was more susceptible to the loss of self, to transferences of her desire onto god substitutes, or god-men as she called them. The task for woman in a godless universe, then, was conceived as continual disengagement from transferential relations without falling out of love, a negotiation of the feminine capacity for receptivity and submission to desire, and the human need for self-assertion. Her own relation to the modern world, one whose structures and forms of authority were no longer underwritten by God, was not to leave the world but to be in it differently, to resist subjection to the social without defying her implication in it. The memoirs are conceived as her attempts to engage in the world without succumbing to its fraudulent claims to authority/inevitability. Her god-men were, as she wrote over and over, the occasion for the coming into being of her desire and her thought, not the source or the ends of them. Hence the increasing importance to her of the symbolic significance of the Father/God, and of the principle of infidelity.

Salomé's memoirs related her development from her God, through her teacher/god-man Hendrik Gillot, by way of Nietzsche to Freud, as an increasing effort to disengage from the desire of/for others without denying the inevitability of mediation itself. It is significant, I think, that she told her own story, in her early fiction as well as in her memoirs (in which the conflicts are tempered, if not erased), in terms of encounters in which she narrowly escapes the death of consciousness, or of desire. She developed those encounters as sites of intra- and intersubjective struggle, indeed as sites of seduction. And she made quite clear that the most significant of all those encounters was her relation to the Dutch reform preacher Hendrik Gillot, whose teaching/preachings of German idealism she claimed to have chosen over religious orthodoxy, on the one hand, and arid rationalism, on the other. It was with Gillot that the adolescent Salomé began her study of the history of Western thought, and she describes his own conception of his project as that of bringing her out of the world of fantasy, childhood, romance, the East, and orthodoxy into the world of rationality, logic, the West. She describes her own deification of Gillot, the erotics of that deification, and the necessity of overcoming it as the paradigm of all subsequent idealizations. It is no surprise that her early fiction, described by many commentators as teeming with desire and youthful passion, without form, plot, or resolution, employs the figure of incest for her expositions of the confrontation of daughter-figures with those fathers in whom she comes to recognize herself.

"Woman," she once wrote, "runs a zigzag path between the feminine and the human."[5] This was not a problem to be solved once and for all, but a conflict at the heart of culture and subjectivity, a conflict that bourgeois feminism, according to Salomé, attempted to solve in two equally unsatisfactory ways. Salomé situated herself in relation to Germany's bourgeois feminisms by insisting on a double-edged polemic against the rationalist/humanist efforts to eradicate difference, and the romantic/metaphysical efforts to elevate femininity by way of its equation with motherhood and (hetero)sexuality. What makes women's lives in all their only apparent banalities significant, according to Salomé, are the ways in which they negotiate the double directionality at the heart of subjectivity from "Fall zu Fall."[6]

At issue were not simply the rationalizations, normalizations, the iron cage of society, but the exclusion of women from the sphere of the social, from the possibility of the elaboration of their desire in the social. The emphasis on the impossibility of a solution, of resolution, is what interests me here, for it suggests that the modern crisis of the incommensurability of desire and language, desire and social positionality, desire and marriage in all of its metaphoric and analogical potential, opens up the very possibility for what Salomé calls woman and her strategic negotiations between resolution and dissolution. Hence, the lack of appeal for her of discourses of apocalypse and heroism that totalized domination in order to totalize liberation in an outside, often known as or conflated with woman, those false alternatives offered by the master narratives of modernism. It is in this context that her objection to what she saw as Nietzsche's totalizations becomes most interesting and clear.

Salomé's study of Nietzsche, published in 1894, was the first major study of his work; it identified three major periods in his thought and identified the middle or realist period as his greatest achievement, that period in which Nietzsche most successfully disciplined his attempts to give life to the idea.[7] Salomé's objections to the late period had to do with what she read as his paradoxical return to metaphysics, a return made inevitable by his totalizing critique of Reason and culture and his privileging of unmediated, instinctual, and autotelic will. The "Übermensch," she wrote, is "pure, timeless conscious power."[8] And Salomé describes this conception as the postulation of the motherless child, identifying this will to knowledge with a will to be god, with a desire to escape the constraints of the social, indeed of the human condition as such, as a paradoxical effect of Nietzsche's profound antimetaphysical claim to life. Despite what she would continue throughout her life to call their fundamental similarity, their religious natures, their *Freigeisterei*, Salomé also continued to claim that to have followed Nietzsche in his totalizing critique of Reason, his contempt for the *Mensch des Geistes*, and in his appeal to unmediated instinctual life would have meant going back in the direction from which she had been moving, back into an exclusion from the social, an isolation, and a masochistic containment in desire.[9] For woman was threatened not only by the mediation and the containment *of* her desire but by a necessarily masochistic containment *in* it, a containment that has the mark not of unbridled nature but of a hopeless and, in the case of Nietzsche's metaphysical turn, willful blindness to one's inevitable mediation through the Other. In an 1899 essay on "woman," Salomé had written that the demise of religion had left woman without a language for articulating the double directionality of the feminine.[10] It is not uninteresting that she should have identified psychoanalysis as providing that language. And perhaps even more interesting that she refused to use its terms consistently, that is, that she insisted, in the words of François Roustang, on turning psychoanalysis into a Russian novel.[11]

Salomé approached Freud and psychoanalysis in 1911–12 at a critical moment in the history of the psychoanalytic movememt. Alfred Adler had left Freud's circle to found an independent psychoanalytic association, Carl Jung's departure was imminent, and internal conflict was at a height. It was also a moment of expansion, of the increasing interest in psychoanalysis outside of the narrow circles to which it had been confined. There is no doubt that Salomé was perceived to be an important because prestigious outsider, and Ernest Jones's perception of her as outsider contrasts significantly with her own conception of herself as part of the brotherhood, albeit with a difference, with the freedom to move in and out of their circles. Salomé would write her memoirs as a lifelong search for the exchange she found in her relation to Freud, the only pedagogical relation that displaced that hierarchical gender divide and inevitable appropriation characterizing other pedagogical exchanges, other all-too-conventional scenes of seduction and tragedy. It is, of course, impossible to explore all of the factors that contributed to that possibility. However, it is significant that Salomé's allegiance to Freud was not her only allegiance at the age of fifty, that their relation was sustained through correspondence, that is, at a distance, and that the position of student was not the only position available to her in relation to the person Freud, or to psychoanalysis. Indeed, it is on the basis of that association that Salomé takes up her own position as analyst and teacher. What concerns me here are the ways in which Salomé negotiated her relationship to psychoanalysis and Freud, and the significance of gender in those negotiations.

Both their unity and their differences were played out on the field of narcissism. From the beginnings of her stay in Vienna in 1912, Salomé used her own difference with Alfred Adler over his conception of the unconscious to support her unity with Freud. "I am absorbed in *Beyond the Pleasure Principle*," she writes to Freud in December 1920, "and you can imagine what pleasure this book has given me, since I was plagued by the worry that you were not in agreement with me on the matter of the passive instinct; and yet it is only from this standpoint that Adler can be conclusively disproved, as I told him in Vienna."[12] Salomé understood the conception of passive instincts to be an advocacy for the unconscious in the face of Adler's overvaluation of the ego. Passivity meant an openness and receptivity to the life that lives through but is neither encompassed by, nor accessible to, the conscious subject—a yielding to that which exceeds and, from a certain point of view, may seem to threaten the ego and its demands for control and coherence. For her, what distinguished Freud's concept of the unconscious from Adler's was its bases in an inarticulable but material narcissism, from within which the ego sets itself apart, but from which it never fully departs. Given this narrative of the development of the ego, sharp distinctions between conscious and unconscious, ego and sexuality, masculine and feminine, active and passive are problematic, and it was this problematic that was at stake for Salomé.

Salomé explains the epistemological importance of Freud's narcissism concept in the following terms:

To hold fast to Freud's present concept of narcissism means to hold fast to psychology's right to its own media and methods no matter what. And that means to be allowed to write, with appropriate obscurity, its personal mark of X, even there where the psychic organization eludes it, instead of defecting into the alien clarity belonging to another side of existence called the physical.[13]

In her critiques of Adler's recourse to simple determinism, Salomé emphasizes the connection between his overvaluation of the ego and his devaluation of femininity and passivity; she rejects his conception of masculine protest as the key to psychic development for reducing sexuality, the unconscious, the feminine to the status of fictions and tools.

Often it is in the very same letters in which she takes up her critique of Adler that Salomé introduces her objections to Freud's own tendency to conceive of the unconscious as contingent upon, even derived from, the ego and its repressions; and she opposes those tendencies for their erasure of the positivity of desire. Her differences with Freud over questions of religion, artistic creation, homosexuality, and ethics always turn on his derivation of those phenomena from inhibitions in development, his conception of them as compensations or compromises. Salomé stood by her conception of the specificity of the development of a presymbolic narcissism and its expression in creative and intellectual as well as "symptomatic" behavior. Far from simply representing compensatory formations in the negative sense, "primitive" religion, infantile preoccupations, artistic production, even neuroses manifested for her the positivity of a desire that has its bases in narcissism. In notes written to Freud about the relation between phantasy and reality, Salomé addresses Freud's explanation of the relationship between artistic expression and repression by arguing that pleasure and creativity are derived not only from the pleasurable opening up of the repressed, but "still more perhaps on account of the objective element in the primal experiences that is regained in this way: precisely those experiences that were not even indirectly reanimated through object-libido, but that are made accessible only under the powerful touch of phantasy to all reaches of the conscious intellect—and in this way extend our personality, hemmed in as it is by object-libido, to spheres that were once its province and that it now regains."[14] Again, a concept of the unconscious that is not subordinated to the demands or the strategies of the ego is fundamental to Salomé's project. And she blames developmental theory for the suppression of that creative, if regressive, direction of narcissism. What was at stake for Salomé was not obscurity or undecidability for its own sake but a challenge to the hypostasization of oppositions that set up rigid and antagonistic boundaries between the primitive and the civilized, between nature and culture, and perhaps most significantly, between sexuality and ego.

In response to what she saw as Freud's tendency to overemphasize the threat posed by sexuality to the ego, Salomé reminded Freud of what she took to be his own argument, that the relation between sexuality and ego has to do with the orientation of the boundary drawn between them. It is because of the rigid line drawn between them in "man" that narcissism's double directionality is clearer in "women." In an essay of 1928 entitled "The Consequences of the Fact That It Was Not Woman Who Killed the Father,"[15] Salomé does what Sarah Kofman was to do somewhat differently fifty years later, namely, she uses Freud's work on narcissism against him.[16] Salomé's 1928 essay is emblematic of her rhetorical/interpersonal strategy of setting herself apart from the terms that she claims unite her with Freud. She and Freud agree that, in the words of Kofman, "woman's enigmatic quality has to do with her affirmative self-sufficiency and indifference, not with the veiling of an inadequacy or lack" (52). "It is no accident," Kofman writes, "that Freud's essay On Narcissism was written in 1914, a time when he was particularly taken with Lou Andreas-Salomé" (50). What Salomé and Kofman emphasize is the difficulty Freud has in sustaining the division he sets up in that essay between masculine anaclitic (ethical) and feminine narcissistic object choices, since the masculine object choice and the male's overvaluation of the object develop by way of the prior narcissistic cathexis of the self, by way of the feminine. Even more problematic are Freud's ultimate ethical condemnation of woman's narcissism and his claim that motherhood provides the appropriate ethical redemption. "The theorist is subject to the same forms of forgetfulness as the little boy" (79), the same fraud, the forgetting which draws too sharp and self-evident a line between unconscious and conscious, desire and autonomy, pleasure and ethics. "All ethical autonomy," writes Salomé in

"Narcissism as Double Directionality," "doubtless constitutes a compromise between command and desire . . . while it renders what is desired unattainable—given the ideal strictness of the value demanded—it draws what is commanded from the depths of the dream of all-encompassing, all sustaining Being."[17] Freud cannot escape narcissism as the ground of ethics or of love, nor can he sustain what Salomé sees as the unnecessarily rigid dichotomy between narcissism and sociality, between self-sufficiency and ethics.

Salomé's essay on the consequences of the fact that it was not the daughter who killed the father begins by explaining her title (*WDF*, 25). The title refers, Salomé reminds her readers, to Freud's proposition that the first human crime (and the advent of culture) was the murder of the father. With this beginning Salomé acknowledges her indebtedness to Freud and her intention to work on woman's difference from within his narrative. The freedom she assumes in order to work both within and against Freud's terms characterizes both the method and the content of the essay. Indeed, the beginning of the second paragraph ventures the suggestion that if Freud's speculation is valid, is "so," then it cannot have been without consequence that the daughter remained free of the son's primal guilt (*WDF*, 25). The "ist es so" (if it is true) marks the hypothetical nature of his and, by implication, her arguments, that which she would have called their symbolic as opposed to their truth value. Our myths, she once wrote to Freud, are that to which we resort when we reach the limit of what we can observe empirically and follow rationally. Following Freud's lead here, Salomé sets out to explain the process through which the son's murder of the father is transformed into a remorseful, deferential deification of the father on the part of the then conformist and obedient son. Salomé appeals to what she sees as the only instance of such deification/idealization accessible in our lived experience, namely, the idealization of the object in erotic love. Again, she takes up Freud's own work on masculine object choice, the aggressive as opposed to the passive type, characterized by an overvaluation of the love object and a dependence for one's sense of self on the reciprocation of that love. Her next move is to suggest that there is no natural basis for such object choice or for such idealization. Nothing prepares us for it in advance, she suggests, since what is prior is that lack of differentiation that Freud, she reminds us, called narcissism. She goes on to explain the lasting effects of narcissism in the relation between psyche and the body. As a consequence of the development of the ego and the separation between subject and object, the body becomes the material limit of our narcissism, in that it comes to mark the boundary between self and other, and is therefore experienced as if it were external to us; it is also the point of contact and connection through which the narcissistic remains at play—the body, then, as *Grenz* and *Bindestrich,* that to which we can have no unmediated relation, but can also not escape. Hence, by analogy, the inescapability of narcissism (*WDF*, 26).

The masculine overvaluation of the object, its ethics, which has no natural basis, according to Salomé, can be said to involve a social intervention into a previously narcissistic state. The renunciation and the forgetting of narcissism require the threat and guilt over incestuous wishes and murderous fantasies. The son's fantasy of murdering the father involves a deep narcissistic wound, since the father is, after all, the son's future. The son, with his murderous omnipotence wishes, is transformed into a remorseful and obedient subject who overvalues the love object even as he misrecognizes what is actually his suppressed desire for a reunion in what he takes to be ethical ideals. The daughter, Salomé argues, need not suppress incestuous wishes so violently, need not fall out of love, at least if we take Freud's mythical narrative seriously (*WDF*, 27); she is not forced, then, to internalize a prohibitive and punitive Law. Here Salomé subtly insists on the often forgotten distinction in Freud's own 1914 "On Narcissism" essay between ego ideal and superego or conscience, making conscience the fate of the male, and an unpunitive ego ideal, the daughter's difference. Salomé's woman is less likely to confuse desire with ethics, and hence her greater sobriety in relation to the Law. The daughter, Salomé writes, resolves her own tendency to idealize the Father through a series of ever more subtle, more refined sublimations without having to murder the father or repress her narcissistic sense of connectedness; hence the more peaceful coexistence of desire and self-assertion (*WDF*, 27). Woman remains more "at home" in her materiality, no matter how sublimated, how spiritualized her relation to it. The sublimations required of her are articulated in terms of a rounding out, a growing and expanding that is horizontal, spatial, that does not depart for a point above or beyond, but reabsorbs the traces of a history that is never renounced. The man who has forgotten the desire at the basis of his ethics and his aspirations reacts more sensitively to external Law, vacillating between guilt and desire, between "natural rebelliousness that would destroy anything in its way" and the impulse to achieve his own worth in the approval of that punitive Other (WDF, 28). For Salomé, the conflict between the desire for total independence from the Father and an equally strong desire to submit to Him explains the ambivalent relations of Freud's sons to their father. And the failure to work through this conflict, which has its basis in an only apparently paradoxical narcissistic desire for unity, makes men blind to their own desires, obliging them to separate mind and body, intellect and erotics, rational and irrational.

If there is lack, then, it is that of the son whose trajectory involves a linear, teleological, sacrificial verticality, the imperative to aspire and achieve with the illusory promise that identification with, and obedience to, the Father will reconstitute the lost whole. "It is no wonder," Salomé wrote elsewhere, "that the male neurotic's desire to be happy is often expressed as a desire to be a woman," to be what she called that "regressive without a neurosis" (FJ, 118). In "Woman as Type," Salomé draws out the paradox that constitutes the daughter's difference and her advantage:

Woman is able to experience what is most vital as most sublimated. This mentalizing, idealizing draws its spontaneity from the fact that, in the transferences of love, their point of departure remains more palpably present for the feminine-unitary nature throughout life. . . . The individual beloved person in all his factuality becomes for her transparent in all directions, a diaphane with human contour through which the fullness of the whole gleams, unbroken and unforgotten.[18]

Salomé concludes her essay on the consequences of the differenes between the sexes, an essay that consistently avoids anatomical determinations, by folding those differences back on themselves. For at the point of furthest development of his masculinity, the man exhibits submission, a giving of himself to his ideal that exposes the feminine-passive, the narcissistic moment that is always at work even in the most apparently total separations. Masculine and feminine approach the border of their difference and tend to become one another (WDF, 28). If the masculine opens out onto the feminine in the drive to achieve, to become the father, motherhood constitutes at least the metaphorical point at which woman can be said to have opened onto the masculine; it combines the feminine capacity for giving with the masculine capacity to create, to protect, and to lead. In motherhood, Salomé argues, woman realizes her sublimated homosexuality. Indeed, motherhood has always elicited the fascination and envy of man both because it transgresses the conventional boundaries of femininity, reaching over into the masculine, and because it is an experience of the body that is denied him (WDF, 29). For that reason, Salomé argues, the mother becomes the essence of that which is inaccessible, and figures for man as a symbol more than a real human being, a symbol of the inseparability, indeed, the ultimate undecidability of all human differentiations, that undecidability, that narcissism that must be repressed if masculine identity is to be secured. Woman exists for man somewhere between the *Kreatürlichem* and the *Überpersonellem,* a position of indeterminacy and a commonplace (WDF, 29). This, of course, is not Freud's ethical mother, not the redemption of woman's narcissism, but its realization, the source of man's fascination and his horror.

Woman's position between the animal and the transcendental, this undecidability, became oppressive, Salomé continues, when the worship of god became the worship of man, and that undecidable figure, that *Mittelding,* was domesticated into the respectable wife. Whereas woman once belonged directly to the *Vater-Gott,* the worship of man and the domestication of woman cut her off from that world of possibility signified by the Father and unfulfillable by any human relation. Penis envy, writes Salomé, a form of desire for equality based in "ressentiment," emerged along with the possibility of the enslavement of woman by man (WDF, 29). It is at this point, she suggests, that woman must struggle against the human male for access to that which is as naturally hers as it is his in its inaccessibility. Salomé's critique here of humanist glorifications of the hu*man* subject is directed at what she takes to be the assumption of a fraudulent complementarity that makes woman his lack and his completion. As soon as woman's access to her own desire is mediated through the human male, as soon as competition with him is her only hope of escape from domestication, the daughter begins to kill the father herself and, with "him," precious parts of herself (WDF, 29).

The essay ends with a discussion of the implications of differences for the relations between the sexes. The only viable relation to the other, according to Salomé, is that based on the furthest possible development of the sexual differences within each one, rather than the projection of difference onto a supposedly complementary and ideal other half. Hence, the significance to her of Freud's notion of bisexuality, understood as a sexual indeterminacy that "can be awakened by the opposite sex, as a consequence of the other's profound approach, his understanding, and his embrace" (FJ, 60–61). So it is, Salomé wrote elsewhere, "that only slightly homosexual men see the universally human qualities in woman and are erotically disposed toward them" as opposed to the more exclusively heterosexual, self-repressive man who prefers the feminine woman in the most circumscribed sense of the word (FJ, 188–89).

Salomé's 1928 essay is typical of her excavations of the internal differences of psychoanalysis, excavations formulated as reminders to Freud of the implications of his own work, perhaps of his own slight "homosexuality." Clearly, Salomé made use of what she characterized as the daughter's good fortune in her relation to Freud, maintaining the privilege and pleasure of speaking in his name without giving herself over to his terms. Salomé avoided war with Freud just as she avoided submission to him by sustaining a relation that she described as one beyond fidelity and infidelity, enabled by her concomitant acknowledgment and destabilization of gender and genre lines—the fact that she refused the exclusive positions of insider and out, that she insisted (in the words of François Roustang) on turning psychoanalysis into a Russian novel, that she contaminated science with the philosophical and aesthetic, even as she credited Freud and psychoanalysis with correcting her tendency toward romantic mystification and hallucinated syntheses.

Notes

1. Alice Jardine, *Gynesis: Configurations of Woman and Modernity* (Ithaca and London: Cornell University Press, 1985), 20–21.
2. Until recently, accounts of Salomé's life were to be found primarily in biographies and accounts of Nietzsche and Rilke, and in two book-length

studies/biographies available in English, H. F. Peters, *My Sister, My Spouse* (New York: Norton, 1962), and Rudolph Binion, *Frau Lou: Nietzsche's Wayward Disciple* (Princeton: Princeton University Press, 1968). Angela Livingstone's more recent biography, *Lou Andreas-Salomé* (London: Gordon Fraser, 1984), does not add substantially new material to Binion's finds, but has the value of a more even-handed and readable style than Binion's reductionist psychoanalytic framework allowed. Cordula Koepcke's *Lou Andreas-Salomé: Ein eigenwilliger Lebensweg* (Freiburg: Herderbücherei, 1982), and her more recent biography, *Lou Andreas-Salomé: Eine Biographie* (Frankfurt am Main: Insel Verlag, 1986), provide lucid and interesting, if general, accounts of Salomé's life and significance.

3. I am influenced in these formulations by John Rajchmann's assessment of the shifts in Foucault's work on modernism from a politics of form to a politics of subjectivity. See John Rajchmann, *Michel Foucault: The Freedom of Philosophy* (New York: Columbia University Press, 1985).

4. Lou Andreas-Salomé, *Lebensrückblick: Grundriss einiger Lebenserinnerungen*, ed. Ernst Pfeiffer (Zurich: Insel Verlag, 1951; Frankfurt am Main: Insel Verlag, 1968; Frankfurt am Main: Insel Verlag, 1979).

5. Lou Andreas-Salomé, "Die in sich ruhende Frau," in *Zur Psychologie der Frau*, ed. Gisela Brinker-Gabler (Frankfurt am Main: Fischer Taschenbuch Verlag, 1978), 285–311. Originally published as "Der Mensch als Weib: Ein Bild im Umriss," *Neue Deutsche Rundschau* 10:1 (1899): 225–43.

6. Salomé develops this conception of an oscillation from case to case both stylistically, by way of reversals, and thematically in "Die in sich ruhende Frau." The strategy and the thematics characterize her fiction as well.

7. Lou Andreas-Salomé, *Friedrich Nietzsche in seinen Werken* (Vienna: Carl Conegen, 1894; Frankfurt am Main: Insel Verlag, 1983).

8. *Friedrich Nietzsche*, 267–68.

9. See in particular Salomé's diary entries for August of 1882, the period she spent in Tautenburg with Nietzsche, in *Friedrich Nietzsche, Paul Rée, Lou von Salomé: Die Dokumente ihrer Begegnung*, ed. Ernst Pfeiffer (Frankfurt am Main: Insel Verlag, 1970). In addition, see Salomé's accounts of life in Berlin with Rée in *Lebensrückblick*.

10. Salomé, "Die in sich ruhende Frau."

11. François Roustang, *Dire Mastery*, trans. Ned Lukacher (Baltimore and London: The Johns Hopkins University Press, 1982).

12. *Sigmund Freud and Lou Andreas-Salomé: Letters*, trans. William and Elaine Robson-Scott (London: Hogarth Press, 1972), 61.

13. *The Freud Journal of Lou Andreas-Salomé*, trans. Stanley A. Leavy (New York: Basic Books, 1964), 111. Cited in the text as *FJ*.

14. *Sigmund Freud and Lou Andreas-Salomé: Letters*, 226.

15. Lou Andreas-Salomé, "Was daraus folgt, dass es nicht die Frau gewesen ist, die den Vater totgeschlagen hat," *Almanach des Internationalen Psychoanalytischen Verlages*, 1928, 25–30. Cited in the text as *WDF*.

16. Sarah Kofman, *The Enigma of Woman: Woman in Freud's Writings,* trans. Catherine Porter (Ithaca: Cornell University Press, 1985). Subsequent page references are cited in the text.

17. Binion's translation of excerpts from Salomé's "Narzissmus als Doppelrichtung," *Imago* 7:4 (1921): 361–86. See Binion, *Frau Lou,* 552; Salomé, 376.

18. Binion's translation of Salomé's "Zum Typus Weib," *Imago* 3:1 (1914): 2–14. See Binion, *Frau Lou,* 555; Salomé, 11.

A View Through the Red Window: Ernst Bloch's *Spuren*

Klaus L. Berghahn

For Axel Stein

PREFACE

At a time when I was still contemplating my topic, I was asked: "What are you working on?" "I am struggling very hard," I answered, "I am preparing my next error." Of course, this is a well-known Keuner story, which Bertolt Brecht aptly called "hardship of the best."[1] This short text has a double function here. It serves as a *captatio benevolentiae,* and it leads into the subject matter of this essay. Brecht's story belongs to a cluster of texts written or published around 1930. Authors and texts that come to mind are: Walter Benjamin's *Einbahnstraße* (One-Way Street, 1928), Siegfried Kracauer's *Die Angestellten* (The White-Collar Workers, 1930) Ernst Bloch's *Spuren* (Traces, 1930), Bertolt Brecht's *Geschichten vom Herrn Keuner* (Stories of Mr. Keuner, 1926–34), Robert Musil's *Nachlaß zu Lebzeiten* (Literary Estate While Alive, 1936), and, as a latecomer, Theodor W. Adorno's *Minima Moralia* (1944). What characterizes these "stories without a story," as Musil once called them, is a combination of observation and reflection, a rare cross between literature and philosophy. They seem to be cognate to Kafka's parables and they border on the essayistic philosophy of the Frankfurt School. Often it is not clear which is more important, the poetic narrative or the didactic commentary, as we can observe in the following example by Brecht:[2]

A Good Answer
A worker was asked in court whether he wanted to use the secular or the religious form of oath. He answered: "I'm unemployed."—"This wasn't just distractedness," said Mr. K. "By this answer he let it be understood that he was in a situation where such questions, indeed perhaps the entire court procedure as such, no longer make sense."

Here the balance between anecdote and commentary tips in favor of the interpretation; the terse shrewdness of the "good answer" gets buried by the heavy-handed explanation.

What we have, then, is a simple prose form with a prevalence for a moral, call it a parable or a fable; not much to it, or so it would seem. But there is more to it than we see at first glance. As an example I have chosen to discuss Ernst Bloch's *Spuren* (Traces), one of the best, yet least known, texts in modern German literature.

TRACES, CRISS AND CROSS

"The title *Spuren* mobilizes primary experiences like reading cowboy-and-Indian stories for philosophical theory," Adorno noted in his review.[3] Indeed, the book contains a remarkable collection of stories that combine storytelling with philosophizing, in keeping with Bloch's *bon mot*: "I know only Hegel and Karl May; everything in between is an impure mixture of both."[4] And there is room for more associations: the trapper and the philosophical pathfinder are joined by a detective: "Something is uncanny, that is how it all starts."[5] The world seems to be full of traces, and the petty details of everyday life in particular contain evidence that something is going on, anticipating things to come. Those things have their meaning, and their stories are part of history, making us aware of an ongoing process. Insignificant things and petty details especially attracted Bloch's attention, as he relates in the only autobiographical piece of *Spuren*, "Spirit, which just forms itself," in which he tells us about experiences of his childhood. One image, that is as inconspicuous as it is mysterious, stands out—the red window:[6]

Eight years old, and the strangest experience was the sewing kit in a shop window on my way to school; it stood between wool and quilt next to feminine needlework, which didn't mean anything to me. But on the sewing box something was painted, with many color dots and spots on the smooth surface, as if the image were coagulated. It showed a cabin, lots of snow and a moon high and yellow on a blue winter sky, in the windows of the cabin glowed a red light. . . . I have never forgotten the red window.

An insignificant red window, painted on a sewing box, becomes the orientation and vanishing point of his life; it expresses a longing for something that has no name yet, a boy's daydream that points to great things to come. Whatever the meaning of this symbol may be— and Bloch is careful not to explain it—it is evidence of a process of self-awareness and self-cultivation that started with the sudden recognition of that image.

The genesis of the book offers another clue to understanding the title *Spuren*. The work belongs to the oldest formation of Bloch's philosophy. (In a footnote to the table of contents of the 1969 edition of *Spuren,* Bloch remarked that these stories originated between 1910 and 1929.) It can be traced back to the essay collection with a Karl May title, *Durch die Wüste* (Through the Desert, 1923), and more important to *Geist der Utopie* (Spirit of Utopia, 1918). Many paralipomena of these two books ended up in *Spuren,* which was published in 1930. It had no impact whatsoever upon its first publication, was not reprinted until 1959, and was finally published as the first volume of Bloch's *Complete Works* in 1969. As is typical for Bloch, he changed the work in its 1969 edition by adding twenty-one stories and altering the introduction. During his lifetime, all of his books were works in progress, and they all contain an introductory section similar to a group of *Spuren* texts that leads into the book and gives it a perspective. The short prose form of *Spuren* seems to be a style as well as a thought process. Even his magnum opus, *The Principle of Hope,* is introduced in this way. Its five famous questions (Who are we? Where do we come from? Where do we go? What do we expect? What expects us?) are followed by *Spuren*-like texts. Since *Spuren* is closely connected with *Spirit of Utopia* and the same narrative structure is used to lead into *The Principle of Hope,* it can be safely assumed (as Adorno does) that the stories in *Spuren*—despite their diversity and colorfulness—have only *one* perspective: they follow and read the traces leading to Utopia, which never comes into sight.

TRACING: MARK THE DETAIL

It is one thing to find traces, but quite another to read and understand them. Bloch does not provide an introduction on how to interpret his texts. These after all are descriptions and stories that can stand on their own and do not need the support of a philosophical tract. Only at the end of the first section is there one text that can be viewed as a preface, since it offers some general advice on how to read the traces in the sand of reality or in the rubble of history. The text is called "Das Merke," which can mean: make note of that. "Pay attention especially to the small things, look into them," is his advice. "Whatever is light and strange, often leads farthest."[7] Bloch's *objets trouvés* include the contents of his pocket when he was a child as well as things that surround us every day. Siegfried Kracauer once observed that Bloch was especially attracted by the "phenomena of indistinct life,"[8] obscure and curious things, the life of fairs and carnival booths. Like his friend Benjamin, Bloch was a flaneur and collector who paid attention to minute detail. Even the trash of history interested him, and there is a lot of trash in our culture; but at the same time Bloch did not want to leave the kitsch and tinsel of the culture industry unnoticed.[9] In this regard, Bloch's *Spuren* is closely connected with his sociopolitical analysis of his times, *Legacy of This Era*. *Spuren* can also be viewed as an example of Bloch's understanding of the literary heritage. He seems to prefer simple and popular forms of narration such as fairy tales, anecdotes, almanac stories, and, above all, pulp novels (*Kolportage*). The pieces of literature that he found and used in *Spuren* are mostly products of low or popular culture. Likewise, he observed with curiosity the disintegration of bourgeois culture. In contrast to Lukács, who smelled the rat of bourgeois decadence in expressionism, Bloch defended the modernist techniques and popular tendencies of this movement. In good old stories and in bad new forms he discovered dreams of a better life and a gleam of hope. He was not willing to yield this heritage to the Nazis for their exploitation.

The meaning of the *objets trouvés* or found stories in Bloch's *Spuren* is not easy to decipher. If Bloch's short prose pieces have a moral, it is not his intention to tell a story for the sake of its moral. Bloch's narratives certainly have a philosophical essence, but they are not the ornament for his philosophy. He describes a thing, or observes a situation, or simply tells a story, and while he talks the listener/reader takes notice without being forced to accept a *fabula docet* solution. His philosophy is part of the narration: he thinks in fables, and he fabulates while thinking. As he follows the traces, he starts a narration of which thinking is a part, as we can see in the following simple story:

The Poor Woman
What are you doing? I asked. I am saving electricity, said the poor woman. She was sitting in the dark kitchen, for a long time now. At least that was easier than saving food. Since there's not enough for everyone, the poor jump in. They're in action for the big shots even if they're resting and left alone.[10]

We have here a simple description of an almost idyllic situation that renders transparent the problems of a class society. The quiet rest in the dark kitchen is evidence of a social process that lies outside the kitchen, overshadowing it. What could be a natural situation becomes unnatural under the conditions of capitalism. The absurdity of the situation is that the poor serve their masters even when they rest.

EMBLEMATIC TRACES

But what do we call these stories? Bloch himself does not give any clue. His book does not have a subtitle that would indicate a genre. It is not organized as an anthology of short stories, nor can its stories be categorized among traditional forms. Granted, many of Bloch's stories are remakes, so to speak, and they remind us of such traditional forms as fairy tales or anecdotes. Bloch, who is not the inventor but merely the narrator of stories, changes their content and form drastically. He uses the found stories as material to work with, and in the process they are given a new meaning. On the part of the critics there is uncertainty as to what to call them: philosophy, or literature, or both? Hans Mayer proposes "philosophical fables," a form of narration that seeks to make a practical philosophy poetically palatable.[11] Traditionally a didactic form like this would be called parable. But these stories are not one-dimensional, nor do they have a moral. They are at best parables without a moral that make the readers notice something, make us aware. Or to adopt a term coined by Lessing: these stories are *fermenta cognitionis,* they stimulate thinking.

Because of their dual nature, narrative/descriptive and reflective, they seem to require an allegorical reading. Traditionally this would mean that the image, the situation, or the story can be reduced to one idea. We have already noticed that this is impossible. But there is another understanding of allegory, defining not just a representation or personification of an abstract concept, but rather a metonymic relationship between image and meaning. For Bloch, as for Benjamin, the allegorical method lies not in projecting a meaning onto a thing; instead, it is discovered in the thing, as a quality that has to be interpreted. In our still unnamed genre, the subjective activity of narration and interpretation corresponds to an objective quality of the world. The narrator finds the world as it is or as it has become; through narration and commentary he disrupts the normal order of things, letting us see them in a new light.

For this allegorical narrative I cannot think of a more appropriate name than *Denkbild,* thought-image, a term coined by Walter Benjamin. In his review of Benjamin's *One-Way Street,* Adorno explains this neologism as an invention of Stefan George, and later in the same text he observes that these prose pieces are riddles that shock the reader into thinking.[12] This is as convincing as it is farfetched. There is, however, a rather simple solution to this riddle: the new genre is as old as the emblem, for which *Denkbild* seems to be an apt German translation. Benjamin, who was an expert on Baroque literature and its imagery, knew what he was talking about when he named his short prose pieces in *One-Way Street* "thought images." They indeed combine *inscriptio* (title), *pictura* (thing, description, image), and *subscriptio* (commentary, interpretation), as is required of an emblem.[13] The tripartite structure and the combination of image and text that constitutes the form of the emblem can also be found in two more recent examples, Benjamin's *Angelus Novus* and Brecht's *Kriegsfibel* (War Primer). Benjamin's famous angel of history received his name and image from a rather insignificant drawing by Paul Klee. The drawing is the *pictura* and the title is the *inscriptio*, while the *subscriptio* can be found in Benjamin's "Theses on the Philosophy of History," the ninth of which reads as follows:

A Klee painting named "Angelus Novus" shows an angel looking as if he were about to move away from something he is fixedly contemplating. His eyes are staring, his mouth is open, his wings are spread. This is how one pictures the angel of history. His face is turned toward the past. Where we perceive a chain of events, he sees only one single catastrophe which keeps piling wreckage upon wreckage and hurls it in front of his feet. The angel would like to stay, awaken the dead, and make whole what has been smashed. But a storm is blowing from Paradise; it has got caught in his wings with such violence that the angel can no longer close them. This storm irresistibly propels him into the future to which his back is turned, while the pile of debris before him grows skyward. This storm is what we call progress.[14]

The text as a whole has become a thought-image. Under the title *Angelus Novus* it combines a short prose description of the drawing with an interpretation. The angel of history looks back on the ruins of history while being driven by a storm, which blows from paradise, into an undecided future he cannot see.

Brecht's *Kriegsfibel* can be regarded as a modern emblem book.[15] It consists of war photographs from *Life* magazine (*pictura*) to which Brecht added a caption (*inscriptio*) and an interpretive four-line verse (*subscriptio*). Brecht wanted his "photograms," as he called them, to be used as didactic material to teach the art of reading pictures and deciphering the hieroglyphs of photojournalism, as we can see in the following example: The picture shows the skull of a Japanese soldier that was propped up on a burned-out tank. Brecht's *subscriptio* reads as follows:

Alas poor Yorick of the jungle tank!
Your head has found no burial plot.
You died by fire for the Domei Bank,
But still your parents owe it a lot.[16]

The picture does not speak for itself; it is ambiguous and needs an interpretation to give it a political and tendentious meaning. For Brecht, it is not enough to be morally indignant about the image; he asks in whose interest Yorick died. The image of horror is transformed into a political statement.

Benjamin's own thought-images are part of his book *One-Way Street,* where the short prose pieces have titles that seem to be lifted from reality, such as "Construction Site," "No. 13," "For Men," "Lost and Found Office." He sketches the physiognomy of places and things and then adds his reflections, which do not explain but rather illuminate the situation and shock the reader into thinking. Bloch was one of the few who reviewed *One-Way Street* and the first to notice the emblematic quality of its prose. He characterized Benjamin as someone who observes and reads the world as if it were a script, a "book of nothing but emblems."[17] Bloch shared with his friend an interest in objects and allegorical narratives that had to be decoded as if they were hieroglyphs. For both, the world was full of traces, which for Benjamin led from the now to promises of the future in the past, while for Bloch they led to a better future.

Now that our stories have a name and a familiar structure, everything seems to be in order. The unfamiliar new forms have been traced back to an old tradition; the new is never as new as it first appears. But is is new nonetheless, for despite formal similarities between emblem and thought-image there are important differences that make the thought-image an expression of modern experience. Emblems make use of a preestablished harmony between image and interpretation; the poet contemplates the meaning that God has inscribed in nature. This harmony cannot be found in thought-images, nor is their imagery based on nature. The material for thought-images is chosen from city life or everyday experiences in a modern society, and it is presented in such manner that tensions and contradictions become apparent. Bloch observes that only such stories make us notice that something is wrong, since we or society are out of balance.[18] Looking back on our examples, we can see how the contradiction within a situation can be amplified by the commentary: the almost idyllic image of a woman sitting in her dark kitchen is contrasted with the necessity of saving money, which—strange to say—helps the rich again.

Thought-images refer to real objects or situations that are produced by man and shaped by society. There is no longer any metaphysical or other emblematic truth hidden behind their appearance, yet they have a social context that has to be explained. When the flaneur/collector discovers these objects, they do not speak immediately; they have to be arranged and interpreted. The problem is very similar to Brecht's observation that a photograph of the AEG factories does not say much about this industrial complex. Pictures say less than the proverb would have it, or, as Benjamin noticed, photorealism can aestheticize even slums and poverty.[19] As we have seen in the case of Brecht's *War Primer*, the images have to be reconstructed, illuminated differently, or just explained by a written commentary (*subscriptio*) to make them emblems of our society that can be read and understood. Thought-images, in contrast to traditional emblems, are concrete objects/situations of a capitalistic society that criticize the social reality they reveal.

It is still not clear what happens between observation and commentary in a thought-image. What mediates between image and thought? With emblems, the mental activity stimulated by the image is contemplation leading to an idea or a moral. With thought-images, readers have to reflect on the true nature of an object or situation (not just accept the appearance); we have to discover their contradictions and criticize them. What we need is a critical theory that can explain why the simple answer by a poor woman in a dark kitchen, "I am saving electricity," is so shocking. A theory is necessary to relate the concrete image to a general concept or to understand the situation of the old woman in the larger context of economic laws (such as ownership of the means of production, working conditions, exploitation, surplus value). The theory that helps decipher the concrete images of capitalist society is called Marxism, and indeed most of the authors who used this prose form are Marxists, of many shades to be sure. This theory criticizes alienated and reified relationships and situations in society, showing that they are historically determined and can therefore be changed. Thought-images, we can now sum up, describe a modern experience, reflect upon it, and return to the experience that is now understood, as the commentary shows. In their best examples thought-images become "dialectical images,"[20] which present, analyze, and grasp a situation in order to change it. Thought-images are not just thought-provoking, they provoke action. Brecht's "Marxist emblems" and Benjamin's "dialectical images" can be considered operative forms that aim at practice. Bloch's *Spuren* belongs to the same genre, even if his stories are sometimes longer and more poetic. The following story (quoted in part) is an ideal example for summarizing the description of the genre:[21]

Forms of Play, Alas

The day wasn't looking very promising.

No money, even Paris gets smaller then. Went into the old workers' pub, there are worse ones that don't cost any less.

But then I saw a man totally engrossed. Having a really good time, innocently, the way it should be. The man opposite me was holding lobster in his worn hands, biting and spitting red shells so that the floor was splattered. But he partook happily of the tender creature inside, once he finally had it, quietly and sensibly.

Here finally was a good no longer disgraced by the bourgeoisie taking their pleasure; the sweat of those who go without, the shame of capital gains was not mingled with the flavor here. Peculiar enough in Paris, where no bourgeois is ashamed of being one, where he not only comfortably but even proudly terms himself a pensioneer. The worker with the lobster awakened other memories as well, of the great breakthrough back then, long ago. Even more, a certain later seemed to start gleaming, when money would no longer bark for goods or wag its tail in them. When we will be spared the thoroughly crazy choice between pure thinking and pure eating.

The situation in the workers' pub is simple enough: a man eats lobster and enjoys it—not much to that. Yet the intellectual who observes and describes him sees it all differently. His commentary not only brings the absent bourgeois into the picture, it also establishes a contradiction between the food of the bourgeoisie and the worker eating it here. The lobster in the stained hands of the worker is, for Bloch, a trace of great things to come. The idyllic moment in the pub becomes transparent for revolutionary history. The worker with the lobster, an emblematic image, reminds Bloch of past revolutions and anticipates a liberated humanity, when there will no longer be a class society based on commodities and money. A tender irony is hidden in the title and the exposition: the critical observer is a displaced intellectual who has to go to a workers' pub because he has no money. There he witnesses a utopian, mouth-watering moment that anticipates his liberation. But alas, this is only a *Spielform*, a form of play!

This story contains everything that is typical for a thought-image: an emblematic structure (title, description, reflection), image and thought mediated by critical theory, and a utopian vision; and yet, one could ask whether this prose is representative of modernism at all. One finds in *Spuren* not only traditional prose forms and allegorical structures but also a conventional narrator and a pragmatic purpose—in short, a closed form with a clear function. What is so modern about it?

MODERNISM WITH PATINA

If Bloch's modernism depended only on his theoretical writings, he could easily be defined as a modernist. His defense of expressionism against Lukács and Kurella, his interest in and writings about surrealism, and his cultural essays in *Legacy of This Era* certainly quality him as one of the leading theoreticians of the "experience of modernity" (Benjamin). But this approach will not do, since it uses the aura of theory to expect or demand modernist prose. As we all know, theorizing well does not guarantee good prose, not even thought-images.

Another approach to defining the modernity of Bloch's texts would be to use the bird's-eye view of the history of ideas. Starting with Schiller's analysis of modern disharmony and alienation, his projected reconciliation, and his theory of modern literature,[22] one could continue with Hegel's skepticism about the possibility of art in modernity: he criticizes the prose of modern life and its abstractness, which make it impossible for the artist to represent the totality of modern experience adequately in art. Philosophy and theory have replaced art, which has become prosaic and partial. But precisely what makes the traditional great art forms a thing of the past (except for the novel) works in favor of the thought-image. Indeed, from this perspective the thought-image can be viewed as the modern form par excellence. It demonstrates the abstractness of life in isolated images and partial situations, and to make sure that the realism of its narrative is properly understood, the theoretical commentary makes the surface of reality transparent by disclosing the underlying social truth. Image, prose, and theory form a dialectical image that makes the prose of life visible and readable. The dilemma of modern art is thus the virtue of the thought-image. But even this legitimation of the thought-image as a modern prose form sounds more convincing in its philosophical abstractness than the textual proof actually is. Therefore we have to go back to the text in order to establish its modernism as a textual quality.

So far we have defined the modernity of thought-images by their emblematic structure, their modern subject matter, and a critical method. But this characterization alone will not suffice to claim Bloch's *Spuren* as a modern text, and there is indeed more sophistication in Bloch's simple stories than meets the untrained eye. To uncover these qualities we have to consider another aspect of Bloch's theory of modernism. Bloch's concept of avant-garde has an aesthetic as well as a political dimension, because it combines new literary techniques with the political interest of the "broad masses." It is very similar to Benjamin's position in his lecture "The Author as Producer" (1934), in which he advanced the radical thesis that "the proper political tendency of a work includes its literary quality."[23] Let us consider this literary quality.

"Truth is concrete." For no other aspect of modern prose does Hegel's *dictum* seem truer than for thought-images. They are based on reality, and their realism is based on theory. The unity of image and thought, the description of an object or situation and reflection about it, guarantees that the reality is interpreted and understood. Only theory and interpretation make reality transparent for truth. Bloch was no friend of documentary literature, be it naturalism or reportage, both of which rely on the immediacy of facts and life. Truly realistic art has to make visible tendencies hidden in reality. To recognize these tendencies, the artist needs what Bloch calls "exact phantasy."[24] Phantasy is the subjective factor that corresponds to the teleological nature of the objective world. The creative process brings out these tendencies; art is *Vor-schein* (pre-appearance) of the real possibility.

These observations are still too general and belong more to the sphere of aesthetics than of poetics. I shall focus now on the modern techniques of which Benjamin speaks in his essay. I have already mentioned that Bloch is in most cases not the author but merely the narrator of found stories. Not unlike Brecht, he changes and transforms the text and material in order to accentuate a new meaning or to demonstrate the possibility of change. For this creative method Bloch coined two verbs, deconstruct and distort (*zerfällen, entstellen*). Modern art and literature distort reality until it is recognizable, which means that they help to understand the underlying truth of society and to discover tendencies that point beyond it.

To demonstrate this modernist technique I have chosen a text from Robert Musil's *Literary Estate While Alive* (1936) that in structure and style comes very close to being a thought-image. "Triedere" (Telescope),[25] as this essayistic narrative is called, describes what happens when we use a telescope to look at things we would not normally observe through a telescope. In this experiment we isolate buildings, things, and people and distort reality beyond recognition. The telescope becomes an "ideological instrument," and the corresponding theory is called "isolation." The normal attitude of looking at things is disrupted and reality loses its contours, its a priori totality. Exposed in this manner, things look strange, alien, and uncanny. We look at reality with new eyes and recognize that its normal, everyday appearance is only one possible side of it. The isolation of things and their distortion produce an alienating effect that is critical and prognostic at the same time. (Bloch may have had something similar in mind when he observed in the preface to *The Principle of Hope* that one needs the strongest telescope to penetrate the presence, the darkness of the lived now. Bloch wants nothing less than to "trieder" time.)[26]

Isolation, fragmentation, and distortion of reality are only one side of modern art, corresponding to another: montage. In the collages of Braque, Picasso, or Schwitters, fragments of authentic life are glued together and challenge the notion of a separation of art and life. Similarly the photomontages of John Heartfield and the "photograms" of Brecht combine picture and text in order to transform the picture and make it readable. Thought-images can be regarded as epic montages; they too combine image and thought in order to decipher the contradictions of reality. *Spuren* as a whole can be read as a montage that brings together things and situations that are far apart and often irreconcilable, as in "Forms of Play, Alas" where a lobster-eating worker, the hat of a bourgeois, and the explosion of a seltzer bottle are read as traces of a revolutionary history that connect the present with the past. One text even uses montage as the theme for a story and contemplates the artistic possibilities of this technique:

The interplay of such an evening is montage, separating the close, bringing together the most distant, just as that appears in such a heightened way in the pictures of the sort drawn by Max Ernst or Chirico. That which is encoded in these things exists there quite objectively, even if the faculty for grasping it more or less accurately is only now awakening, mediated by the social earthquake. Painters, as mentioned, and poets have gone ahead in these lateral connections of things, very broadly spread.[27]

The cross-connections of things and the reading of traces, criss and cross, open up the hollow spaces of reality, discover possibilities and tendencies that otherwise would have been overlooked.

In an essay of 1931, "Poesie im Hohlraum" (Poetry in a Hollow Space), Bloch deals with the disintegration of bourgeois culture and its heritage, and he speaks about the necessary work of a "dialectical avant-garde" that uses this heritage and transforms it for its own purposes.[28] This could be "the birth of utopia out of the spirit of destruction."[29] Among the forms that could be used and transformed, he includes the "subversive fairy tale," the revolutionary use of "pulp novels," "surrealism," and the utopian surplus of distorted masterworks. Of all these forms and techniques, which he used himself in *Spuren,* surrealism seems to be the most interesting, since this style uses the isolation of things (*objets trouvés*) and the montage of fragments as a creative method to disrupt the normal order of things and to take a fresh and critical look at reality. That which has a shocking effect in pictorial/figurative arts is difficult to imitate in literature, yet Bloch believes that there is something like surrealist thinking and writing. In his review of Walter Benjamin's *One-Way Street,* he characterizes the surrealistic perception of the world as consisting of interest in details and fragments, interruption, cross-connection, and improvisation. The whole book is a "montage of fragments," and correspondingly the philosophical interpretations are fragments too. It lies outside the sphere of traditional, systematic philosophy, and Bloch characterizes it as philosophical "improvisation" and "revue." What is missing, he criticizes, is a "concrete intention": "Even one-way streets have a destination."[30] In contrast, Bloch's *Spuren* has a material tendency.

Bloch's concept of the avant-garde includes two elements easily forgotten in the discussion of advanced, highly cultivated modernism: popularity and tendentiousness. "Today the artist can be considered an avant-gardist," he writes, "only if he succeeds in making the new art forms useful for the life and the struggle of the broad masses; otherwise glittering alloy is nothing but old iron. It is wrong to think that the gap between the old avant-garde and the masses is insurmountable."[31] Both tendencies, however mediated, are present in *Spuren*. Bloch's narrative style may be confounded, but at the same time it is spontaneous and has the quality of oral storytelling. His narration leads to thinking, yet his philosophy is neither academic nor esoteric. The political tendency is not as strong as our selection of examples suggests, but the utopian vision is present in most of the stories, if one deciphers the traces correctly.

Finally, thought-images no longer adhere to the principle of autonomy in art. In contrast to poetic images and/or symbols that rest in themselves and stimulate contemplation, thought-images confront the reader with reality and provoke an answer, if not change. Their critical theory and didactic function render the question of disinterested pleasure superfluous.

The important question "Should one act or think?" that makes many practical philosophers blush receives from Bloch a tolerant answer that does not overburden theory:

One can also ask whether the thinker is doing anything at all. He lifts up something of that which exists by writing it. He seeks to make a few things brighter by showing where they're going.[32]

It is not up to philosophers and writers to change the world. To make things dance, nothing less than a revolution would be necessary. Until then, writers are critical observers who describe and interpret the world with the hope of changing it. "Thinking has to open this window," Bloch continues, and maybe this is the proper image for the philosophical observer who was once fascinated by a red window. "This secret window," Bloch concludes, "is the convex lens for the utopian material the earth is made of."[33]

Notes

I would like to thank my colleague Jim Steakley for translating the texts of Bloch and Brecht.

1. Bertolt Brecht, *Gesammelte Werke* (Frankfurt am Main: Suhrkamp, 1967), 5:377.

2. *Ibid.*, 5:389.

3. Theodor W. Adorno, *Noten zur Literaur II* (Frankfurt am Main: Suhrkamp, 1961), 131.

4. Gert Ueding, *Glanzvolles Elend* (Frankfurt am Main: Suhrkamp, 1973), 187.

5. Ernst Bloch, *Literarische Aufsätze* (Frankfurt am Main: Suhrkamp, 1965), 242.

6. Ernst Bloch, *Spuren* (Frankfurt am Main: Suhrkamp, 1969), 63 f.

7. *Ibid.*, 16.

8. Siegfried Kracauer, "Zwei Deutungen in zwei Sprachen," in *Ernst Bloch zu ehren,* ed. Siegfried Unseld (Frankfurt am Main: Suhrkamp, 1965), 146.

9. Bloch, *Spuren,* 17.

10. *Ibid.,* 21.

11. Hans Mayer, "Ernst Blochs poetische Sendung," in *Ernst Bloch zu ehren,* 21–30.

12. Theodor W. Adorno, "Benjamin's 'Einbahnstrasse,'" *Über Walter Benjamin* (Frankfurt am Main: Suhrkamp, 1970), 55.

13. Albrecht Schöne, *Emblematik und Drama im Zeitalter des Barock* (Munich: Beck, 1964), 18–30. See also Heinz Schlaffer, "Denkbilder," in *Poesie und Politik,* ed. Wolfgang Kuttenkeuler (Bonn: Kohlhammer, 1973), 137–54.

14. Walter Benjamin, "Theses on the Philosophy of History," *Illuminations,* ed. Hannah Arendt (New York: Schocken, 1969), 257 f.

15. Bertolt Brecht, *Kriegsfibel* (Berlin: Aufbau, 1955).

16. *Ibid.,* 44.

17. Ernst Bloch, "Erinnerung," in *Über Walter Benjamin: Mit Beiträgen von Th. W. Adorno, E. Bloch, et al.* (Frankfurt am Main: Suhrkamp, 1968), 17.

18. Bloch, *Spuren,* 16.

19. Walter Benjamin, "The Author as Producer," *Reflections,* ed. Peter Demetz (New York: Harcourt Brace Jovanovich, 1978), 229 f.

20. Walter Benjamin, *Schriften I* (Frankfurt am Main: Suhrkamp, 1955), 489.

21. Bloch, *Spuren,* 22 f.

22. Jürgen Habermas, *The Philosophical Discourse of Modernity* (Cambridge: MIT Press, 1987), 45–50.

23. Benjamin, "Author as Producer," 221.

24. Bloch, *Literarische Aufsätze,* 137.

25. Robert Musil, *Prosa, Dramen, späte Briefe,* ed. Adolf Frisé (Reinbek: Rowohlt, 1957), 492 ff.

26. Ernst Bloch, *Das Prinzip Hoffnung* (Frankfurt am Main: Suhrkamp, 1973), 1:11.

27. Bloch, *Spuren,* 167.

28. *Ibid.,* 133.

29. Ernst Bloch, *Erbschaft dieser Zeit* (Frankfurt am Main: Suhrkamp, 1973), 371.

30. Ernst Bloch, *Vom Hasard zur Katastrophe* (Frankfurt am Main: Suhrkamp, 1972), 324.

31. Bloch, *Spuren,* 202.

32. *Ibid.,* 71 f.

33. *Ibid.*

Walter Benjamin's Collector: The Fate of Modern Experience

Ackbar Abbas

COLLECTOR AND MODERNIST

(1)

Is it possible that the largely dated figure of the collector has anything to tell us about the experience of modernity? Walter Benjamin, himself a passionate collector, has this to say: "The figure of the collector, more attractive the longer one observes it, has not been given its due attention so far. One would imagine no figure more tempting to the romantic storytellers. The type is motivated by dangerous though domesticated passions."[1] This is a provocative characterization of the collector, which places him in a paradoxical social space: one that is dangerous and domesticated at the same time. It is, as we shall see, the social space of modernity. For if the romantic storytellers have neglected the collector, modern writers have not. From Flaubert onwards, a number of literary, philosophical, anthropological, and art historical texts—not least of which are Benjamin's own writings—focus attention on the collector figure, specifically in its relation to modernity. It is as if collector and modernist, two social metaphors, were tied together, back to back, all the more strongly for the ties being negative ones.

(2)

Two contemporary texts introduce the difficult relations between collector and modernist: John Fowles's *The Collector* and Lévi-Strauss's remarks on the film version of the novel. In Fowles's novel,[2] the collector is a lonely and uneducated young man, Frederick Clegg, who abducts a sophisticated and beautiful art student, Miranda Gray. Miranda is an advocate of modernity. "I love, I adore *my* age" (24), she writes in her diary. Her chief strategy for freeing herself is to educate Frederick and to bring him up to date with the modern world: "We'll make you into someone really modern. Someone really interesting to meet" (91). Modernism sees itself as enlightenment capable of containing the mythic chthonic violence of the collector's destructive passion. The opposition between modernist and collector is emblematic of the opposition between enlightenment and myth, that is, of myth as a form of reversion to the past that does violence to modern life.

Complications in the text disturb without developing this simple opposition. For example, in the relation between captor and captive, it is the captor who is diffident and differential, and the captive who is demanding and domineering. Running parallel to Frederick's physical violence is the equally palpable violence of Miranda's modernist discourse. Miranda's "education" of Frederick consists largely of her referring to books he has not read, pictures he has not seen, facts he does not know. In its opposition to the violence produced by retrogressive myth, modernism too becomes violent and imbricated in its own myth: in Fowles's novel, modernism is not an agent of enlightenment but a mode of domination. Miranda's rejection of the collector figure is as clichéd as her criticism of photography: "When you draw something it lives and when you photograph it it dies" (58).

Lévi-Strauss's response to the William Wyler film version of the novel is a covert defense of the collector against the modernist. It comes in a passage where Lévi-Strauss is voicing his disappointment with Picasso and modern art. The story, Lévi-Strauss writes, gives "a complete reversal of an authentic value system . . . the healthy attitude—forgetting about legality—is rather that of the hero who reserves his passion for real objects . . . whereas the very symbol of the artificial contemporary taste is illustrated by the heroine, who for her part, lives only through art books."[3] Here Lévi-Strauss presents modernism as enlightenment gone wrong. It went wrong at the moment when it began to lose touch with "real objects," with nature; and when in the experimentations of modern art it went in pursuit of chimerical forms of knowledge and experience.

Lévi-Strauss's critique of modernism can be related to his own study of myth, which can be regarded as an attempt to preserve modes of knowledge and experience that are in danger of disappearing. That is why he believes that anthropology could with advantage be re- named "entropology." In his critique of modernism, the myth of en- lightenment is replaced by the enlightenment of myth. However, it is a critique that simply repeats, in reversed form, the sterile opposi- tions—between knowledge and experience, the critical and the dog- matic, freedom and coercion—that appear when modernist and col- lector confront each other in Fowles's novel. We shall have to look elsewhere for more productive ways of situating the collector.

(3)

A different way of approaching the relation between the collector and modernism is to give an account of the conditions that led to the collector's arrival on the historical scene. Two such accounts, both written in the thirties, may be mentioned. One is by the art historian Martin Wackernagel and the other is by Walter Benjamin.[4]

Wackernagel studies the rise of the collector in relation to changing patterns of patronage in Renaissance Florence. He shows that the collector is a new historical type that is clearly distinguishable from the patron, as well as an index of the changing social conditions of artistic production. The older generation of patrons, on the one hand, ordered an art object "that appears desirable and necessary for a par- ticular place in a church space or in their own house"; the collector, on the other hand, is interested in the artwork "for itself on account of its creator, its particular artistic qualities, or other noteworthy characteristics."[5] In other words, with the collector's appearance, whether as cause or as effect, the art object begins to lose its root- edness in place and prepares itself for its future career on an art mar- ket of potential buyers.

Moreover, Wackernagel shows that the rise of the collector was possible only because certain documented changes in social attitudes toward art and artists had already occurred. As E. H. Gombrich puts it, "The emergence of a deliberate patronage of 'art' . . . is impos- sible without the idea of 'art.'"[6] These changes include: the gradual separation of a realm of "art" from "craft"; the shift in social status of the artist, from "servant" to "genius"; the artist's aspiration toward emancipation from patronage; and finally, the development of a doctrine of the autonomy of art, which served as justification for valuing art objects for their own sake. These changes would seem to give Renaissance Florence some of the key features of societal and aesthetic modernity, with which the rise of the collector is correlated.

Indeed, Wackernagel's view of Renaissance Florence is not only that it has produced the modern but that it should remain the *model* for the modern. His book ends with the dubious plea that the conditions of Renaissance Florence that "produced" so much great art should be duplicated today, as they constitute almost "an ideal picture of desirable artistic conditions in general."[7] This is where the limits of Wackernagel's historical approach become apparent. His approach, because it is fixated on an "ideal picture," can situate neither the collector nor modernity.

By contrast, Benjamin's account of the social conditions that produced the collector differs from Wackernagel's not only in that he focuses on a different time and place—Paris in the nineteenth century instead of Florence in the fifteenth—but also, and more important, in the way he reads cultural history. Wackernagel studies the collector from the point of view of art history; Benjamin studies art history from the point of view of the collector.

We can pick up Benjamin's account of the collector in the section of his exposé of the Arcades Project entitled "Louis-Philippe or the Interior."[8] Under the rule of Louis-Philippe begins the momentous division of life into private and public spheres. A new and ambivalent social space emerges. There is a spatial division into the living space and the place of work, or the interior and the office. Corresponding to this spatial division is a psychic division: the office is where the private citizen takes "reality" into account, while what he requires of the interior is that "it should support him in his illusions" (*CB*, 167). In the interior, the private citizen takes refuge, suppressing both social and business preoccupations. "From this sprang the phantasmagorias of the interior" (*CB*, 167). In the anonymity and privatization of the interior, and without the high social profile of the Renaissance collectors, the modern collector now appears: the etui man. "The interior was the place of refuge of Art. The collector was the true inhabitant of the interior" (*CB*, 168).

What is the collector's relation to objects in the interior? On the one hand, he hides behind objects, glorifies them, *fetishizes* them; he succumbs, Benjamin says, to "the sex-appeal of the inorganic" (*CB*, 166). The "phantasmagoria of the interior" derives therefore from what Lukács calls "a *specific* problem of our age," the problem of commodity fetishism.[9] On the other hand, the collector is engaged exactly in a struggle *against* universal commodification. His possession of objects strips things of their commodity character; but, Benjamin immediately adds, it is a "task of Sisyphus." The collector confers on objects "only a fancier's value, rather than use-value" (*CB*, 168). In other words, the collector saves objects only by turning them into Art. In the process, however, art turns into mere objects of contemplation; hence the uneasy relation between art and commodity fetishism.[10] One illustration of this point is provided by the history of Taste.

As Benjamin presents it, the history of Taste is not a history of the progressive refinement of the human sensorium.[11] Benjamin links Taste surprisingly with the history of commodity production. The importance of Taste increases in direct proportion to the consumer's *declining* awareness of the commodity's social and technical conditions of production, that is, the less one knows about a product, the more important Taste becomes. Taste is a highly ambiguous response to the commodity. On the one hand, it bathes the commodity in a "profane glow"; on the other hand, Taste is a "more or less elaborate masking" of the consumer's "lack of expertness" (*CB*, 105). The collector's relation to objects cannot but be affected by this history of Taste.

Finally, Benjamin links this problematic of Taste and certain attitudes to language. Thus together with the interior, commodity fetishism, and Taste, language makes up the forth and perhaps the most ambiguous element that situates the collector for Benjamin. "In *l'art pour l'art*," he writes, "the poet for the first time faces language the way the buyer faces the commodity on the open market. He has lost his familiarity with the process of its production to a particularly high degree" (*CB*, 105). In this quotation on language, "production" refers of course to *sign-production*. The type of poet Benjamin is describing operates in a linguistic field where signifiers generate only other signifiers in an infinite but closed series. There is nothing urgent enough to require the *coining* of words; it is simply a matter of choosing among words that are already there in accordance with the poet's taste. A "literature without an object," a *poésie pure,* now appears, to find its culmination in Mallarmé. It is as if poets like Mallarmé go to language in order to *lose* the object. What should be noted here is again the nuanced way in which the esoteric poet, like the collector, is seen: Benjamin is arguing that a "literature without an object" can be at the same time a sign of the poet's *unawareness* of his class position and a sign of his *repudiation* of the causes of his own class (*CB,* 106). Esoteric poet and collector resemble each other in that both inhabit an ambiguous social space.

(4)

Thus, while Wackernagel traced the rise of the collector in a heroic era, Benjamin describes his survival in an era of little deeds. However, in Benjamin the anonymity of the collector is balanced by the near ubiquity of the type: in an age where public and private spheres remain so clearly separated, everyone is more or less a collector. We shall have to return to Benjamin's account of the collector later. For the moment, it is worth trying to see how the ambiguity of the collector figure can be used as a way of reading a number of the canonic texts of literary modernism, in each of which the collector figure makes a brief but dramatic appearance. In every case, the figure's ambiguity threatens to subvert the text's major assumptions.

Consider the relation between collecting and writing in Flaubert's *Bouvard and Pecuchet.* In chapter 4, the eponymous heroes are represented briefly as collectors. They assemble a collection of phallic symbols:

At one time towers, pyramids, candles, mile-posts, and even trees had the significance of Phalluses—and for Bouvard and Pecuchet everything became a phallus. They collected the swing-bars of carriages, legs of arm-chairs, cellar bolts, chemists' pestles. When anyone came to see them, they asked: "What do you think that's like?"—then confided the mystery; and if the visitor protested, they shrugged their shoulders pityingly.[12]

Here the novel parodies the naïve illusions of the collector. The more specific the classification—in this case, "phallic symbols"—the more the heterogeneity of things becomes manifest. The collector is confronted by fragments that are impossible to arrange into any conceptual or temporal order. Cultural history is unwittingly revealed as a history of ruin, randomness, and disorder.

Yet there is something unconsciously ironic about Flaubert's critique of collecting when one thinks about Flaubert's own mystique of writing. For Flaubert, as *Bouvard and Pecuchet* shows, it is no longer "fine writing" that the modern writer is concerned with but resistance to the temptations of fine writing. From this perspective, the self-conscious writer is not so different from the naïve collector: he too tries to make something out of the rubbish-heaps of history, turning compositions out of compost. Collector and modern writer, the parodied and parodist, are in fact engaged in the same impossible enterprise. The collector is not the modern writer's antithesis, but a poor disreputable relative, a Cousin Pons. What Flaubert's textual practice entails, almost as a necessity of its production, is the suppression through parody of the collector.

It is appropriate therefore that *Bouvard and Pecuchet* begins and ends (as Flaubert's notes show) with "copying." Copying, it turns out, is like collecting, in the sense that it is not a simple antithesis of "writing" but a caricatural double of it. The copyist is the true saint of modern literature. Bouvard and Pecuchet will aspire to copying again after they have reached a point when they have "no more interest in life."[13] A "literature without an object" now comes into view. In Flaubert, the self-conscious modern writer, unable to criticize himself, criticizes two caricatures of himself, the copyist and the collector.

Nietzsche's second essay in his *Untimely Meditations* of 1874, entitled "On the Uses and Disadvantages of History for Life," also has a portrait of the collector. This portrait is a striking grotesquerie that comes in the course of his discussion of "antiquarian history." Nietzsche speaks there of "the repulsive spectacle of a blind rage for collecting, a restless raking together of everything that has ever existed. Man is encased in the stench of must and mould; through the antiquarian approach he succeeds in reducing even a more creative disposition, a nobler desire, to an insatiable thirst for novelty, or rather for antiquity and for all and everything; often he sinks so low that in the end he is content to gobble down any food whatever, even the dust of bibliographical minutiae."[14] This presentation of collecting and antiquarian history as pathological is just a specific instance of Nietzsche's criticism of "historical culture" in general: historical culture is not "real culture," but only a "kind of knowledge of culture" (78). In the essay, Nietzsche's major criticism of "we moderns" is that *knowledge is pursued without relation to real needs.* Knowledge therefore becomes abstract, reified, and loses its transformative ability, that is, it cannot "serve life."

Scattered through the essay are a number of anatomies of such modern types, all of whom can be implicitly related to Nietzsche's collector. These are all figures of alienation: the art connoisseur, whose "hatred of the great and powerful of their own age is disguised as satiated admiration for the great and powerful of past ages" (72); the "walking encyclopedias," whose empty heads are crammed with dead knowledge (79); the cultural tourists who "race through art galleries and listen to concerts"—"pleased with everything" (98); the epigones, born gray-haired, who live out an ironic existence as "antiquarians and gravediggers" (104); and finally, the summation of all the above, the educated barbarian, "the historical-aesthetic cultural philistine" (117).

If historical culture, where the collector is placed, is responsible for the pathology of modernity, then the first step toward a cure would involve a critique of history. Yet Nietzsche's elaboration of such a critique, like Flaubert's elaboration of the aesthetic, implicitly requires us to rethink the position of the collector. The critique comes in its most powerful form in a late section of the essay, where the nineteenth-century fascination with history, a legacy from Hegel, is revealed as nothing more than "a naked admiration of success," as well as an idolization of the power of the status quo. Nietzsche insists therefore that "greatness ought not to depend on success" (113). In other words, there is a history other than that written by the victors. But Nietzsche does not just argue the case that history does not serve life; he also argues the case that certain modes of life *deform* history. Such a revaluation of history now casts a new light on the activity of collecting. What Nietzsche had called the antiquarian's lack of "discrimination of value" and "sense of proportion" (74) can now be seen not just as the antiquarian preservation of a dead past but also as the collector's *recovery* of all the objects and values that have failed to "make it" historically. In Nietzsche as in Flaubert, two exemplars of modernity, the dismissed figure of the collector returns unrecognized to haunt the argument.

Conrad's *Lord Jim* gives us a much more attractive portrait of the collector in the figure of Stein. Midway through the narrative, Marlow goes to visit Stein to ask his advice on Jim's case. This Stein has been many things—revolutionary, adventurer, merchant—but we see him chiefly in his latest role as a "learned collector," whose collection of beetles and butterflies—what Marlow the noncollector calls "a few bushels of dead insects"[15]—has made him famous. The scene is structured like a medical consultation, and it ends with the collector's diagnosis of Jim—"He is romantic"—and the famous prescription—"to the destructive element submit yourself." However, when Stein tries to explain in a more discursive mode "the destructive element," he ends in confusion. What then is the collector's own relation to the destructive element?

When Marlow visits Stein, he finds him absorbed in his collection and in writing up his descriptive catalogue. "I respected the intense, almost passionate, absorption with which he looked at the butterfly, as though on the bronze sheen of these frail wings . . . he could see other things, an image of something as perishable and defying destruction as these delicate and lifeless tissues" (158). Stein tells Marlow how he caught the specimen on a day of great personal fulfillment: "On that day, I had nothing to desire" (161). Yet this autobiographical fragment of Stein's reads like a cautionary tale: we learn immediately that friend, wife, child, and victory over his enemies, the sources of his fulfillment, are taken away as easily as a match blown out by the wind. Only the butterfly remains, the collector's treasured object. Is the butterfly treasured because its perfection consoles the collector for what has been lost? Or does the butterfly, on the contrary, serve to remind the collector that human and natural history follow very different courses? Lévi-Strauss once said that we should study men as if they were ants. Against Lévi-Strauss, Stein the collector never forgets that entomology is not anthropology, and that fulfillment and perfection are not necessarily the end products of human history.

Though Conrad gives the collector a positive role, the collector in *Lord Jim* is nevertheless an ambiguous figure. For all his collector's wisdom, Stein is not more adept at dealing with the destructive element than Jim himself. In the novel, action and reflection remain mutually exclusive. On the one hand, action is blind, the result typically of a sense of duty or a fixed code of conduct. On the other hand, reflection is purely negative, producing not solutions but dissolutions—witness the confident Brierly's mysterious suicide. Caught in between, experience is simply benumbing. In *Lord Jim,* the collector is ultimately an isolated choral figure, stammering conundrums on the sidelines of history.

EXPERIENCE IN MODERNITY

(1)

As modernists, Flaubert, Nietzsche, and Conrad underline, though less tendentiously than Fowles, the "dangerous though domesticated passions" of the collector. In Flaubert, it is the danger of a classification that reduces the heterogeneity of experience; in Nietzsche, it is the threat of knowledge being increasingly reified and so losing its ability to "serve life"; in Conrad, it is the ironic spectacle of the collector's object of desire producing a narrative of desire whose theme is the impossibility of desire being fulfilled. These texts may be taken to be representative of a certain direction in modernism, where an intense longing for experience goes together with an even more intense suspicion that authentic experience under modern conditions is somehow not available. The figure of the collector focuses and exacerbates these tensions in modernism: even when rejected the collector figure cannot be quite dismissed. Adorno, another anti-collector, makes some paradoxical remarks in *Minima Moralia* that could be read as a kind of oblique commentary on the texts we have been considering so far. In a section entitled "Auction," he deals in passing with the vicious dialectic of collecting and concludes with the following sentences: "What beauty still flourishes under terror is a mockery and ugliness to itself. Yet its fleeting shape attests to the avoidability of terror. Something of this paradox is fundamental to all art; today it appears in the fact that art still exists at all. The captive idea of beauty strives at once to reject happiness and to assert it."[16]

Adorno's remarks, though they deal only with the emancipatory potential of art and not that of collecting, can with a slight shift of emphasis suggest how Benjamin sees the collector figure. While Adorno, like other modernists, sees an antithesis between art and collecting, Benjamin sees a homology: collecting too is at once an attempt to avoid experience and to confront it. In this sense the collector figure is not merely dangerous but also "more attractive the longer one observes it." It is as if the whole complex question of experience in modernity were somehow hidden in the folds of the collector figure, waiting to be uncovered.

To uncover the full implications of the collector figure, one has to follow certain methodological procedures. Benjamin's point of departure, what he calls "the materialist method," is "the object riddled with error . . . and [the materialist method] cannot present this object as mixed or uncritical enough" (CB, 103). Hence, Benjamin's figure of the collector is not a Florentine prince like Lorenzo de' Medici, or his modern avatars, the princes of industry; rather, it is the traumatized, privatized, and impotent individual, the etui man of the interior. Benjamin's reflections on the fate of modern experience are closely related to the *transformation* of this poor figure of the collector. It is necessary therefore to examine Benjamin's category of experience as a way of situating the rest of the discussion on Benjamin's collector figure.

(2)

Experience is a central but complicated category in Benjamin. Some of its complexities can be seen in his important essay "Some Motifs in Baudelaire." This essay starts off with the deceptively simple question: Why do modern readers find lyric poetry difficult to read? This could only be because lyric poetry is no longer in rapport with modern readers' experience, which suggests therefore that the structure of their experience has changed. Benjamin goes on to formulate the nature of this change as follows: what characterizes modern experience is its inability to assimilate the experience of modernity. This is the paradox of the modern also alluded to in the texts of Flaubert, Nietzsche, and Conrad; the difference is that Benjamin formulates the paradox only as a first step to unraveling it.

In his discussion of Bergson, he shows that Bergson's "philosophy of life" attempts to lay hold of "true" experience, in a situation where experience is becoming increasingly standardized and denatured, by making the important connection between experience and the structure of memory. It is memory that makes true experience possible, and memory itself is not so much a collection of isolated facts as it is the site of a convergence of "accumulated and frequently unconscious data" (*CB*, 110). However, the problem with Bergson's approach, as Benjamin sees it, is that it is unhistorical: his project of laying hold of experience proceeded by shutting out the most important experience of all, the experience of "the inhospitable and blinding age of big-scale industrialism" (*CB*, 111). As a result, Bergson does not give us any *image* of modern experience, but something quite different. "In shutting out this experience," Benjamin writes, "the eye perceives an experience of a complementary nature in the form of its spontaneous after-image" (*CB*, 111). Bergson is one example of a curious modern phenomenon: an obsession with authentic experience going together with an inability to assimilate it.

What of experience in Proust? Proust takes over Bergson's placement of experience in memory, not in nature; but he introduces an important distinction within memory itself, distinguishing between voluntary and involuntary memory. What Bergson called the *mémoire pure* is now Proust's *mémoire involontaire,* while voluntary memory is placed in the service of the intellect. The difference between the two modes of memory is the subject of the first part of Proust's novel. The narrator's conscious attempts to recall his childhood at Combray proved to be futile; but the taste of the madeleine dipped in tea vividly summoned back the past to him. Proust therefore concludes that the past is "somewhere beyond the reach of the intellect, and unmistakeably present in some material object (or in the sensation which such an object arouses in us), though we have no idea which one it is. As for that object, it depends entirely on chance whether we come upon it before we die or whether we never encounter it" (*CB*, 112).

Involuntary memory summoned up by some material object is then Proust's way of taking hold of experience. There are suggestive parallels here with the activity of collecting, especially if we remember that both Swann and Marcel's grandmother are interested in collecting.[17] However, the point to stress now is that Proust also says that the availability of the right object, and hence of experience, depends entirely on chance. For Benjamin, however, chance cannot be a satisfactory basis for experience: "It is by no means inevitable to be dependent on chance in this matter. Man's inner concerns do not have their issueless private character by nature" (*CB*, 112). What Proust perceives as chance needs therefore to be historicized. Benjamin does this by referring to Freud's concept of shock defense in *Beyond the Pleasure Principle*. Freud is used to psychologize and also to historicize Proust's concept of involuntary memory.

The essential point Benjamin derives from Freud is that, in any individual psyche, becoming conscious and leaving behind memory traces are not compatible with each other; or to put this in Proustian terms, only what has *not* been experienced consciously and explicitly can become memory. If consciousness is no longer receptive to experience, what does it do? It protects against stimuli, defends the psyche against shock. When shock defense as a response to experience has become the norm, experience not only becomes incommunicable, resulting in silence and privatization; it also splits up into two kinds. Benjamin distinguishes between, on the one hand, specific experiences lived through, and assigned a precise point in time by consciousness and held there, which he calls *Erlebnis*; and, on the other hand, experiences that have managed to enter memory and are not located at specific moments in time, which he calls *Erfahrung*.

We see now why experience is so difficult to lay hold of: it follows a very involved path, crossed by many false trails. The path to experience first leads off into memory, which bifurcates into voluntary and involuntary memory, ending with the concept of experience itself being split into two. But though the path is labyrinthine, it is still negotiable, and writers like Proust and Baudelaire succeed in negotiating it, hence their importance for Benjamin. He concedes that both writers bear the marks of an age of the isolated individual, starved of all but sterile experiences. Under the sway of the age, Proust was led to postulate an absolute split between voluntary and involuntary memory, and spoke of recovery of the past as a matter of chance. However, Proust's activity as a writer shows that even involuntary memory can be summoned up by a practice or a ritual—of the image, of storytelling—and this changes its nature. In this way, Benjamin says, voluntary and involuntary recollection "lose their mutual exclusiveness" (*CB*, 113) and chance loses its supremacy. Similarly, Baudelaire's writing clearly registers shock experience. His poetry has a large measure of consciousness and moments of *fright* that mark the points where the shock defense has been breached; but Benjamin concludes that Baudelaire's poetry manages to give what has been lived through (*Erlebnis*) the weight of an experience (*Erfahrung*) (*CB*, 154).

(3)

Benjamin works out the category of experience through discussion of writers like Proust and Baudelaire. These writers in their artistic practices managed to find a way through to experience. What of the activity of collecting? Benjamin's argument, as I shall now try to show, is that certain practices of collecting, like certain textual practices, are alternative means of laying hold of experience in modernity. In his presentation of the collector figure, Benjamin sometimes plays with the note of nostalgia, but his argument is not a nostalgic one. Furthermore, it should be noted that the implications of collecting come out not only in the few essays and fragments that directly address themselves to the subject but also obliquely in the whole range of Benjamin's literary and philosophical essays. The crucial question, however, is the following: can collecting and writing as cultural practices really be compared? It seems that in Benjamin's essays some definite comparisons between writing and collecting can indeed be reconstructed. I shall focus on three major areas of comparison.

The first such area centers on the concept of *possession*. It concerns the relation of the writer to the image and the collector's relation to the object: the writer possesses experience through the image, the collector through ownership of the object.

Benjamin argues for the importance of the image to the writer in an essay on Proust,[18] the details of which we shall have to forgo. In this essay, Benjamin traces a trajectory that leads from Proust's "frenzied quest for happiness" (*Ill.*, 205), through memory, boredom, dream, and resemblances, to the image: "Proust could not get his fill of emptying the dummy, his self, at one stroke in order to keep garnering that third thing, the image" (*Ill.*, 207). The image shows the way back to experience and allows "the true surrealist face of existence" (*Ill.*, 207) to break through.

What is the nature of the literary image? It is important to see that for Benjamin the image does not establish identities but produces similarities. This is true of the Proustian image as well as of the Baudelairean image. In "A Berlin Chronicle," Benjamin states that no image satisfies Proust. This is because the Proustian image is an image that, like a fan, can be unfolded "and only in its folds does the truth reside."[19] The image does not fix experience but allows it to unfold, as memory itself is unfolded. Another example: in "A Berlin Chronicle," the city of Paris is an important image; but Paris is an image of straying, or better still, *the image-as-straying*. "Not to find one's way in a city may well be uninteresting and banal. . . . But to lose oneself in a city . . . that calls for a different schooling. . . . Paris taught me this art of straying" (R, 8–9). Benjamin's autobiographical fragment itself, we note, is contructed out of street images.

While the Proustian image is structurally analogous to memory, the Baudelairean or dialectical image is in counterpoint to it. The dialectical image intermingles the new with the old (R, 148). It is not an unfolding image but a static one. Statis is the result of being pushed in different directions by the ambiguities of the age. "Ambiguity," Benjamin writes, "is the pictorial image of dialectics, the law of dialectics seen at a standstill. This standstill is utopia and the dialectical image therefore a dream image" (R, 157). Because it is frozen in time and dream, the dialectical image interrupts the flow of consciousness and removes itself from experience as *Erlebnis*. The significant moments in Baudelaire are "days of recollection, not marked by any experience" (CB, 139). Thus in Baudelaire it is by means of the dialectical image that *Erlebnis* is transformed into *Erfahrung*.

Different though the image in Proust and in Baudelaire is in its constitution, there is a similarity in one respect: no image satisfies Baudelaire either. His is preeminently an allegorical art. Benjamin follows André Gide in observing that there is "a very calculated disharmony between the image and the object" (CB, 98) in Baudelaire. "His images are original by virtue of the inferiority of the objects of comparison" (CB, 99). In Baudelaire, as in Proust, it is precisely the "calculated disharmony" put into play by a specific practice of the image that allows the image to be a means of coming into possession of experience, and so avoiding the sterilities of an imageless world.

The writer's relation to the image is important too because it suggests a way of explaining the rather puzzling matter of how Benjamin sees the collector's relation to objects. In the essay "Unpacking My

Library," Benjamin says that "for the collector . . . ownership is the most intimate relationship that one can have to objects" (*Ill.*, 67). It is as if under certain conditions, the experience of possession could be transformed into the possession of experience. How is this transformation achieved? For Benjamin, such a transformation is achieved by *rethinking the nature of ownership*. Like the literary image, ownership has its subtler aspects. For example, analyzing how books come into the collector's possession, Benjamin speaks about the collector's "tactical instinct" (*Ill.*, 63). The tactics for acquisition include borrowing books and not returning them; or systematically failing to read them; or inheriting them. Even the most obvious means of acquiring books, buying them, has its tactics, which differ when one buys at bookstores, or from catalogues, or at auctions. But "the most praise-worthy method" of acquiring books is "writing them oneself" (*Ill.*, 61). Beneath the whimsicality, then, possession becomes a matter not of contingency but of strategy. A second aspect of ownership that Benjamin stresses is the importance of the "personal owner": "[T]he phenomenon of collecting loses its meaning as it loses its personal owner. Even though public collections may be less objectionable socially and more useful academically than private collections, the objects get their due only in the latter" (*Ill.*, 67). Benjamin is not, however, elaborating an ideology of the private self here. He makes the same point in the essay on Fuchs, and there he adds an explanation: "The collector's passion is his divining rod and turns him into a finder of new sources" ("Fuchs," 250). That passion led Fuchs to study "scorned and apocryphal matters" ("Fuchs," 252) such as caricature, pornography, and the problematics of "mass art." These two aspects of ownership can now be compared to the writer's use of the image. Ownership is firstly a question of strategy, of allowing a process to unfold; secondly, it is an interruption: not in the sense that the private owner takes objects out of circulation but in the sense that he takes objects that *are* out of circulation and confronts cultural history with them.

Cultural history provides a second area of comparison between writer and collector. Both mount a critique of cultural history as the unproblematic accumulation of "treasures" from the past.[20] There is a convenient figure in Baudelaire that combines the attitude of writer and collector to cultural history: this is the figure of the *chiffonnier*, the ragpicker. Of this figure, Baudelaire writes: "Here we have a man who has to gather the day's refuse in the capital city. Everything that the big city threw away, everything it lost, everything it despised, everything it crushed underfoot, he catalogues and collects" (*CB*, 79). Benjamin calls this description "an extended metaphor for the procedure of the poet in Baudelaire's spirit" (*CB*, 80). We must not understand Baudelaire's description in a pathetic sense. What is implied by the ragpicker figure is a view of culture that places "master-pieces" back within the historical conditions, often bloody, that make them possible. Culture cannot afford to forget the underside of culture, though what is passed on as culture is established very much on the basis of such a forgetting. This is why Proust's literary activity effects a paradoxical reversal: it *begins* with a forgetting (*Ill.*, 204). It contests culture as a forgetting by a forgetting of culture. Benjamin's comment on "The Destructive Character" provides a gloss on Proust and cultural activity in general: "[H]ow immensely the world is simplified," he writes, "when tested for its worthiness of destruction" (*R*, 301).

The collector's relationship to cultural history is defined by his concern for the fate of the object, yet such a concern too has its "destructive" side. What is the object's fate? Benjamin writes that "for a true collector the whole background of an item adds up to a magic encyclopedia whose quintessence is the fate of his object" (*Ill.*, 60). In the essay on Fuchs, this "whole background" that makes up the object's fate is specified as the historical conditions of production and reception of the object, its "pre- as well as post-history" ("Fuchs," 226). By contrast, cultural history fetishizes the art object, and so isolates it from its "fate." That is why the collector is opposed to it. "For cultural history," Benjamin concludes, "lacks the destructive element . . . cultural history, to be sure, enlarges the weight of the treasure which accumulates on the back of humanity. Yet cultural history does not provide the strength to shake off this burden in order to be able to take control of it" ("Fuchs," 234). Only a different kind of historical consciousness , "a consciousness of the present which explodes the continuum of history" ("Fuchs," 227), could turn the past from a burden to a possession, and so ensure its transmissibility.

This brings us to a third area of comparison between writer and collector, which involves exactly the question of the transmissibility or communicability of experience. Here the focus seems to fall not on the allegorists Proust and Baudelaire but on the relation between the storyteller Nikolai Leskov and collecting. As the collector is concerned not to reify the art object, so the storyteller is concerned not to reify the story. Storytelling does not aim "to convey the pure essence of the thing, like information or a report. It sinks the thing into the life of the storyteller, in order to bring it out of him again. Thus traces of the storyteller cling to the story the way the handprints of the potter cling to the clay vessel" (Ill., 91–92) and, we might add, the way marks of the collector cling to the object. Storytelling is a medium in both senses of the word, as is collecting.

What we find here is not nostalgia for the "handmade" in a prefabricated world. Benjamin realizes of course that traditional storytelling is an artisan mode of communication that thrived under certain social conditions that have now largely disappeared. There is no question of reviving storytelling in its traditional form in spite of remarks about seeing "a new beauty in what is vanishing" (Ill., 87). What storytelling represents rather is a mode of communication in touch with experience, and the question is whether similar modes of communication are still available. An answer may be suggested by noting that what Benjamin says about Leskov is not so different from what he says about Proust and Baudelaire. As Benjamin presents it, storytelling as a mode of communication is not opposed to allegory, to which it is in fact quite close, but to information. For example, a storyteller is described as someone who has "counsel" for his readers; but counsel is seen as "less an answer to a question than a proposal concerning the continuation of a story which is just unfolding. To seek this counsel one would first have to be able to tell the story" (Ill., 86). "Story" here is not unlike the unfolding image. Similarly, the contrast between the mode of information and the mode of storytelling is analogous to the contrast between consciousness and memory: information is shot through with explanation and does not survive the moment when it is new, while the story arouses astonishment and thoughtfulness and is open to interpretation and renewal.

Can collecting too be regarded as "a way of telling," a way of transmitting experience through objects rather than through verbal language? Benjamin describes the collector's attitude to his possessions as stemming from "an owner's sense of responsibility toward his property. Thus it is, in the highest sense, the attitude of an heir, and the most distinguished trait of a collection will always be its transmissibility" (*Ill.*, 66). The idea of "responsibility" provides the important link between storytelling and collecting. Unlike information, storytelling is a responsible mode of discourse in that it can proceed in response to the listener's questions. It has an improvisatory air. The relation of storyteller to story is not one of mastery. Similarly, the collector responds to objects and in this way opens them up to interpretation. Objects acquire a history and become the material means by which this history is passed on. In "The Destructive Character," Benjamin writes: "Some pass things down to posterity, by making them untouchable and thus conserving them, others pass on situations, by making them practicable and thus liquidating them. The latter are called the destructive" (*R*, 302). Benjamin's collector finally steps out of the etui of the interior, emerging as "the destructive character."

(4)

To summarize the direction of the argument so far: In Benjamin, the collector is a deeply paradoxical figure. He is a modern figure who stands in opposition to some of the dominant tendencies of modernity. In a situation where experience is difficult to lay hold of, the collector, like the writer, manages to find a way through to it. The collector, one is almost tempted to say, has the capacity to articulate experience, to give experience a language. The question that must now be raised is how such a positive account of the collector can be squared with Benjamin's views on language. For example, the following chilling sentence from his essay on translation seems to put a limit to the possibilities of communication: "No poem is intended for the reader, no picture for the beholder, no symphony for the listener" (*Ill.*, 69). My concluding remarks will deal with the relation between the collector and Benjamin's philosophy of language and will try to show how collecting can offer a perspective on language as well as on history and modernity.

The sentence from Benjamin is quoted by Paul de Man in his last lecture, which takes as its text Benjamin's essay on translation.[21] It is the starting point of a highly intriguing reading that understands Benjamin's text as saying that it is impossible to translate. De Man develops this reading by showing the errors, often surprisingly elementary ones, that highly competent translators make when they translate a text on translation. What these errors of the translators show, de Man argues, is not their lack of linguistic competence or the fact that translation is necessarily secondary, hence imperfect, in relation to the original. Their errors reveal that there was always already something impure in the language of the original itself. A translation may "disarticulate the original" only to find that "the original was always already disarticulated" (de Man, 36). In other words, errancy belongs not only to the translation but also to language itself. As translation gives us no true image of the original, so language gives us no true image of things. Language, de Man understands Benjamin to be saying, is a field of permanent disjunctions, where we find a necessary "nonadequation of symbol to a shattered symbolized" (de Man, 44). It is this errancy of language, de Man concludes, that Benjamin calls history—which is neither human, nor natural, nor phenomenal, but "purely a linguistic complication" (de Man, 44). History is not even temporal: only temporal metaphors make it seem so. It is necessary, de Man argues, to go through this linguistically "nihilistic moment" in order to understand history, that is, what history is not.

De Man's essay is an economical way of approaching Benjamin's philosophy of language, partly because de Man warns against using Benjamin facilely as an emblem of hope, and partly because de Man's own critical style, with its insistence on the errancy of language, can be compared at so many points with Benjamin's. But there is an important difference of emphasis. In his later writings, Benjamin associates language with the "mimetic faculty," the capacity to recognize and produce similarities, a faculty seen, Benjamin says, not only in children's play but in all the higher human functions. At first sight, the "mimetic faculty" seems like a regressive view of language, as the collector seems like a regressive figure. We shall have to show firstly in what way the "mimetic faculty" as Benjamin conceives it is not a naïve view of language, and secondly, in what ways it differs from modern theories of language like de Man's and what the implications of these differences are.

Benjamin's discussion of the mimetic faculty makes the crucial point that this faculty has changed over the course of time. Our capacity for perceiving similarities has decayed compared to ancient peoples' whose magical rites we no longer comprehend because we are incapable of seeing the similarities and correspondences that they saw. Benjamin is concerned not with mourning the decay of this faculty but with tracing the course of its historical transformation. He does so by introducing a distinction *within* the mimetic faculty between sensuous similarity and nonsensuous similarity. Sensuous similarity is tied to perception and is a capacity that has largely decayed in us moderns; nonsensuous similarity is the modern form of the mimetic faculty and is tied to verbal language.

The mimetic faculty historicized as nonsensuous similarity is therefore not a naïve concept. It shows clear affinities, as Benjamin's discussion of it elsewhere suggests, with the idea of language as a structure of differences, and in this regard it can be compared with the de Manean view of language. Yet at a crucial point, Benjamin's "doctrine of the similar" is not quite a "doctrine of difference." Language, as Benjamin sees it, is indeed a structure whose origins are lost in time, and in this sense, language must always be understood as a more or less synchronic differential structure—but it is a synchronic structure *with a memory*. In the folds of its differences, traces of real experience are preserved: that is why Benjamin calls language "the most perfect archive of nonsensuous similarity."[22] Though language conceived in this way does not give us, as de Man would point out, a perfect view through its symbols of the "shattered symbolized," it does give us a sense of it, an experience of it.

We can invoke now, for the last time, the collector as a figure that can help us sort out the issues of experience and modernity that arise again out of Benjamin's discussion of language. Language as "mimetic" connotes for Benjamin language as a medium of experience. Seen in this way, language is always something that not only can be, but also has to be, read. This applies to the most "obvious" texts, as well as to those linguistically self-reflexive texts that annihilate the image, suspend narration, and derealize experience. On the question of reading, the collector provides again a point of departure for reflection. The collector is always a reader, an interpreter of the fate of objects. Benjamin calls collectors "the physiognomists of the world of objects" and "interpreters of fate" (*Ill.*, 60–61).

It is important, however, not to give the notion of reading and interpretation too passive a meaning. "To read what was never written" (R, 336): this is how Benjamin sees the function of reading. This is the kind of reading that Fuchs the collector may be said to exemplify when he chose to collect neglected objects for study. Furthermore, such a notion of reading can be correlated with a nonreductive concept of experience: linked to language and not merely to perception, experience becomes not just a response to the self-evident facticity of the world but a "profane illumination . . . that perceives the everyday as impenetrable, the impenetrable as everyday" (R, 190). Understood in this way, reading is not only a form of interpretation; it is also a form of prophecy, a way of taking hold of the future. It is a form of action in the world.

It is really on the question of the future and not merely as is often assumed on the question of the past that Benjamin's figure of the collector finally speaks. What is the collector's relation to the past and to the future, to history and to modernity? We can approach this set of issues once more by way of de Man, who gently chides those critics who think that Benjamin subscribes to "the pathos of history" by means of which "one looks back on the past as a period that is lost, which then gives you the hope of another future that may occur" (de Man, 38). To deconstruct such pathos, de Man presents history in Benjamin as "purely a linguistic complication." However, one of the conclusions we can draw from a study of Benjamin's collector figure is that linguistic complications are never pure; they are inscribed in what can only be called a politics. One of Benjamin's most important insights on the relation between past and future, arrived at in part through a reflection on the problematics of collecting, is that as the past itself can be rewritten, so that the past does not lie safely in the past, so the future too, the not yet written, does not lie safely in the future. As he puts it, "*even the dead* will not be safe from the enemy if he wins" (Ill., 257). If this is indeed the case, then language, memory, and experience, these constituent elements of our modernity, are the genuine sites of a cultural politics: both a politics of resistance to the potential erosion of language, memory, and experience in modernity; and a politics of anticipation alert to emancipatory strategies.

The collector can finally be compared to what Benjamin calls "the destructive character." Like the "destructive character," the collector positions himself "at crossroads"; because he sees "nothing permanent" or sacrosanct, "he sees ways everywhere" that can lead to action. Furthermore, "because he sees a way everywhere, he has to clear things from it everywhere. Not always by brute force; sometimes by the most refined" (R, 302–3). In this description of the destructive character, Benjamin's double characterization of the collector as attractive and as motivated by "dangerous though domesticated passions" receives its most suggestive gloss.

Notes

1. Walter Benjamin, "Eduard Fuchs: Collector and Historian," in *The Essential Frankfurt School Reader,* ed. Andrew Arato and Eike Gebhardt (New York: Urizen Press, 1978), 241. Hereafter cited in the text as "Fuchs."

2. John Fowles, *The Collector* (London: J. Cape, 1976). Page references cited in the text.

3. Claude Lévi-Strauss, *Structural Anthropology,* trans. Monique Layton (Harmondsworth: Penguin, 1978), 2:179.

4. A recent comprehensive history of art collecting can also be mentioned: Joseph Alsop, *The Rare Art Tradition: The History of Art Collecting and Its Linked Phenomena* (New York: Harper and Row, 1982). Though Alsop stresses the relation among art collecting, art history, and the art market, his argument moves in a different direction from Benjamin's. See also Susan Stewart, *On Longing: Narratives of the Miniature, the Gigantic, the Souvenir, the Collection* (Baltimore and London: Johns Hopkins University Press, 1984), esp. pp. 151–69.

5. Martin Wackernagel, *The World of the Florentine Renaissance Artist,* trans. Alison Luchs (Princeton: Princeton University Press, 1981), 249.

6. See Gombrich's essay, "The Early Medici as Patrons of Art," in *Norm and Form* (London: Phaidon, 1978), 36.

7. Wackernagel, *World,* 370.

8. In Walter Benjamin, *Charles Baudelaire: A Lyric Poet in the Era of High Capitalism,* trans. Harry Zohn (London: New Left Books, 1973). Hereafter cited as CB.

9. See G. Lukács, *History and Class Consciousness,* trans. Rodney Livingstone (London: Merlin Press, 1971), 84.

10. Cf. Horkheimer and Adorno's reading of the "Sirens" episode of the *Odyssey* as illustrating the process by which "the enjoyment of art and manual labor break apart as the world of prehistory is left behind." In Max Horkheimer and Theodor W. Adorno, *Dialectic of Enlightenment* (New York: Herder and Herder, 1972), 32–34.

11. See *CB*, 104–6.

12. Flaubert, *Bouvard and Pecuchet*, trans. T. W. Earp and G. W. Stonier (New York: New Directions, 1971), 131.

13. *Ibid*, 347.

14. F. Nietzsche, *Untimely Meditations*, trans. R. J. Hollingdale (Cambridge: Cambridge University Press, 1983), 75. Subsequent page references cited in the text.

15. Joseph Conrad, *Lord Jim* (Harmondsworth: Penguin, 1949), 155. Subsequent page references cited in the text.

16. Theodor W. Adorno, *Minima Moralia*, trans. E. F. N. Jephcott (London: New Left Books, 1974), 121.

17. See Marcel Proust, *Swann's Way, Part One*, trans. C. K. Scott Moncrieff (London, New York: Modern Library, 1922), 19–20 and 51–53.

18. In Walter Benjamin, *Illuminations*, trans. Harry Zohn, ed. with an introduction by Hannah Arendt (New York: Harcourt Brace and World, 1973). Hereafter cited as *Ill.*, with page references in the text.

19. Walter Benjamin, *Reflections*, trans. Edmond Jephcott (New York: Harcourt Brace Jovanovich, 1978), 6. Hereafter cited as *R*, with page references in the text.

20. Cf. Alsop, *The Rare Art Tradition*, chapter 5, "The Siamese Twin," where he discusses the Italian *rigattieri* or junk dealers of the eighteenth century, particularly one Fra Carlo Lodoli, and how their collecting activities subverted the Vasarian canon of art.

21. Paul de Man, " 'Conclusions' Walter Benjamin's 'The Task of the Translator,' Messenger Lecture, Cornell University, March 4, 1983," in *Yale French Studies* 69 (1985): 25–46. Hereafter cited as "de Man."

22. Walter Benjamin, "Doctrine of the Similar," *New German Critique* 17 (Spring 1979): 68.

Index